Communication, Advocacy, and Work–Family Balance

This book presents an understanding of work–family balance for working adults belonging to a number of different family structures (e.g., single and/or childfree adults, LGBT couples, families with female breadwinners). It contends that the family structure should serve as a way of thinking about diversity (i.e., race, gender, age, family) in the U.S. workplace. It also argues that—in addition to accommodations occurring through workplace policy—the negotiation of work–family balance happens as a result of self-advocacy that occurs in everyday communication about family at work. Relaying the stories of a number of different working adults belonging to a variety of different family structures, it explores the range of obstacles faced in the attempt at balancing work and family life, generates informed ideas for eliminating barriers commonly experienced in balancing work and family, and problematizes enduring assumptions regarding gender roles and the myth of steadfast public and private spheres.

Jenny Dixon (Ph.D., University of Missouri) is an Associate Professor and Chair of the Communication and Media Arts Department at Marymount Manhattan College, USA. Dr. Dixon is featured in *Journal of Applied Communication Research*, *Communication Quarterly*, and *The Electronic Journal of Communication*. Jenny's research explores workplace diversity through the consideration of family structure.

Routledge Research in Communication Studies

Communication, Advocacy, and Work–Family Balance

Jenny Dixon

Routledge
Taylor & Francis Group

LONDON AND NEW YORK

First published 2017 by Routledge

2 Park Square, Milton Park, Abingdon, Oxfordshire OX14 4RN

52 Vanderbilt Avenue, New York, NY 10017

*Routledge is an imprint of the Taylor & Francis Group,
an informa business*

First issued in paperback 2019

Library of Congress Cataloging-in-Publication Data
CIP data has been applied for.

ISBN: 978-1-138-12618-3 (hbk)
ISBN: 978-0-367-87652-4 (pbk)

Typeset in Sabon
by codeMantra

Contents

Acknowledgments

I'm foremost indebted to the organizational, family, and interpersonal communication scholars who had the intellectual precision to recognize work–family balance as a discursive process. The invaluable insight of Dawn Braithwaite, Patrice Buzzanell, Kathleen Galvin, Erica Kirby, and Caryn Medved shaped and drove this project.

A pursuit of this size requires time and resources that simply aren't readily available. This project would not have been possible without the daily support, direction, and mentorship of my friends and colleagues at Marymount Manhattan College. In addition to the Department of Communication and Media Arts and the MMC Leaves and Fellowships Committee, I thank Katie LeBesco, Peter Naccarato, and especially Laura Tropp for their sage advice and unwavering encouragement throughout this project.

I would also like to thank my friend, colleague, and undergraduate advisor, David Scott. In tracing the lineage of my ability to succeed in academics, it all started with the time and energy he invested. Also, I thank my MA advisor, Tim Steffensmeier, whose energy and thirst for academic pursuit is, thankfully, contagious. And to Debbie Dougherty, who pushed me harder than I thought I could go. I'm learning, all the time, that I'm better for it. I don't care to imagine who or where I would be without the scholarly influences and opportunities imparted to me by these thoughtful and talented mentors.

I would like to thank the fun, snarky, bold, and waggish characters who agreed to lend their voices to this project. Anytime someone sets a recorder in front of you and asks you to complain about work, you are agreeing to take a risk. I cannot begin to express my gratitude to the people who entrusted me with their stories, perspectives, and opinions.

And to my students at MMC, who will be in the working world that this project seeks to improve, your sassy tenacity should not be tied to an office desk.

I'm intellectually inspired and emboldened by the vision and fortitude of my writing group: Leah Anderst, Ivone Margulies, Peter Schaefer, and Jill Stevenson. Thank you for withstanding the early drafts and for your brilliant editorial suggestions.

And thank you to my friend and colleague MJ Robinson, for your round-the-clock support. Let's never be up, writing, at 3 a.m. ever again. "Such fun."

Finally, and from the bottom of my heart, I thank my wonderful and diverse family for loving me, centering me, and allowing me to fall off the earth for a year and a half. I thank my domestic partner, David Minsky, my best friend, Emily Rauscher, my Avuncle Cedric, and my cats, Moochie and Emily. And most of all, I thank my mom, Barbara Dixon. You're fierce, BD!

Introduction

Leslie is mostly contented. She works at a government agency called Children and Family Services (CFS) with six other co-workers. On the whole, she likes her job, and she knows not to take it for granted as she is frequently and subtly reminded by her qualified yet un(der)employed friends from college. One aspect of her job that she feels most fortunate about is the people she works with.

Co-workers Maria and Lisa come to work most days with new stories about their kids—moments of cuteness, milestones in development, times of frustration, and so on. Maria is married to a moderately successful small business owner and views her earnings as a supplement to her husband's income, and Lisa is a single parent with no correspondence with her children's father, aside from the occasional, although not dependable, child support payment. Joel also works at CFS. He has kids and, although he doesn't talk about family life to quite the extent of Maria or Lisa, he has been known to attribute sleepy days to sleepless nights of tending to childhood illnesses or eradicating monsters from bedroom closets. And then there's Nora. In her early 20s, Nora is the youngest in the work group and is often gently chided by her colleagues for crossing professional boundaries as she drops details of weekend parties and occasional hookups. When slightly chastised for her sultry disclosure, Nora rationalizes her stories with rhetorical questions such as, "How am I supposed to find someone if I don't put myself out there?" … missing the point that it isn't her search for a future husband that makes her co-workers uncomfortable but rather her choice to share explicit details of the hunt. Jeremy, the only gay man in the department, feels accepted but occasionally tokenized. He regularly shares stories of restaurants he and his fiancé, Vlad, have visited, and responds to his colleagues' adventures in parenting with tales of the epic cuteness of their beloved schnauzer, Parker. In his mid-60s, Trent is the oldest co-worker at CFS. His kids have grown up and left home, leaving him and his wife contemplating retirement and beaming at the prospect of grandchildren.

All of the employees count themselves lucky to work in an environment where everyone generally gets along. However, two moments of contention have recently occurred: In one instance, Maria wanted to take time away from work so that she could attend her middle child's school play, all the while Jeremy wanted to take a half day to spend time with his sister while she was in town, on business. The other conflict surfaced when Trent needed to go to a doctor's appointment, at the same time that Joel had a sick child at home. Decisions needed to be made quickly since there was no way of anticipating a chest cold. Nobody wanted to cause anyone else to make sacrifices when it comes to being there for family, nor did anyone want to be pegged as uncommitted to work. There must be a full staff, five of the seven employees, at all times. Customarily, each day, one person has the day off. How does it all get sorted out?

Back to mostly-contented Leslie: Everyone describes Leslie as "really nice," though nobody in the office knows much about her. She asks about people's weekends, "awwws" and "oh mys" over new school pictures, and laughs at the funny stories her co-workers share about their home lives. Leslie cares about her co-workers and her interest in their lives is genuine. As a single woman with no children, no pets, and limited extended family, Leslie feels she has very little to add to workplace conversation. She frequently gives up her days off to cover for colleagues who need to be away. Usually she is glad to do it, although sometimes she gets the feeling that it has become her expected role to pick up the slack. Leslie has a friend—Kris—with whom she is very close, but she doesn't mention Kris at work because her friendship doesn't really seem to "count" as family.

This vignette illustrates the politics of family and work–family balance conflicts that occur daily in workplaces in the United States.

- There are three parents of school-age children in the workplace, a married woman in a dual income home, a single mother relying on her own earnings to raise her children, and a man whose marital status is unknown. While their shared experience of raising children brings them closer together, personally they are all negotiating parenthood from different subject positions and with different resources. Company policies provide them with a guide to what they are entitled to and how they are officially supported with flextime, but their specific workplace environment requires interpersonal negotiations and is complicated by other issues on both macro and micro levels.
- Of the three parents of school-age children, Maria and Lisa are cisgender women, and Joel is a cisgender man. Though the three colleagues bond over the shared experience of parenthood, gendered assumptions of parenting cast a different set of expectations on Maria and Lisa, compared to Joel.
- One employee is viewed by the others as just starting out in adulthood. Her workplace impropriety is excused due to her young age

and the fidelity of her narrative to find a life partner. Though Nora's search for a future husband resonates with many young women's, we are left to ponder whether co-workers would be equally tolerant of her behavior if she rejected the (long-term) coupling narrative.

- Two employees need time away from work; Maria would like to attend her child's school play, and Jeremy would like to spend time with his sister. Though Maria's request for accommodation was granted, it is important to reflect on why and whether it should have been.
- A greater stalemate occurs when two employees need accommodation for medical reasons. Trent's appointment, versus Joel's need to care for a sick child, perhaps tips the scale for Joel. After all, couldn't Trent just reschedule? Would it be inappropriate of Trent to ask why Joel's wife couldn't care for the child?
- And finally, there is an employee who brings no narrative of familial attachment to the workplace. How is Leslie impacted by her lack of contribution to the conversations about family at work?

None of these conundrums has a definitive answer. Instead, each illustrates potential assumptions about family structures and identities that are enacted in workplace cultures.

***

Work–family balance research within the communication discipline has traditionally examined the process of negotiating work and family obligations (Kirby & Buzzanell, 2014). This research has generally assumed family to be an unquestioned and uniform construct. But what happens when we see family as dynamic, multi-faceted, and politically charged? *The personal is political* is a powerful and important slogan to come from second-wave feminism. Simply put, it argues that personal decisions such as (but certainly not limited to) the division of household labor is a social and cultural matter, not to be reduced to a private, in-home, negotiation.

This book argues that the *familial is political*. Specifically, the process of negotiating work and family balance is enmeshed in the politics of what it means to have a family. We see these politics in our mediated messages as well as in our own everyday conversations.

The negotiation of work and family in the U.S. is a ripe topic of conversation and it is not confined to the traditional *opposite-sex spouses and kids* archetype. NBC news anchor Jenna Wolfe and NBC correspondent Stephanie Gosk, in 2014, welcomed their second child. Jenna wrote a blog, *(Baby) Food for Thought* (2013), that covered universal topics such as morning sickness as well as questions unique to same sex parents, such as what the child will call each parent. In another example,

Rosie O'Donnell cited a recalibration of priorities as her reason for leaving *The View* back in 2015 (Chasmar). Specifically, the single mother of five's stated reason for leaving was to devote more time to her children. Both examples point to a flexible, inclusive world in which diverse family structures are equally valid and everyone can adjust work–family balance needs as they see fit.

Though these examples indicate that the U.S. has a script for talking about non-traditional family, two important factors should be noted: First, given their wealth and social status, celebrities have more flexibility to make work–family balance choices. Rosie O'Donnell can leave *The View* to focus on her five children; Lisa, the single mom with two kids we met in the opening vignette, doesn't have that luxury. Second, there is an important distinction between being non-traditional and positioning non-traditional status as equally worthy of accommodation. For example, an employee, in his mid-40s, who is single and therefore perceived to be "without a family" probably isn't going to be marginalized in the workplace ... at least not until he tries to measure the worth of his personal time against that of his coupled and child-raising colleagues.

Just as we shouldn't see celebrity life choices as a mirror reflection of our own work–family balance options, we should also be wary of work–family balance as depicted in popular time management and self-help books. In the popular press, work–family balance appears to be largely myopic, with (likely straight) male professional success to be the ultimate goal for us all. In a *New York Times* best-selling book, *Decide*, Steve McClatchy (2014) only vaguely acknowledges the family aspect of negotiating one's time. He explains that balancing work and life obligations means delegating tasks. As his example, McClatchy recalls a time in which he asked his wife to hire a personal assistant (for him). Throughout the book, the challenge of balancing work and family is missing as family obligations are completely silenced, save for when family is depicted as an unequivocal means of supporting work goals. Similarly, *The Experiment*, which claims to present a "revolutionary way" to "achieve work-life balance," depicts *life* as a static and oversimplified variable (Anderson, 2014). In the opening scenario, a fictional character named Dennis is forced to take public transportation to work after determining that his car wouldn't start. Usually his wife would take him to work under these circumstances, but they had recently separated. Fortunately, his assistant, Cindy, was able to pick him up at the station when his train arrived. Unlike *Decide*, which provided "practical" advice (e.g., make a list of what you want to do with your day and do the most important tasks first), *The Experiment* advocates changes in attitude, ultimately plugging the services of a life coach. Dennis realizes he's been spending too much time stressing about work, calls his wife, and (spoiler alert) offers to spend some time with his children, thereby setting their relationship back on course.

In both books, work–life balance is framed with work taking the higher priority and family as incidental and willing to yield to work obligations. Additionally, both books tout advice for navigating work–family balance with men assumed to be the workers and women serving in supportive roles. In *The Experiment*, Dennis relies on Cindy to coordinate his busy schedule and offer help when needed. While Dennis voices appreciation for Cindy, her availability is nonetheless taken for granted as something all readers enjoy.

I'd love to say that these two examples are obscure titles, found buried in a dusty stack or filed on the discount shelf. But these books were among the top five listed on Amazon.com when I searched "work–family" and "balance." They were the top two when searching for books published in 2014 or later.

Though cringe-worthy, the gendered assumptions in these books point to an added dimension for thinking about the politics of family: Diversity of family includes not only structure (i.e., what persons make up a family) but also role distribution (i.e., who is supposed to do what tasks to sustain the family). Family role expectations gain complexity when we consider that ideology and practice do not seamlessly overlap (Franco et al., 2004; Lucas-Thompson & Goldberg, 2015). For example, two adults within a family may claim to value egalitarian roles in which housework, childcare, financial contributions, and other obligations are equally shared. However, the actual norms of this family may reflect divisions of labor congruent to traditional gender ideologies (Hochschild, 1989; Lucas-Thompson & Goldberg, 2015).

The opening narrative provided several examples of the politics that may occur in the workplace that are related, in one way or another, to family identity. Some families are celebrated, some are accepted, some take on narrative form in regular installments of workplace conversation, and some go unrealized. The celebration of Jenna and Stephanie's growing family and Rosie's choice to put a greater focus on motherhood speaks to the acceptance of diverse family structures.[1] But are these family structures and life trajectories also celebrated among employees in the labor force, the corporate offices downtown, or the service industries? Perhaps the better question might be, *how are diverse family structures valued differently compared to the traditional opposite-sex spouses and child family form?*

Purpose

Considering work–family balance in relation to the construction of family identity holds important implications for (a) the scope of what is meant by *honoring diversity*, (b) the reconsideration of gender roles as presently reinforced or otherwise encouraged in the workplace, (c) the capacity for organization members to relate to one another, and

(d) the ways individuals *do* work–family balance. Diversity has become what Kenneth Burke would call a god term—a word with an inherent potency, signifying concepts and ideas that one would unequivocally embrace (Burke, 1984). Workplaces claim to value diversity and scholars call for research exploring ways for making workplaces (more) accepting and equitable. Generally, when we think about diverse workplaces, we go to the mainstays of gender, race, and sexuality. We might even delve into age, class (perhaps blue- vs. white-collar workers) and (dis)ability. This book positions family structure as a component of diversity. Just as the experience of navigating work and family obligations is different for men and women (Mills, 2014), these obligations are also different for working adults with and without children, with and without elderly parents to care for, etc. But family structure—as a phenomenon distinguishable from sexual orientation and gender identity—has yet to be added to the lexicon of what it means to be diverse.

Viewing family through the lens of diversity makes clear the capacity for the familial to be political. Family politics, within the workplace, may be thought of in terms of acceptance and equality. Acceptance accounts for whether employees belonging to a certain family structure are welcomed into the workplace. Thankfully, workplaces are becoming more and more accepting of lesbian, gay, bisexual and transgender (LGBT) employees (although it would be a grave mistake to assume that we have arrived at a place of unequivocal and unwavering acceptance). Likewise, single and childfree employees are all but undoubtedly accepted in the workplace, as are female breadwinners and other members of families that reject traditionally gendered distributions of labor. Employees who care for family of choice[2] aren't likely to be shunned from the workplace, but their familial attachments may not be held in esteem as a family bound by more traditional criteria.

In addition to considering acceptance, it is also important to think about how work–family balance opportunities and constraints vary by family structure. It's not good enough to be accepted as a work colleague. Rather, employees' family structures must be valued as having equal worth as any other and the unique needs of those structures must be equally worthy of accommodation. For example, in the opening vignette, Leslie is technically allowed the same leave opportunities as her co-workers, yet she feels that taking time off for herself isn't feasible because it doesn't involve caring for others. There may be policies that assure equal work–family balance for all employees; however, it has been established that just because a policy exists doesn't mean we can use it (Kirby & Krone, 2002). It is important to illuminate situations in which employees belonging to diverse family structures have unique constraints when navigating work–family balance, such as the inability to use a workplace policy, or the inability to compare work–family balance obstacles with other employees.

In addition to broadening our scope of workplace diversity, this project seeks to further dismantle the assumption that balancing work and family is a women's issue. Recall the self-help books; each featured a man's perspective as well as an oversimplified notion of balancing family obligations. Could this oversimplification of family be due to the notion that navigating the intricacies of family life is a woman's obligation? As will be elaborated below, the history of work–family balance research parallels the history of women in the workplace. Unfortunately, social and interpersonal discourses still assign women the task of balancing work and family, far more so than men. This is unfair to everyone: just as women are assumed to be responsible for household labor, men's work–family balance obligations are silenced or perhaps deemed emasculating. It is important to consider how otherwise traditional family structures become non-traditional when common gender roles are reversed or rejected.

Furthermore, considerations of varying family structures present us with opportunities to *relate*. Many of our core work–family balance goals are the same. For example, 90 percent of working adults are concerned about spending too little time with their families (Sutton & Noe, 2005). Additionally, whereas different employees have different sensibilities with regard to self-disclosure, it's safe to say that employees want to work where their non-work lives don't have to be actively hidden. In addition to the common need to know that we are spending enough time with our families and that we don't have to expend energy building and maintaining a metaphorical closet, we all want a fair opportunity to balance work and family. Basically, we all want the fulfillment and dignity that comes from knowing we're accepted and afforded equal opportunities (as well as equal constraints). As Kirby and Buzzanell (2014) aptly state, "fulfillment and dignity are shaped by access, agency, and opportunities to implement work-life choices" (p. 352). This exploration of work–family balance will illuminate how this fulfillment and dignity are sought and the constraints that make them an unattained reality.

Finally, though this is not a *how to* or a *best practices* book, *Communication, Advocacy, and Work–Family Balance* does explore how people manage work and family obligations. In doing so, you will hopefully come away with a pragmatic new perspective about work–family balance. Perhaps most importantly, this book serves as a prompt for awareness of the constraints faced by our fellow employees and will ideally spark dialogs within as well as outside of the workplace.

Communicating Work–Family Balance

Seeing as this project focuses on the communication of family identity in the workplace and the discursive processes through which we advocate for family at work, it stands to reason that *Communication,*

Advocacy, and Work–Family Balance occurs within the lineage of the communication discipline. However, many academic disciplines contribute to what is known about work–family balance. The *Work and Family Research Network* functions under the primary charge of networking work–family scholars across an array of disciplines. The creation and sustainment of such a group speaks to the widespread interest in the topic of balancing work and family. It also speaks to the contributions that scholars from differing disciplines can make. Research from disciplines including psychology, sociology, management, and family studies have played an indispensable roll in the shaping of this book.

A major inspiration for this project comes from the work of Lotte Bailyn, a Professor of Management at MIT, who took the traditional value system that gives work primacy over family and literally turned it upside down. Specifically, Bailyn (2006) dares to propose a workplace norm in which personal needs shape the way we do work and the way in which commitment to work is communicated. *Communication, Advocacy, and Work–Family Balance* uses Bailyn's emphasis on personal need as a salient aspect of the workplace as a foundational assumption. Bailyn's work is also exceptionally influential in that it emphasizes that work–family balance is an issue of equal constraints as well as equal opportunities. It is because of Bailyn's work that this book considers not only the search for equality in work–family balance opportunities, but also calls for change in workplace cultures so that diverse families no longer experience unique constraints.

Another source of foundational influence is the work of sociologist Kathleen Gerson. Her book *The Unfinished Revolution* speaks to how young adults make sense of family trajectory. Namely, Gerson's (2010) work illustrates how the criteria for happy families are changing from being bound to a particular structure (e.g., wedded parents) to pursuing particular goals (e.g., living with financial independence). The present volume uses this departure from the structure-bound notions of family as a prompt for exploring how working adults of all family structures communicate family into being within the workplace.

Building from Bailyn's deconstruction of work–family priorities as they often occur within the workplace, and Gerson's depiction of a future of family in which goal attainment undermines structure, the next step is to consider how family identity is constructed in the workplace and how we might advocate for more family-friendly value systems. Specifically, *Communication, Advocacy, and Work–Family Balance* focuses on the communication processes through which family identities are presented and/or negotiated in the workplace. This project also presents these family identities as the basic catalyst for taking advantage of opportunities and alleviating constraints (Kirby et al., 2003). Nestled under the umbrella of communication studies, this project gives primary focus to the assumptions and expertise found in family communication and organizational communication disciplines.

The family communication discipline focuses heavily on the role of communication in defining family, analyzing communication processes within and beyond family units, managing privacy, relational development, etc. (Rogers, 2006). This project takes up the call of focusing on the diversity of family structures while leaning on the lineage of family communication research that shapes what "counts" as family and how the question of "what is a family?" is determined. Central to the role of communication in developing what it means to be family is the concept of discourse dependency.

Family communication scholar, Kathleen Galvin, explains that, "[a]s families become increasingly diverse, their definitional processes expand exponentially, rendering their identity highly discourse dependent" (p. 3). In other words, the status of family depends, in part, on communication with outsiders as well as within the family (Galvin, 2006). The more a family deviates from the traditional "opposite sex spouses and child[ren]" construct, the more a communicated construction of family status is necessary. For example, the familial relationship of mother and (biological) child is not likely to be disputed. There are other relationships in which familiarity is mostly taken for granted, but a little bit of discursive construction is needed. A step-parent may communicate about his stepdaughter in such a way to indicate that she *is* his daughter. Adoptive parents often have to communicatively reinforce their parental connection to their children. Finally, a family of choice may require the most discourse in an attempt to construct that the family is indeed a family, despite the fact that no one is bound by traditional ties such as biology or law. Essential to the purpose of this book is how family is created through discourses that occur in organizational settings such as the workplace.

Organizational communication scholarship focuses on communication as it occurs within organizational settings as well as how organizations are "built" through communicated meaning-making. The claim that we use communication to shuffle our day-to-day work and family obligations is self-evident. When we sheepishly ask for the afternoon off, when we ask the sitter if he's available to watch the kids, and when we ask a neighbor to check our mail while we're away on a business trip, communication happens. What might not be quite so obvious is the idea that we negotiate work–family balance through everyday self-disclosure in the workplace. Work–family balance research is an important line of inquiry within the organizational communication discipline. And while, as discussed above, work–family balance is an interdisciplinary issue, Kirby and Buzzanell (2014) explain that "[o]rganizational communication scholars ... provide a unique point of difference by focusing on *how* communication constitutes work-life phenomena" (p. 251). *Communication, Advocacy, and Work–Family Balance* will illustrate the *how* of constituting work and family balance by considering two functions of discursive discourse: affirmation and self-advocacy.

Most people enjoy talking about family while at work. Talking about family serves to affirm one's familial station in life. Going back to the opening narrative, Maria and Lisa talk about their kids at work, because child rearing has been deemed an acceptable aspect of one's life course. Their ability to talk about it openly affirms that they have made good choices. (Even when they are complaining about the difficulties of children, they are still affirmed through sympathy and support.) Nora, on the other hand, gets less affirmation because partying doesn't receive the same affirmative response as childrearing. Granted, this could be largely dependent on one's workplace. The staff of the local pizza chain might be more likely to congratulate a partying lifestyle than the Children and Family Services office. Regardless of the given workplace, families are communicated—and, therefore, represented—into being.

Navigating family and work requires establishing identity. Specifically, one has to construct an identity within the workplace that acknowledges one's family. Kirby and Buzzanell (2014) argue that work–life communication may be viewed through the process of *constructing (gendered) (working) identities*. We construct our identities as we advocate for work–family balance needs, and we advocate for work–family balance needs through the constructions of our identities. As has been established thus far, these identities are gendered and they are also *familied*— or serve to constitute the sort of family structure an employee belongs to. Accepting that identities are constructed through the process of work–life balance serves as a worthy starting point for considering how the construction of one's family identity is inextricably bound to navigating work–family balance. With "work–family" established as its own unique point of scholarly focus, the importance—and intricate nature— of creating one's familied identity is explained.

In addition to affirming one's familial station in life, talking about family while at work serves as a site for self-advocacy. When frequently mentioning family at work, something akin to character development occurs. Even though one probably never says, "I went out with my partner, Stanley—remember that when he has to have triple bypass surgery," we use everyday communication about family to make family familiar. Therefore, when Stanley needs some extra attention, the people who serve as gatekeepers to work–family balance needs are accommodating you as well as a person they know (or feel they know). This self-advocacy can become tricky when one cannot communicate family into being to the extent that other co-workers do.

Terminology

It may be apparent, by now, that I have been using the term *work–family balance*, all the while referencing works that refer to *work–life balance*. My choice to use the former is both political and slightly arbitrary. Early research exploring the attempt of balancing work and non-work obligations was referred to as "work–family" balance (e.g., Ashforth et al., 2000). However, in 2003, the National Communication Association's Organizational Communication Division's Article of the Year established "work–life" (Kirby et al., 2003) as a more comprehensive label (Kirby & Buzzanell, 2014). The majority of subsequent communication studies have followed suit (e.g., Hoffman & Cowan, 2010; Tracy & Rivera, 2010).

The choice to return to work–family balance, for this project, is not a critique of the shift away from this term. Because this book focuses specifically on the politics of developing family identity in the workplace, it makes sense that *family* would be the term of focus. Perhaps this book creates a precedent for a conceptual splitting of research areas: Research on work–life balance would concentrate on a work and non-work dichotomy in which "non-work" includes family but also other forms of non-work commitment, such as volunteer work, jury duty, etc. Work–family balance would focus specifically on the enactment, primacy, and assumptions of work and family obligations, in particular. This salient contrasting of two otherwise interchangeable terms is a political choice in that it serves to allow clarity for the unique obstacles of communicating family and family needs in the workplace.

At the same time, choosing work–family balance is somewhat arbitrary and even contradictory to the thesis of the project. In a notebook, I made a list titled "non-work, non-family obligations." The list reads, "self care, taxes, hobbies, friends, bills, leisure time, spiritual growth, house upkeep." Let me emphasize that this was a brainstorming activity. Not only are there many other items that could be added to this list, I'm somewhat embarrassed that "taxes" came before "friends" and "spiritual growth." The purpose of making this list was to reflect on what I'm leaving out by studying work–family balance. Taxes, bills, and house upkeep could easily be extensions of family obligations. Leisure time and hobbies may or may not be enjoyed with family members, and friends—as will be discussed in the next chapter—can be conceptually indiscernible from family. So that leaves self-care. The care of one's self can be just as much for the sake of the family as it is for one's own general wellbeing. So all of the non-family, non-work obligations have some sort of impact on the wellbeing of the family. It is in this sense that choosing work–family over work–life is somewhat arbitrary.

A note is also needed about balance. I chose the term balance, not because it aptly describes our day-to-day experiences but because it is an ideal. Other terms are used throughout the literature, each serving its own descriptive purpose: Work–family management (Golden & Geisler, 2007) refers to our addressing the competing obligations of work and family. Conflict (Carlson & Perrewé, 1999) describes this vying for our attention. Though far more literature focuses on competing obligations, work–family facilitation (Wayne et al., 2007) or enrichment (Munn & Greer, 2015), accounts for ways in which work and family are mutually nourishing. Balance was selected because it focuses, albeit optimistically, on the end goal. Work–family conflict will always occur as will the necessity for management.

Collecting Experiences/Methodology

Borrowing the language of Arlie Hochschild (2016), the research conducted for this book is "'exploratory' and 'hypothesis generating'" (p. 247). My analytic focus is on family as a component of diversity and work–family balance as a site of family structure-based inequality. In addition to culling scholarly and popular insights to develop ways of thinking about families as emblems of diversity, stories, perspectives, and ideas yielded from semi-structured qualitative interviews (Croucher & Cronn-Mills, 2015) also shape the experience of balancing work and family reported in this book. Following Hoffman and Cowan (2010), the present study examines work–family balance experiences across a variety of workplace contexts, showcasing obstacles unique to some organizations but not others.

Work–family balance experiences were gathered through a primary and a supplementary dataset. The primary dataset formed from 26 interviews conducted expressly for this project. A supplementary dataset, from a previous study examining LGBTQ (Lesbian Gay Bisexual Transgender and Queer) and single/childfree workplace identities was also analyzed (Dixon & Dougherty, 2014). All data were collected with Institutional Review Board approval.

Criteria for participation in both the primary study (as well as the supplementary dataset) were very broad to match the diversity sought for understanding the intricacies of work–family balance in relation to family structure. All participants were 18 years of age or older and worked outside the home for a wage.[3] In the primary study, a relatively even representation was attempted of participants who identify as (a) single and/or childfree, (b) LGBTQ, (c) female breadwinners, (d) belonging to a family of choice, or (e) belonging to the now-dominant "dual earner, with child(ren)" structure.[4] Of course, many participants fell into multiple categories and gave voice to multiple chapters.

Though even greater diversity would have been ideal, the primary dataset includes an assortment of family structures, ages, ethnicities, sexual orientations, and occupations. Thirteen (50%) participants identified being single,[5] 19 (73%) were childfree, 13 (50%) were LGBTQ, four (15%) identified as female breadwinners, six (23%) reported belonging to a family of choice, and four (15%) belonged to a dual-earner household, with one or more children. Ages ranged from 24 to 61, with a mean age of 38. Though the majority of participants were white (17; 65%), the experiences of working adults from a variety of racial/ethnic backgrounds were actively solicited: Three (11.5%) Hispanic, three (11.5%) African American, one (4%) Puerto Rican, one (4%) Jewish participant, and one (4%) Native American[6] shared their work–family balance stories for this project. Fourteen (54%) participants identified as straight, four (15%) were gay, two (8%) were lesbian, five (19%) bisexual, one (4%) identified as queer, and none were transgender. Fifteen (58%) participants identified as female, ten (38%) identified as male, and one (4%) participant was genderqueer. Participants had acquired varying levels of education: Three (11.5%) reported a high school diploma as their highest degree completed, four (15%) earned an Associate's degree, nine (34.6%) earned Bachelor's degrees, five (19.2%) had Master's degrees, one (4%) had an MD, and four (15%) earned Ph.D.s. A broad range of occupations is represented in the interview data including bartender, cab driver, college professor, and social worker. Three participants were freelance artists. Initially, I felt that the freedom afforded to freelance professionals did not meet the criteria of the study because these participants didn't report working regular hours nor did they have a dedicated superior. However, I decided to include freelance experiences so as to gain insight on how work–family balance constraints occur despite such flexibility. Time spent in participants' occupation at the time of the interview ranged from eight months to 30 years, with a mean duration of 7.6 years. Interviewees lived in Georgia, Illinois, Nebraska, New Jersey, and New York at the time of their interviews.

The supplementary dataset also represents diverse perspectives. Though family structure was not included in the demographic questionnaire, participants' diverse family structures were explained in many of the interviews. Ages ranged from 19 to 65 with a mean age of 34. Twenty-one (35%) participants identified as straight, ten (16.6%) were gay, seven (11.6%) were lesbian, 16 (26.6%) were bisexual, and six (10%) were transgender. Thirty (50%) women contributed to this dataset as well as 28 (46.6%) men, and two (3.3%) who were genderqueer. Fifty-two (86%) identified as white, three (5%) Native American, three (5%) Asian American, one (2%) African American, and one (2%) Hispanic participant contributed to this dataset. Educational backgrounds included two (3.3%) participants with high school diplomas, one (2%) with an Associate's degree, 24 (40%) with a Bachelor's degree, 11 (18.3%) with a Master's degree, and six (10%) with a Ph.D.[7] Interviewees lived in Alaska, Indiana, Kansas, Maryland, Missouri, Oklahoma, and Texas at the time of the interviews.

Participants in both datasets were recruited through snowball sampling and word of mouth. Interviews for the primary project were also recruited through Craig's List postings. Participants were offered monetary compensation for their time and insight, however many elected to participate without compensation. Interviews took place in person, on the phone, and via Skype. In-person interviews took place in coffee shops, on college campuses, in libraries, and in participants' homes. All participants were provided with a consent form, detailing the purpose and procedure of the study. To maintain confidentiality, all participants were asked to select a pseudonym. In several instances, a pseudonym was provided for them. All additional identifying details were changed as necessary.

Interview questions, asked in the primary study, varied based on the reported family structure of the participant being interviewed. For example, when speaking with a participant who was single, questions focused on how the identity of being single is created in the workplace. A list of questions asked of all primary study participants is provided in the appendix. Interviews that formed the supplementary dataset included questions that focused on gender and sexual identity in the workplace. However, topics of work–family balance and family structure frequently emerged and ultimately prompted the primary study. Though participants' stories of current work–family balance experiences were preferred, past experiences and comparisons across different workplaces were included in the analysis. Primary study interviews ranged in duration from 26 to 74 minutes, with a mean interview time of 40 minutes. Interviews yielding supplementary data ranged from 18 to 132 minutes with a mean time of 42 minutes. All but two interviews were audiotaped. In two instances, malfunctions with the digital recorder resulted in relying on interview notes. In one instance, a participant requested a copy of the interview transcript to approve prior to being included in the analysis process. The participant approved of the transcript.

As Tracy (2013) astutely observes, interviews are just as much about constructing meaning as they are about "mining data gems" (p. 132). In this project, the construction of meaning occurred through the development of themes that emerged through thematic analysis (van Manen, 1990, 2002). Themes are presented in the book in various ways. For example, the culture of care is a theme explained in Chapter 5 that emerged from interview data with women. In Chapter 3, themes that emerged through interviews with single and childfree participants are presented in relation to the work of Casper, Weltman, and Kwesiga (2007). Not every passage from interview data provided in this book is an exemplary representation of an emerging theme. In some cases, participants provided thought-provoking ideas and experiences that were not typical but were nonetheless relevant and worthy of inclusion. With these instances, mention of the infrequency of the perspective was made.

Despite dividing the chapters by distinct identity categories, analysis occurred with the understanding that no experience rooted in family structure occurs in a vacuum. Intersectionality represents the idea that social identities mediate one another (McDonald, 2015) and acknowledge a "simultaneous process of identity" (Holvino, 2010, p. 249). Data analysis occurred with the understanding that the social identities attributed to family (e.g., single, breadwinner, etc.) are created in relation to one another and in relation to other social identities (e.g., age, race, etc.). Though not every composite of intersectional identities could be accounted for, attempts were made to draw connections to the simultaneous process of identity construction that occurred with the construction of family structure. For example, considering the role of LGBTQ identity in work–family balance can be enriched by considerations of age, race, etc.

Finally, a note on including interview passages: I include the age and occupation of each participant as they are represented within the text. Additional information is provided when pertinent to the chapter in which the participant's words are showcased. For example, Joy is included in both Chapter 4: Balancing LGBTQ Identities and Chapter 5: Balancing Gendered Obligations. In Chapter 4, I mention that Joy is a 45-year-old film editor who is a lesbian. In Chapter 5, I replace *lesbian* with *woman*. My intention is not to compartmentalize identities but rather to exercise brevity in introducing each passage.

Chapter Preview

Chapter 1: Perceptions of Family

There is no typical family structure in the US. In a briefing prepared for the Council on Contemporary Families, Cohen (2014) describes the movement away from the traditional family form as "an explosion of diversity, a fanning out from a compact center along many different pathways" (p. 1). By this he means that there is no single type of family taking a commanding lead over the archetypal norm. Owing to the emergent kaleidoscope of family structures, disagreement occurs among co-workers and between co-workers and management regarding what "counts" as family, and who is eligible for work–family balance accommodations (Dixon & Dougherty, 2014). Several questions bear addressing about the extent to which notions of family diverge and the impact this divergence has on the everyday obstacles of working adults. First, do academic conceptualizations of family reflect the "explosion of diversity" explained by Cohen (2014)? And in what ways do academic notions of family intervene in the daily lives of working adults? Second, does communication within workplaces honor diverse family structures? Does a threshold of acceptance occur in which some families (e.g., stepfamilies) are taken seriously but others (e.g., families of choice) are not? And finally, are the families of workplace members who are in charge of refereeing work–family balance requests (e.g., managers) just as diverse, with regard to family structure, as other organizational members? Chapter 1 explores each question with the goal of illuminating a divergence among family structures, workplace discourses, and common managerial perspectives.

Chapter 2: Ambiguous Expectations & Precarious Prospects

Just as it is impossible to describe families using specific and concrete criteria, it is equally unreasonable to describe the workplace in any absolute fashion. Workplace cultures can be contradictory, fragmented, and contrived, making it difficult to determine the extent to which affirming and advocating for family needs is allowed. Workplace expectations can be equally unclear. Mumby (2012) provides characteristics delineating the Fordist from the post-Fordist workplace. Named after Henry Ford of the Ford Motor Company, the Fordist workplace values efficiency and productivity; workplace members actively identify with their workplace and view employment as a life-long commitment. Fordist notions align with what we might think of as modernity and the product of the Industrial Revolution.

The post-Fordist, or postmodern, workplace is characterized, in part, as a work environment with a more flexible organizational structure (e.g., decisions-making delegated to a work team or committee as opposed to an individual person of authority). This chapter will argue that the norms and expectations of workplaces are difficult to navigate, not necessarily because of an ushering in of a postmodern work environment, but because modern and postmodern ideals often co-exist. This co-existence occurs despite largely contradictory expectations of organization members. For example, a postmodern work environment blurs boundaries of what it means to be "at work" by allowing for telecommuting. However, being physically present (referred to at times as putting in "face time") is a highly valued modernist notion in many workplaces (Bailyn, 2006). This presents ambiguity as workers allowed to work from home are left to wonder whether doing so will result in negative consequences (e.g., being perceived as less committed than co-workers who commute to work). Workplace expectations only gain ambiguity when considering the frequency with which adults change careers within a given lifespan, as well as workplace cultures that vary by career/vocational genre (i.e., blue-collar, white-collar, and the emergent "no-collar"). This chapter examines modern and postmodern work–family balance expectations in order to set the stage for considering the task of navigating work and family obligations from a diversity of family structures.

Chapter 3: Balancing a Lingering Compulsion

Considering the unique obstacles of work–family balance for single and childfree working adults unearths a lingering compulsion. In other words, despite the growing number of working adults who are single and do not have children (Daly, 2014), we are actively encouraged to wed and procreate (DePaulo, 2006). These expectations extend into the workplace—even in spaces in which the criteria for "professional" generally exclude personal matters. How does everyday communication function to reinforce coupled and child-raising working adults as being more deserving of accommodation than their single and childfree counterparts? Chapter 3 employs Casper et al.'s (2007) framework for examining opportunities for creating work–family balance equality.

Chapter 4: Balancing LGBTQ Identities

Chapter 4 explores the unique barriers of work–family balance for LGBTQ working adults. This chapter builds from the assumption that families containing one or more LGBTQ working adults are basically the same as families containing only straight, cisgender counterparts. Despite experiential similarities, research shows that LGBTQ working adults face unique obstacles (Dixon & Dougherty, 2014). For many LGBTQ workplace members, to negotiate time with family is to communicate sexual identity in the workplace. As Woods (1993) explains, straight families are seen as a social construction, while gay and lesbian families are seen as a sexual construct. Inequalities with regard to family leave policies are also an issue. Workplace cultures of sexuality, the decisions about disclosing sexual orientation and gender identity, and the contradictory nature of policy and interpersonal communication (Compton, 2016) are each important points of consideration. This chapter couples existing research about work–family balance for LGBTQ working adults with the findings gathered from interviews to explore how work–family balance for LGBTQ working adults is (and might be) achieved.

Chapter 5: Balancing Gendered Obligations

At the start of the twenty-first century, only one-third of families followed the male breadwinner model (U.S. Bureau of Labor statistics, 2008). Amid her development of elements to describe the experiences of female breadwinners, Meisenbach (2010) found that breadwinning is bound to gender identity. Research seems to indicate that while an increasing number of women are becoming breadwinners of their respective households, we should not assume that a seamless role reversal—nor a matching change in gender ideologies—is taking place. The purpose of this chapter is to explore gendered obstacles to work–family balance.

Exploring the themes of *the culture of care* and *the male success model*, this chapter looks primarily to the work of Hochschild (1989), Meisenbach (2010) and Medved (2016a, 2016b) to look at the gendered nature of negotiating non-work obligations (such as the negotiation of household labor), and performing workplace commitment (such as constructing the identity of the driven businesswoman).

Chapter 6: Balancing Family of Choice

Family of choice can include longtime neighbors, friendships that inspire feelings of kinship, and relationships with people described as being "like a sister/brother/etc." Labeled in communication research as fictive (Lucas & Buzzanell, 2006) or voluntary kin (Braithwaite et al., 2010), I prefer to use *family of choice* because it lends a sense of legitimacy withheld in the word "fictive" and it relays a certain sense of affection missing in the word "kin." Family of choice is built when someone chooses to regard someone with familial love and care (Dixon, 2015). Despite its step away from traditional notions of family, family of choice is communicated largely in relation to those traditional structures (e.g., a substitute following the death of a traditional family member or filling needs unmet by the traditional family). It can be assumed that comparing family of choice to traditional family constructs serves as a way of legitimizing the latter. The purpose of this chapter is to explore why, and within what contexts, people form family of choice, and how integration of family of choice into work–family balance may hold implications for how friendships and the greater community are prioritized.

Conclusion

The final chapter serves to synthesize the findings illustrated throughout the book and especially Chapters 5–6. Specifically, the conclusion will explain the means through which working adults construct family identity in the workplace and discuss the role this construction plays in balancing work and family obligations. Furthermore, this chapter will summarizes and provides commentary for methods of balancing work and family as mentioned throughout the book. Finally, closing remarks on the implications of considering family as a construct of diversity—in relation to the findings provided throughout the book—will be provided.

Notes

1 Even among celebrities, there are limits to what family structures are accepted. For example, the coupling of actors Sarah Paulson and Holland Taylor has been under scrutiny, not because they are a same-sex couple, but because of the 32-year age difference between them (Vulpo, 2016).

2 Family of choice is defined, in Chapter 6, as "those persons perceived to be family, but who are not related by blood or law" (Braithwaite et al., 2010, p. 390), and is built when someone chooses to regard someone with familial commitment and care (Dixon, 2015).
3 Important insight could be yielded from exploring the balance of family with volunteer work. However, due to the already deleteriously broad research design, I elected to limit participants to those who, theoretically, didn't have the luxury to simply leave the work environment in the event the attempt at balance became too hectic.
4 This allowed for informative comparisons among discourse-dependent and non-discourse-dependent family structures.
5 The definition of single was left to the interpretation of the participant. However, in most cases, participants who identified as single were both unwed and not in a romantic relationship.
6 Ethnicity and gender were reported based on an open-ended demographics questionnaire in which participants filled in (or I asked and filled in) their ethnicities and gender identities. This was done to avoid suggesting that a participant choose a category with which they do not identify.
7 Some participants elected not to report the highest level of education achieved.

References

Anderson, R. M. (2014). *The experiment: Discover a revolutionary way to manage stress and achieve work-life balance.* San Diego, CA: Executive Joy! Publishing.

Ashforth, B. E., Kreiner, G. E., & Fugate, M. (2000). All in a day's work: Boundaries and micro role transitions. *Academy of Management Review*, 25(3), 472–491. doi: 10.5465/AMR.2000.3363315.

(Baby) Food for Thought (2013, June 12). Jenna Wolfe: What will the baby call you and Steph? And 14 more questions I'm always asked [Web log message]. Retrieved from www.today.com/parents/jenna-wolfe-what-will-baby-call-you-steph-14-more-6C10292325 (accessed July 20, 2015).

Bailyn, L. (2006). *Breaking the mold: Redesigning work for productive and satisfying lives* (2nd ed.). Ithaca, NY: Cornell University Press.

Braithwaite, D. O., Bach, B. W., Baxter, L. A., DiVerniero, R., Hammonds, J. R., Hosek, A. M., ... Wolf, B. M. (2010). Constructing family: A typology of voluntary kin. *Journal of Social and Personal Relationships*, 27, 388–407. doi: 10.1177/0265407510361615.

Burke, K. (1984). *Permanence and change: An anatomy of purpose* (3rd ed.). Los Angeles: University of California Press.

Carlson, D. S. & Perrewé, P. L. (1999). The role of social support in the stressor–strain relationship: An examination of work–family conflict. *Journal of Management*, 25(4), 513–540. doi: 10.1177/014920639902500403.

Casper, W. J., Weltman, D., & Kwesiga, E. (2007). Beyond family-friendly: The construct and measurement of singles-friendly work culture. *Journal of Vocational Behavior*, 70, 478–501. doi: 10.1016/j.jvb.2007.01.001.

Chasmar, J. (2015, February 8). Rosie O'Donnell leaving "The View" again after split from wife. *The Washington Times.* Retrieved from www.washingtontimes.com/news/2015/feb/8/rosie-odonnell-leaving-the-view-again-after-split-/ (accessed July 20, 2015).

Cohen, P. (2014, September 4). Family diversity is the new normal for America's children: A briefing paper prepared for the Council on Contemporary Families.

Compton, C. A. (2016). Managing mixed messages: Sexual identity management in a changing US workplace. *Management Communication Quarterly*, 30(4), 415–440. doi: 10.1177/0893318916641215.

Croucher, S. M. & Cronn-Mills, D. (2015). *Understanding communication research methods: A theoretical and practical approach*. New York: Routledge.

Daly, N. (2014, September 11). Single? So are the majority of U.S. adults. *PBS Newshour*. Retrieved from www.pbs.org/newshour/rundown/single-youre-not-alone/ (accessed April 10, 2016).

DePaulo, B. (2006). *Singled out: How singles are stereotyped, stigmatized, and ignored and still live happily ever after*. New York: St. Martin's Press.

Dixon, J. (2015). *Family*arizing: Work/life balance for single, childfree, and chosen family. *Electronic Journal of Communication*, 25(1–2).

Dixon, J. & Dougherty, D. S. (2014). A language convergence/meaning divergence analysis exploring how LGBTQ and single employees manage traditional family expectations in the workplace. *Journal of Applied Communication Research*, 42(1), 1–19. doi: 10.1080/00909882.2013.847275.

Franco, J. L., Sabattini, L., & Crosby, F. J. (2004). Anticipating work and family: Exploring the associations among gender-related ideologies, values, and behaviors in Latino and White families in the United States. *Journal of Social Issues*, 60(4), 755–766. doi: 10.1111/j.0022-4537.2004.00384.x.

Galvin, K. M. (2006). Diversity's impact on defining the family: Discourse dependence and identity. In L. H. Turner & R. West (Eds.), *The family communication sourcebook* (pp. 3–20). Thousand Oaks, CA: Sage.

Gerson, K. (2010). *The unfinished revolution: Coming of age in a new era of gender, work, and family*. New York: Oxford University Press.

Golden, A. G. & Geisler, C. (2007). Work–life boundary management and the personal digital assistant. *Human Relations*, 60(3), 519–551. doi: 10.1177/0018726707076698.

Hochschild, A. (1989). *The second shift: Working families and the revolution at home*. New York: Penguin Books.

Hochschild, A. (2016). *Strangers in their own land: Anger and mourning on the American right*. New York: New Press.

Hoffman, M. F. & Cowan, R. L. (2010). Be careful what you ask for: Structuration theory and work/life accommodation. *Communication Studies*, 61(2), 205–223. doi: 10.1080/10510971003604026.

Holvino, E. (2010). Intersections: The simultaneity of race, gender and class in organization studies. *Gender, Work & Organization*, 17(3), 248–277. doi: 10.1111/j.1468-0432.2008.00400.x.

Kirby, E. L. & Buzzanell, P. M. (2014). Communicating work-life issues. In L. L. Putnam & D. K. Mumby (Eds.), *Sage handbook of organizational communication* (2nd ed., pp. 251–374). Thousand Oaks, CA: Sage.

Kirby, E. L. & Krone K. J. (2002). The policy exists but you can't really use it: Communication and the structuration of work/life policies. *Journal of Applied Communication Research, 30*, 50–77. doi: 10.1080/00909880216577.

Kirby, E. L., Golden, A. G., Medved, C. E., Jorgenson, J., & Buzzanell, P. M. (2003). An organizational communication challenge to the discourse of work and family research: From problematics to empowerment. *Communication Yearbook, 27,* 1–43.

Lucas, K. & Buzzanell, P. M. (2006). Employees "without families": Discourses of family as an external constraint to work–life balance. In L. H. Turner & R. West (Eds.), *The family communication sourcebook* (pp. 335–352). Thousand Oaks, CA: Sage.

Lucas-Thompson, R. G. & Goldberg, W. A. (2015). Gender ideology and work-family plans of the next generation. In M. J. Mills (Ed.), *Gender and the work-family experience: An intersection of two domains* (pp. 3–20). New York: Springer.

McClatchy, S. (2014). *Decide: Work smarter, reduce your stress, and lead by example.* Hoboken, NJ: Wiley.

McDonald, J. (2015). Organizational communication meets queer theory: Theorizing relations of "difference" differently. *Communication Theory, 25*(3), 310–329. doi: 10.1111/comt.12060.

Medved, C. E. (2016a). The new female breadwinner: Discursively doing and undoing gender relations. *Journal of Applied Communication Research, 44*(3), 1–20. doi: 10.1080/00909882.2016.1192286.

Medved, C. E. (2016b). Stay at home fathering as a feminist opportunity: Perpetuating, resisting, and transforming gender relations of caring and earning. *Journal of Family Communication, 16*(1), 16–31. doi: 10.1080/15267431.2015.1112800.

Meisenbach, R. J. (2010). The female breadwinner: Phenomenological experience and gender identity in work/family spaces. *Sex Roles, 62,* 2–19. doi: 10.1007/s11199-009-9714-5.

Mills, M. (2014). *Gender and the work-family experience: An intersection of two domains.* New York: Springer.

Mumby, D. K. (2012). *Organizational communication: A critical approach.* Thousand Oaks, CA: Sage.

Munn, S. L. & Greer, T. W. (2015). Beyond the "ideal" worker: Including men in work-family discussions. In M. J. Mills (Ed.), *Gender and the work-family experience: An intersection of two domains* (pp. 21–38). New York: Springer.

Rogers, L. E. (2006). Introduction: A reflective view on the development of family communication. In L. H. Turner & R. West (Eds.), *The family communication sourcebook* (pp. xv–xx). Thousand Oaks, CA: Sage.

Sutton, K. L. & Noe, R. A. (2005). Family-friendly programs and work–life integration: More myth than magic? In E. E. Kossek & S. J. Lambert (Eds.), *Work and life integration: Organizational, cultural, and individual perspectives* (pp. 151–169). Mahwah, NJ: Lawrence Erlbaum Associates Publishers.

Tracy, S. J. (2013). *Qualitative research methods: Collecting evidence, crafting analysis, communicating impact.* Hoboken, NJ: Wiley Blackwell.

Tracy, S. J. & Rivera, K. D. (2010). Endorsing equity and applauding stay-at-home moms: How male voices on work-life reveal aversive sexism and flickers of transformation. *Management Communication Quarterly, 24*(1), 3–43. doi: 10.1177/0893318909352248.

U.S. Bureau of Labor Statistics (2008). Women in the labor force: A databook (Report 1011). Retrieved from www.bls.gov/cps/wlf-databook-2008.pdf (accessed January 9, 2015).

van Manen, M. (1990). *Researching lived experience: Human science for an action sensitive pedagogy.* New York: University of New York Press.

van Manen, M. (2002). *Writing in the dark: Phenomenological studies in interpretive inquiry.* London, ON: Althouse.

Vulpo, M. (2016, May). Sarah Paulson thinks people should be able to love "whomever they f—king well please." *E News.* Retrieved from http://www.eonline.com/news/762039/sarah-paulson-thinks-people-should-be-able-to-love-whomever-you-f-king-well-please (accessed March 21, 2017).

Wayne, J. H., Grzywacz, J. G., Carlson, D. S., & Kacmar, K. M. (2007). Work–family facilitation: A theoretical explanation and model of primary antecedents and consequences. *Human Resources Management Review, 17*(1), 63–76. doi: 10.1016/j.hrmr.2007.01.002.

Woods, J. D. (1993). *The corporate closet: The professional lives of gay men in America.* New York: The Free Press.

1 Perceptions of Family

Before investing too much time considering non-traditional (or maybe newly traditional) family structures, it is important to consider what the traditional family looks like. When I think of the traditional family, I think of what might be described as "the old normal." The old normal takes us to the 1950s, when there was one television in the house, Sears Roebuck sold shiny new labor-saving devices, man and wife had clear familial roles, and abiding by those roles trumped any curiosity toward another life path. Siblings Billy and Suzie played baseball and doted over dolls (respectively, of course) while the household churned on as the substance of social and financial stability. And all of this visualization occurs in black and white, indicating that most if not all of what I assume to know about 1950s family came from the preserved television programming of that era.

Then there is the new normal. When thinking of the new normal, our minds might go to the mainstay of television shows such as *Modern Family* (2009–present), which depict gay/gay adoptive parenting, step-parenting, and an intergenerational relationship. Another sitcom, *Casual* (2015–present), disrupts the expected linearity of family development as a bachelor brother and divorced sister live, once again, under the same roof. Shows such as these are part of a sitcom trend (see also the short-lived yet aptly named *The New Normal* (2012–2013) and the also defunct *One Big Happy* (2015), which was about two best friends, a lesbian woman and a straight man, who decide to have a baby together).[1] Watching *Modern Family*, we might pat ourselves on the back for laughing at the mishaps of a gay couple as they go through the tribulations of raising an adopted child. Or we might think ourselves delightfully progressive for not tsk-tsk'ing at the age difference between Gloria and Jay.[2] The synopsis of *One Big Happy* gives us another sequence of events that asks us to accept a new family structure. Namely, we experience the inevitable calamity of a man living with two women, one carrying his child and the other his newly wedded wife. Is the trend of non-traditional family structures, within the situation comedy genre, an act of activism or easy comedy? Perhaps in the same way I only see the old traditional family archetype in black and white, these new programs are creating new portraits of the normal American family. This time, in color.

But surely television isn't our only means of reflecting on the American family as it is, or how it should be. Idealistic sloganeering of what it means to be a family and to espouse "family values" is a mainstay of American politics. "Family values" is something of a conceptual panacea, bandied about in politics with the logic that the sanctity and wellbeing of the family is not something a political opponent could disagree with. It also makes plain that the family—as a concept—is something to be defended. But I'm less concerned with what politicians have to say about family, as it all seems to be a smattering of generalities. Instead, it might be more useful to consider the political consequences of candidates' families. Following Hillary Clinton's announcement that she would run in the 2016 presidential election, Fox News political analyst Brit Hume provided a list of the candidate's strengths and weaknesses for running a campaign (Raw Story, 2015). In the first item in a list of "baggage" that won't work in Clinton's favor, Hume asks, "do Americans really want another four years of the Clintons and their weird marriage?" Now, rather than dismissing Hume's rhetorical question as a partisan slight, it would be more interesting to consider what might possibly make Hillary's marriage to Bill "weird." Is it because Hillary and Bill are a power couple? Is it because she chose not to divorce Bill following the scandal? (And now, with Donald Trump in the White House, we find ourselves watching to see what roles Trump's family members will play amid laws against nepotism within presidential administrations [Zarroli, 2017]). Though people had questioned inviting four to eight years of "The Clinton Dynasty," a "weird marriage" and a dynasty are two different phenomena. Would a "weird marriage" have gotten in the way of our "family values"?

In a distinct contrast to an objectionable marriage, 2004 Presidential Candidate Ralph Nader had the audacity to run as a single man. DePaulo (2006) points to Chris Matthews' interview with Nader on the political television program *Hardball*. In discussing whether incumbent George W. Bush was irresponsible, Matthews rationalizes that Bush "raised two daughters; he's had a happy marriage." And asks Nader, "Isn't he more mature in his lifestyle than you are?" Matthews continues, "you haven't exactly grown up and had a family and raised them and seen them off to college … He's had a happy marriage. Isn't that a sign of maturity that you haven't demonstrated?" (DePaulo, 2006, p. 127). Based on DePaulo's (2006) summary, it sounds like Nader held his own in the interview. But Matthews's seamless stitching of family and responsibility reflects a usually subtle assumption that those who form traditional family structures are somehow more capable people. Following this interview, we're left to feel that to be a capable leader (of the United States, at least), one must not only be familied but properly familied.

Clearly in the world(s) of media and politics, there are depictions of what a family is and what it should be. Is *Casual* indeed normal? Does being married and having a "non-weird" marriage instill a level of personhood indispensable if one is to run for president of the United States? What happens when we turn away from the mediated messages and simply look around? Is everyone being normal enough? And are those of us pushing the boundaries of what it means to have a family in some sort of precarious state of perpetual definition? This chapter surveys how we think about family by considering what the typical family looks like, examining academic and popular notions of family, and exploring how family is built and maintained in the workplace.

Kaleidoscopic Families

It is of no great surprise that the traditional family archetype is no longer the most common configuration. A married couple with one or more children in a male bread-winning family no longer characterizes the majority. In a briefing prepared for the Council on Contemporary Families, Cohen (2014) describes the movement away from the traditional family depiction as "an explosion of diversity, a fanning out from a compact center along many different pathways" (p. 1). By this he means that there is no one family structure taking a commanding lead as the neo-traditional norm. In the 1950s, 65 percent of children under the age of 15 lived with two, married, parents with the father as the head of the household and the mother out of the workforce (Cohen, 2014). Today, the most common family structure is the dual-earner household, yet only 34 percent of children under 15 live in such a household. Almost a quarter of children (23%) live with a single mother, another 22 percent live with married parents, and the remaining 21 percent live either with a single father, one or more grandparents, or no parents (Cohen, 2014). It is no longer possible to point to a "typical" family.

Of course, families need not be defined in relation to whether there are children present. Slightly over half of adults in the United States are unmarried (PBS, 2014). Additionally, 28.9 percent of women aged 30–34 are childfree (US Census, 2014). The significance of cohabitation and the importance of access to legal marriage for LGBTQ couples has been examined (Haas & Whitton, 2015). I'm sure there are numbers available for just about any family structure. But to claim to have an exhaustive set of numbers would delimit how family is defined. For example, I recently spent Mother's Day with my half-brother's half-brother, who isn't my biological brother (half or otherwise; it's kind of a riddle). Admittedly, I doubt there are statistics indicating how many other people did that.

As if the variety of family structures wasn't enough, it is important to consider the potential for individual families to change structures as the life course progresses. A simple consideration of what it means to get married, have children, or come to have stepchildren may render this statement obvious. But the propensity to change family structures, as opposed to stages in a given family trajectory, is a neo-traditional construct. Returning to the 1950s family archetype, you stick to what you're dealt. Women who grew disenchanted with their familial duties would be diagnosed mentally unstable and sometimes given shock treatment (Coontz, 2000). And while the move from courtship to engagement to marriage to kids may count as change, it pales in comparison to the varying family structures we might find ourselves in, now. People not only go from married to single, they go from being in opposite-sex relationships to same-sex relationships (and back again). Blood relatives may go away for long periods of time and then come back again, causing a long-term but nonetheless transient shift on one's family arrangement.

So what about young adults with eyes cast on starting a family? The diverse and transient nature of family leaves young adults with "no well-worn paths to follow" (Gerson, 2010, p. 7). But such clear paths may not be necessary, anyway. Kathleen Gerson (2010) interviewed 120 young women and men between the ages of 18 and 32 to understand how family upbringings influence perceptions of what a family should be. She presents the case that the current generation of young adults is more focused on how well their parents met the challenges of providing economic and emotional support than on what form their families took. For example, rather than seeking to determine whether it's "better" to grow up in a two-parent household, Gerson's participants generally considered the meaning and contexts of their parents' marital statuses. It was just as possible to be a happy child of divorce, or a discontented child of two married, biological parents. In short, it was more important to be happy than to be typical. And as we see more and more indications of the kaleidoscopic family, young adults may approach family formation with contentment, rather than structure, in mind.

This stance that family structure pales in comparison to contentment strikes a sharp contrast to the 1950s archetype, mentioned at the beginning of this chapter. While the kaleidoscopic family leaves us with no "right" path, the 1950s family was delightfully predictable. Well ... perhaps not *delightfully*. There are compelling arguments that this idyllic model family genre never existed in the first place (Coontz, 2000). To be sure, the 1950s was "a pro-family period if there ever was one" (Coontz, 2000, p. 24) and hailed as the most basic institution of society. But, as historian Stephanie Coontz explains in great detail in *The Way We Never Were*, the would-be idyllic 1950s family was far from perfect. Women were relegated to housework and thankless jobs,[3] while racism was rampant and largely unquestioned.[4] Furthermore, despite the postwar economic boom, 25 percent of Americans were poor—this in the midst of a hiatus in the food stamp program. Coontz said it best: "*Leave it to Beaver* was not a documentary." (p. 29).

Even though the traditional family archetype of the 1950s might not have been as steadfast as we would like to think, the notion of an idyllic family genre not only endures but provides a value-charged contrast to the unpredictable and unapologetic kaleidoscope of family structures. This tension can be seen in political messages propagating family values, everyday conversation (e.g., "when are the two of you going to get married?"), and, of particular importance to this book, within the workplace. But what attempts have been made to reconcile the varying ways that we might think of family? What happens when we try to define family?

Academic and Lay Notions of Family

How scholars choose to define "family" influences social assumptions of what can "count" as family (Floyd et al., 2006). Put another way, conceptualizations of family create parameters for research. In doing so, academic notions of family can inform clinical practice, shape policy and social justice activism, and serve as an indication of what is "normal." These notions are extended in a number of different ways including articles, books, TED Talks, and college curricula. With the expert power of defining family, scholars have the important responsibility of examining multiple family configurations. As Baxter et al. (2009) caution, "when the research community defines 'family' along traditional lines, this definition functions to marginalize our understanding of alternative family forms" (p. 186). Owing to the influential power of academic representation, and the liability of leaving some families in the dark, it makes sense that scholars would seek to develop broad and inclusive definitions.

And they do. Particularly in the family communication discipline, communication (as one might guess) is a foundational criterion. For example, Turner and West (2013) define family as

> a self-defined group of intimates who create and maintain themselves through their own interactions and their interactions with others; a family may include both voluntary and involuntary relationships; it creates both literal and symbolic internal and external boundaries; and it evolves through time.
>
> (p. 8)

This definition is nothing if not broad and inclusive. Baxter and Braithwaite (2006) define family more concisely as, "a social group of two or more persons, characterized by ongoing interdependence with long-term commitments that stem from blood law *or affection*" (emphasis added; p. 3). These definitions suggest that a family is a family if the family members say so. Or, perhaps, a family is a family if members communicate as a family. In addition to composing definitions, scholars also develop family types, accounting for family structure (e.g., stepfamily), conformity orientation (i.e., the extent to which family members feel they must emphasize similarity in attitudes, beliefs, and values), types of couples (e.g., unmarried cohabitating couple), etc. Though an exhaustive review of family typologies is beyond the scope of this book, Turner and West (2014) provide a summary of family types that have made a significant impact in shaping the way family communication scholars approach family research. At first blush, it's hard to see a problem with these definitions, especially if they do, indeed, provide endorsement to families whose status as a family might otherwise be doubted. But these definitions raise the question of what a family *isn't*.

A review of family communication literature points to three obstacles in employing a broad definition of family: First, there is a paradox in that "the broader the definition of family, the less distinctive the concept of family becomes" (Floyd et al., 2006, p. 37). Consider the possible criterion of in-dissolvability. Families are often regarded as involuntary and difficult, if not impossible, to dissolve (Afifi, 2006). Of course, families *can* dissolve insofar as couples can break up or divorce and elect to sever all ties, or siblings can become estranged. If we assert that families can be voluntary (as Turner and West [2014] do) how do we distinguish family from friendship? Are we choosing to pretend to be un-dissolvable? Or, considering Baxter and Braithwaite's (2006) stance that families require "ongoing interdependence," are we saying that a family is un-dissolvable until such time that it dissolves, and then it's not a family anymore?

A second challenge with broad definitions of family is that they are difficult to operationalize in research. As Whitchurch and Dickson (1999) and later Floyd et al. (2006) point out, even scholarship that begins with a broad conceptualization of family tends to revert back to traditional "opposite-sex spouses and children" assumptions when operationalizing the term. For example, gay and lesbian couples are often excluded from surveys generally intended to explore families (Allen et al., 2000). Furthermore, family of choice—while accounted for in the sample definitions provided above—has been omitted from family communication research (Braithwaite et al., 2010; Braithwaite & DiVerniero, 2014 are two exceptions). Despite a lineage of research that does not mirror the diversity accounted for in a broad and inclusive definition of family, scholars have begun to recognize the importance of exploring non-traditional family structures (Kurdek, 2004; Soliz, Ribarsky, Harrigan, Tye-Williams, 2010). For example, Kurdek (2004) examines how processes thought to constitute a "healthy relationship" (e.g., social support) extend across gay, lesbian, and straight couples, alike. It stands to reason that diverse family structures have a unique and important impact on the way we think about family—especially if they were sufficiently represented in family research.

Third, Floyd et al. (2006) warn that the degree of breadth used in these definitions risks ignoring socially engrained motivations for behavior. Consider common social arenas you've occupied: school, work, other work, etc. In each space, would you see a glowing endorsement of the idea that family is defined by communication? If you refer to your dog as your child—and (while acknowledging that you at no point gave birth to a Schnauzer) earnestly feel an enduring parental feeling toward the dog, do you think Sonia in the next cubicle, who has five kids, would agree? The necessity to at least nod to the limitations of existing social constellations of family can be found in Floyd et al. (2006), who provide three lenses through which to consider parameters of family: The *role lens* holds that relationships are familial insofar as partners feel and act like family. The *sociolegal lens* asserts that family is constituted by enactments of law and regulation. And the *biogenetic lens* focuses on the ability to successfully procreate. We aren't intended to choose a lens but rather acknowledge that each holds social influence. By accounting for the social positioning of each lens, we step away from the *we're family because we say we're family* stance mentioned above and acknowledge the implications of a *we're family if* you *say we're family* viewpoint.

Perhaps another way of considering the social influence in defining family is to consider institutionalization as a property of family, itself (White & Klein, 2014). Baxter and Braithwaite (2006) explain institutionalization as the idea that the family "is recognized as a legal institution and as such has normalized connections with other institutions such as schools, the workplace, and government agencies" (p. 2). So perhaps the strength of the communication-based definition of family is largely dependent on the willingness of those around us to communicate agreement. So, what are the odds of attaining such agreement, particularly with regard to a broad and inclusive definition of family? What do non-academics consider to be family?

Several studies have been conducted in the last quarter century that seek to illuminate what people, in general, consider to be family. In Sweden, Trost (1990) conducted a survey in which he developed 16 scenarios, each depicting a constellation of people, and asked participants to indicate whether the scenario involved a family. In this study, separated and divorced parents, and gay and lesbian couples did not count as family. But that was a long time ago. In 2009, Baxter et al. replicated the study, sampling predominantly white American females in their early twenties. Findings seemed to nod to traditional notions of family (e.g., a straight couple was more likely to be identified as family than a gay couple), however, defining family relied largely on the frequency with which the families were said to communicate with one another. These updated findings are important to the consideration of family definitions in that communication *helped* define family, yet a straight couple was more likely to be seen as a family than a gay couple. This points to another layer of complexity: In addition to the question of, *what is a family?* there may also be a question of *what family structures are more familial than others?* It is perhaps this disparity that illustrates the need to examine family as it is constructed in social arenas such as the workplace.

Defining family presents a paradox: scholars would do well to craft broad and inclusive definitions and research designs to match them. And yet, exceptionally broad definitions fail to account for the social construction of family and the challenges that occur when there is disagreement as to what counts as family. If laypersons perceive certain features of family (e.g., marriage) as being more important than others (e.g., mutual interests and goals), these features make for powerful symbolic resources when members go about the business of building family identity. The question, now, to consider is how the symbolic resource of family translates into privileged accommodations within the realm of work–family balance. In other words, do the broad definitions of family crafted by scholars, and the increasingly inclusive notions of family espoused by lay people, in general, extend to the work–family balance needs of the workplace?

Notions of Family Within Workplace Cultures

Most academic notions of family allow for some constructive license on the parts of the family members. Seeing as academic definitions of family both influence, and are influenced by, lay assumptions, it is important not only to consider popular definitions and hierarchical schemata (i.e., what families are *more family* than others), but also how these definitions and schemata occur in everyday interactions and decision-making. One could use White and Klein's (2014) language by asking how families come to be defined through institutionalization. Or rather, by asking what role the workplace plays in the construction of family. Here, we consider the capacity of the workplace to shape the meanings of family, the political implications of participating in the meaning-making process, and why employees might choose to excuse themselves from this process by keeping their family life private.

Most people *enact family* in the workplace. A simple Google search of the word *enact* yields two definitions: (a) to make a bill or other proposal into law, and (b) to act out, as on a stage. The former definition sounds brazenly optimistic for our purposes, as if family is defined through seamless fiat power. The second definition suggests that by enacting family, we're pretending. Is it a matter of practicing the latter definition until the former one—symbolically, at least—comes to fruition? Referencing the work of Karl Weick, Clark (2002) explains that enactment occurs when "an individual engages with an environment to organize it, make sense of it, and create possibilities for action within it" (p. 24). Enactment assumes that each person's environment includes both elements that are beyond the person's control as well as opportunities for choice. So, in defining family in the workplace, we can choose the extent to which we communicate family identity but we cannot control the extent to which communication successfully integrates family into the workplace culture. Weick (1979) would argue that we communicate the possibilities and constraints in our environment into being. This makes for a nice theoretical foundation to consider how the definitions and schemata of family are created and constrained in the workplace.

The idea of enacting our ideals in the workplace suggests that our communication holds influence. Fairhurst and Putnam (2004) delineate among three ways of thinking about organizations and communication[5]: First, an organization may be thought of as an entity separate from communication. In this sense, organizations contain communicated messages and those messages generally reflect the goals, norms, and overall culture of the workplace. Second, workplaces may be thought of as a "perpetual state of becoming" in that they are continually shaped by communication (Fairhurst & Putnam, 2004, p. 5). In this way, known as the relativist view, communication makes the organization. What we think of as "the workplace" is the sum total of communicatively constructed ideas, values, and realities. Third, organizations may be thought of as grounded in action and anchored in social practices and discourse. This perspective, known as the realist view, presents a social reality that is separate from its actors. Rather than choosing which perspective best suits our needs, Fairhurst and Putnam (2004) assure that discourse and organizations can be best understood by considering each perspective. With this in mind, let's see what happens when we apply the possibility of enacting family in the workplace, using these three perspectives.

With the first perspective, we walk into organizations with preexisting definitions of family. Family might be discussed and celebrated among employees, or it might be only rarely mentioned. Work–family balance policy may exist and employees choose whether they will use it. Simple enough. With the second perspective, "family" is based on the talk that occurs within the workplace. There might (or might not) be policies, but the worth and usability of these policies is based on what is communicated about them. Finally, the workplace might be a tapestry of preconceived notions about family. Communication may or may not add to the tapestry, depending largely on the clout of the people engaging in the conversations. Each perspective seems plausible in accounting for how family is defined in the workplace. But to what extent is talk about family an aspect of workplace communication?

Different workplace cultures have different acceptable scripts for non-work-related conversation. (A different way of looking at it would be to say that different scripts come together to form different workplace cultures.) Anyway, the existence of communication about family in the workplace is indicated in the interviews conducted for this project, as well as for a project preceding it (Dixon, 2011). Specifically, I asked participants to share with me popular topics of discussion that occur in the workplace, other than work itself. Many of the responses fed into stereotypes about the occupation the person belonged to. For example, a construction worker told me that his fellow workers would talk about attractive passers by. I guess I could have seen that coming. Several members of restaurant staff reported various discussions about dating and partying. But, it was explained to me, this sort of banter is confined to a certain, younger, age group. Though asking what people talk about at work yields a number of largely occupation-bound or employee-age-bound responses, the most common topic spanning age, occupation, and any other demographic is family.

People generally enjoy talking about family at work. As Andy, a 35-year-old musician from New York remarked about the people with whom he works, "we bond by talking about family." Indeed, several participants discussed, with happiness, the experience of talking about family at work. Referring to "border-crossers" as people who talk about work with family members, and/or talk about family to co-workers, Clark (2002) states that, "given the relative invisibility of a border-crosser's other-domain activities, conversation may be a primary way that their other-domain activities have importance and meaning" (p. 27). Clark (2002) found that communication about family at work (as well as communication about work while with family) results in greater work satisfaction, and higher satisfaction with family/home activities. Owing to Fairhurst and Putnam's (2004) three ways of linking communication and organizations, we might look at it as bringing our family stories to work with us to brighten someone's day, gain sympathy, relate to co-workers, etc. With this perspective, the organization is no different after our talk. Taking the relativist perspective, we might see our talk about family as a means of contributing to what family is (not to mention the level of disclosure that is acceptable in a workplace). Or, employing the realist perspective, we might see talk about family as something that occurs in relation to pre-existing systems of meaning about family. Let's focus on the latter two possibilities. Ideally, talking about family at work comes with at least two advantages: Affirmation and self-advocacy.

Affirmation serves to make us feel good about our familial station in life. From the relativist perspective, talking about family affirms family in that it creates the meaning of family. If you don't talk about your partner—according to this relativist bend—this person, and perhaps the possibility of his or her relationship with you, doesn't exist within the workplace setting. Relatives are relative. If you've been sharing stories about your now teenaged nieces since they were born, it's not likely to become weird. I mean, sure, all of the nice people could transfer out of your workplace and be replaced by a pack of niece-haters. But I don't see that happening. With the realist perspective, talk about family serves to affirm family in that it seeks to influence the broader social systems that dictate what (or, more accurately, *who*) family is and is not. One might think of it in terms of campaigning for acceptance into the aforementioned tapestry. If you're the only single person in your work area, the idea that your best friend is your family may take some discursive trailblazing.

In addition to talk about family serving as a means of affirming one's personal definition of family, it also serves as a means for self-advocacy. Whereas affirmation serves to contribute to communicative meaning-making in the present, self-advocacy attends to one's future (as well as present and ongoing) needs. When we talk about family, in the workplace, we humanize them. By talking about family, we are able to materialize our non-work lives. Relativists would think of this as a set of building blocks for work–family balance: To be in this work environment is to have an awareness of one another's non-work needs. Realists, on the other hand, might view self-advocacy as an occasionally (or maybe perpetually) futile attempt.

Very little is known about the material benefits of affirming one's family and advocating for family needs at work. Wayne, Musisca, and Fleeson (1999) examined ways in which work facilitates meeting family-related needs and vice versa. They define facilitation as, "occurring when participation in one role is made better or easier by virtue of participation in another role" (p. 109). It occurs when participation in one role leads to privileges, resources, security from failure, etc. Facilitation also occurs when social support in one area empowers another. The overall purpose of Wayne et al.'s (1999) study was to determine what personality characteristics (e.g., agreeableness) could predict whether family roles can facilitate work demands and whether work facilitates family life (as well as what characteristics instigate conflict). These considerations are beyond the scope of this book. However, the facilitative effects of talking about family at work are intriguing. The idea that workplace communication can facilitate work–family balance is essential to considerations of enacting family identity within the workplace. For example, if two co-workers develop a supportive working relationship that is founded on the shared experience of having twin boys, the experiences of one's home life have potentially nourished the workplace. Having this common dialog has made work more pleasurable. At the same time, talking about the boys affirms the experience of raising twins (not that it's generally contested[6]) and allows both employees to advocate for future twin-related work–family balance accommodation. Facilitation works both ways.

Thus far, I have suggested the potential for defining family in the workplace and the possibility for work–family balance benefits as a result of doing so. But we don't all talk about family at work. Furthermore, the idea that work–family balance is a matter of affirming our familial status and regularly advocating for ourselves is a gross oversimplification.

Josephine, a 33-year-old college admissions councilor, speaks to the intricacies of communicating family into being:

> I'm a very private person, but there were things I wanted to talk about in order to explain my time off. And they know I don't have children, they know that I don't have a spouse. You know I, I felt like I needed to tell them about my personal situation in life and all my family obligations in order to ... for them to allow me to take this time and for them to respect it. But it gets a little aggravating. You know, I feel like another co-worker, for example, everyone knows she's married and has a child, and all she has to say is something like, "oh, my son has a sore throat" and she doesn't have to divulge her family history to get her time off. She just has to say, "my son isn't feeling well," and they're like, "oh, okay, go home." And I have to go into the whole situation of my mom doesn't know how to drive and she has diabetes, and her blood sugar is low and my dad's working full time. You know, I have to give this life story of my own personal life and my family's trials and tribulations in order for them to be like, "oh, okay, take the day." And other people don't have to go into these long stories about why they need the day off. It's uncomfortable.

Josephine shares not only the uncomfortable amount of disclosure required to attempt to enact and affirm her family, but she also draws a comparison between herself and her co-worker, who she feels has a family narrative that is far more recognizable, and therefore, requires less discourse dependence (Galvin, 2006, 2014).

In addition to working adults, like Josephine, who have to discursively go the extra mile to communicate their families into being, some feel they are unable to communicate about family at all. For example, though some women relish the opportunity to talk about their children, they may feel reluctant to discuss motherhood at work for fear of being considered less committed to their careers (Farley-Lucas, 2000). Similarly, a gay employee may choose not to talk about his partner or child. This person may not be "in the closet" but rather have a general preference to not draw attention to his personal life. In these two examples, definitions of family are not disputed but rather muted. Finally, ambiguity as to whether talk about family is appropriate, or (unspoken?) rules that only seasoned co-workers can engage in such talk, can also make defining family at work all the more trying. There are so many different workplace cultures in the U.S. and around the world that it is impossible to describe, definitively, the political consequences of talking about family at work. Adding an additional layer of complication to the enactment process is the idea that attempts at affirmation and self-advocacy might be met with resistance.

Divergence

It is important to consider the potential for disagreement in workplace definitions of family. These disagreements may not be readily evident because they do not generally take the form of verbal arguments. Consider the previous example of a gay man who chooses not to talk about his husband: If the workplace climate suggests that having a same-sex partner is somehow less than having an opposite-sex partner, for many, the best course of action is no action at all. Most of us go our entire lives without seeing an argument over what counts as family (at work, at least), and yet disparities readily and pervasively exist.

Language Convergence/Meaning Divergence (LC/MD) is a useful theory for considering definitions of family as constructed by the workplace (Dougherty et al., 2008). When we hear the word *family*—be it in the workplace or anywhere else—we aren't likely to respond with "Ummm … what's that?" However, owing primarily to the realist notion of communication and organizing, individual definitions of family may clash with what LC/MD refers to as meaning clusters—a holistic description for a given concept or phenomenon. Other common meaning clusters might be "marriage," "success," or "conflict." These terms can mean different things to different people, yet we don't often take the time to explore potential disparities. Dixon and Dougherty (2014) found that in many workplaces, the dominant meaning cluster for *family* was that of opposite-sex spouses and children. Affirming one's family structure is an uphill—if not a Sisyphean—climb if meaning clusters do not account for said structure. It stands to reason that being left out of the dominant definition of having a family presents sizable challenges to work–family balance.

In addition to unearthing dominant family-related meaning clusters within organizations, Dixon and Dougherty (2014) found that employees whose families existed outside of the cluster did not count as family and/or did not qualify for family-grade accommodation. LGBTQ, single, and childfree employees are often expected to yield to the work–family balance needs of their traditional-familied counterparts. This is what happens when self-advocacy cannot occur. This yielding may not be apparent to employees who meet the traditional family meaning cluster. Workplaces that claim to value diversity may fall short when the needs of employees belonging to diverse family structures are overshadowed by the needs of those belonging to the "opposite-sex spouses and child(ren)" meaning cluster.

If we agree with Clark (2002) that talk about family at work gives families importance and meaning, then it makes sense that the inability (or even reluctance) to talk about family would give way to inequalities with regard to negotiating work–family balance. Though communication among co-workers is an important site for affirmation and self-advocacy, defining family at work gains even more complexity when considering the role of managers, and others who serve as "gatekeepers" to work–family balance accommodation.

Notions of Family and Managerial Perspectives

This chapter—and indeed this book—offers very broad definitions of family. Owing to the family communication scholars cited thus far, family is pretty much who we say it is. And the previous section established that when we are in spaces in which ideas of family may be different—like workplaces—we have the daunting task of enacting family. The process of enacting family can be difficult, if not virtually impossible, when our family is outside the accepted meaning cluster. Yet another factor to consider is the role of workplace leadership in refereeing the definition of family as well as gatekeeping work–family balance opportunities.

First-level managers as well as upper-level bosses, CEOs, and business owners make a significant impact on the organizational culture of work–family balance. Employees are less likely to intend to leave their organizations and are more likely to report higher organizational commitment if they perceive greater managerial support for work–family roles and if other employees also feel this support (O'Neill et al., 2009). In addition to appreciating managers who are supportive of family balance needs, employees also benefit from managers who serve as work–family balance role models. Psychologists Anna Koch and Carmen Binnewies (2015) use social learning theory to examine the positive effects of supervisors who role model healthy work–home balance practices. Their findings indicate that the role modeling power of supervisors plays a significant role in the overall work satisfaction of employees. As we will see in Chapter 2, employees may be less likely to take time off for fear of missing an opportunity for promotion (either actual or symbolic), or being seen as less than committed. Managers who use work–family balance policies may, in doing so, reassure employees that taking time off isn't a sign of non-commitment to one's work.

Managers also play an important role in communicating when (if ever) it is okay to use work–family balance policy. The usability of policy is contingent on the endorsement of senior management as well as the assurance that one will not be punished—either immediately or in the long term—for taking time off. Many employees feel that before they can use family balance policies, they must be assured that management agrees with the policies (Drew & Murtagh, 2005). Research indicates that management is not always forthright or consistent with regard to communicating acceptable or unacceptable reasons to put family before work (Kirby, 2000; Medved, 2004). For example, a manager might emphasize the importance of bracketing time away from work, and also emphasize meeting work deadlines to the neglect of other obligations (Kirby, 2000).

These mixed messages only gain ambiguity when there is a question as to whether specific reasons for taking time off are considered legitimate.

From our earliest school days, we are instilled with the distinction of excused and unexcused absences (Dixon & Liberman, 2015). Notions of acceptable and unacceptable reasons for taking time off from work vary by workplace and also by various members of management. In search of factors that might predict whether managers would grant work–family balance-related accommodation, Powell and Mainiero (1999) conducted a study in which they asked participants with managerial experience to respond to fictitious vignettes. In each scenario, employees request an alternative work arrangement (e.g., unpaid time off, working part time on Tuesdays, etc.). They found that requests were most likely to be honored if they (a) interfered minimally with the daily conduct of work; (b) if the requester is less skilled or currently working on a relatively unimportant task; (c) if requesters do not serve in supervisory roles; and (d) the reason for the request is considered short-term or to require less overall commitment. Though these findings are hardly generalizable to all workplaces, they do highlight the capacity for the giving and withholding of accommodation to be unjust.

Thus far, this section has veered slightly off course insofar as any employee, regardless of family structure must experience the workplace culture in relation to management's sensibilities and navigate mixed messages and other forms of ambiguity. However, conceptualizations of family become paramount when considering that negotiating work–family balance requires strategy. For example, Medved's (2004) research on the everyday routines of work–life balance unearths an instance in which a participant explains feeling the need to be evasive about why or for how long she is taking time off from work. This need to engage in strategic ambiguity is due to remarks, made by management, indicating that the amount of time taken is not necessary. In this instance, the participant explains needing to take time off from work to care for her one-year-old daughter, to which her boss replies, "we're very busy." Medved's example represents an aforementioned common constraint: Many women try to avoid pointing to parenthood when navigating work and family obligations for fear of being considered less than committed or less driven. So—consider the added layer of strategy that would go into taking time off to care for a family member who isn't considered family by those granting accommodation.

Perhaps the most telling means of determining whether management will honor work–family balance needs is to consider the personal family life that management espouses. Tracy and Rivera (2010) explored women's organizational challenges by talking to male managers and executives about gender roles and work–life balance. The authors interviewed 13 male "gatekeepers," each of whom held an upper-management position, was a CEO, or owned his own company. Coining the *privatization of work–life policy*, the authors found a strong connection between executives' personal preferences with regard to wives and children in the private sphere and general hesitancy toward progressive work–life policy and women's participation in the public sphere. In other words, most participants had stay-at-home wives and limited professional aspirations for their daughters, segueing to a limited understanding of the worth of work–family balance policy (Tracy & Rivera, 2010).

Tracy and Rivera (2010) discuss the potential for aversive sexism in which managers voice support for equal pay and treatment for men and women, and yet allow unequal treatment to occur in the workplace. An understanding of aversive behavior may best be established with a look at racism: Although some people think racism is a thing of the past,[7] aversive racism continues to operate within organizations without explicit or deliberate references to overt racism. This, in turn, affects the implementation and use of affirmative action policies including decisions about hiring, firing, and promotion. So, just as Tracy and Rivera (2010) uncovered aversive sexism, which is comparable to aversive racism (Dovidio & Gaertner, 2004), it is likely that this aversive behavior can be extended to notions of family. In other words, even though a manager might laud the importance of diversity in the workplace, this importance doesn't extend to the day-to-day needs of diverse employees.

The authors state that women may benefit from finding bosses whose spouses work and who envision their daughters or future daughters-in-law working. This makes sense. It also makes sense that working adults belonging to non-traditional families would benefit from having a boss of the same family make-up. For example, one could assume that LGBTQ working adults would benefit from bosses who are also LGBTQ—especially if said boss matched letters with the employee (e.g., both were transgender). But what are the odds of this happening, and who is in a position to be picky?

Managers, business owners, and other gatekeepers are central to the development of workplace cultures that foster work–family balance. Their function as role models as well as their capacity to be opinion-leaders carries significant weight in whether one's family structure gets to "count" as family in the workplace. Just as working moms may strategically choose not to point to parenthood as their reason for needing time off, so too might employees belonging to non-traditional families seek to avert attention away from the family they are trying to balance. This may be counter-intuitive when the goal—as stated earlier in this chapter—is to communicate family into being.

Conclusion

The normal family, as we now know it, is a kaleidoscope of structures, roles, and trajectories, with no predictable make-up and no clear message of what a family should be (Galvin, 2004). Family communication scholars provide broad definitions of family, with the hope of creating inroads in understanding the unique needs of varying family configurations. However, a paradox exists in which exceptionally broad definitions fail to establish a boundary demarcating family from other relationships. Lay notions of family are broadening as well, though the opposite-sex spouses and child(ren) endures as the structure most likely to be identified as family. Adopting the work of Karl Weik, we can make strides in enacting family in workplace settings, perhaps with one or more of Fairhurst and Putnam's notions of the relationship between communication and organization in mind. However, attempts at family affirmation and self-advocacy are challenged by divergent notions of what it means to have a family. Managers and other gatekeeping workplace members play an accentuated role in the processes of defining family and (dis)allowing accommodations. Furthermore, policy gatekeepers are often influenced by their own familial sensibilities, resulting in possibilities for aversive discrimination. The next chapter explores (post)modern workplace expectations that serve as the impetus for work–family balance challenges, particularly for employees whose enactment of family is challenged.

Notes

1 The non-traditionality thickens when the man impulsively marries a woman before learning that his lesbian friend has become pregnant, creating a comedic and unlikely triad.
2 I would be interested to see if we would be equally accepting of a much older, professionally successful, woman marrying a young, attractive, and financially dependent man.
3 Coontz (2000) also explains that by the mid-1950s, advertisers' surveys reported on a growing tendency among women to find "housework a medium of expression for … [their] femininity and individuality." In the same decade, when Redbook's editors asked readers to provide them with examples of "why young mothers feel trapped." They received 24,000 replies (Coontz, 2000, p. 37).
4 Some 10,000 African Americans worked at the Ford plant near Dearborn, MI, but they weren't allowed to live in Dearborn (Coontz, 2000; Shapiro, 1988).
5 Fairhurst and Putnam (2004) use the term discourse rather than communication. They distinguish between little-d discourse, which refers to the everyday talk and social practices and the big-D Discourse, which encompasses the general and enduring systems of thought. Big-D-Discourses are formed by constellations of talk, ideas, and modes of reasoning that make up the ways in which we make sense of things. Both phenomena are at play in this chapter's discussion of the role of communication within organizations.
6 Although it could be. As the next paragraph mentions, female employees sometimes feel the need to keep quiet about parenting responsibilities so as not to appear less than committed to work obligations (Farley-Lucas, 2000).
7 Owing to the recent wave of racial injustice, such as the incident in Ferguson, MO and the impending "Muslim Ban" (Wilkie, 2017), the population of people who think racism no longer occurs may be newly narrowed.

References

Afifi, A. L. (2006). Forward: Variations and challenges. In D. O. Braithwaite & L. A. Baxter (Eds.), *Engaging theories in family communication: Multiple perspectives* (pp. xi–xviii). Thousand Oaks, CA: Sage.

Allen, K. R., Fine, M. A., & Demo, D. H. (2000). An overview of family diversity: Controversies, questions, and values. In D. H. Demo, K. R. Allen, & M. A. Fine (Eds.), *Handbook of family diversity* (pp. 1–14). New York: Oxford University Press.

Baxter, L. A. & Braithwaite, D. O. (2006). Introduction: Metatheory and theory in family communication research. In D. O. Braithwaite and L. A. Baxter (Eds.), *Engaging theories in family communication: Multiple perspectives* (pp. 1–16). Thousand Oaks, CA: Sage.

Baxter, L. A., Henauw, C., Hulsman, D., Livesay, C. B., Norwood, K., Su, H., ... Young, B. (2009). Lay conceptions of "family": A replication and extension. *Journal of Communication and Family*, 9(3), 170–189. doi: 10.1080/15267430902963342.

Braithwaite, D. O. & DiVerniero, R. (2014). "He became like my other son": Discursively constructing voluntary kin. In L. A. Baxter (Eds.), *Remaking "family" communicatively* (pp. 175–192). New York: Peter Lang.

Braithwaite, D. O., Bach, B. W., Baxter, L. A., DiVerniero, R., Hammonds, J. R., Hosek, A. M., ... Wolf, B. M. (2010). Constructing family: A typology of voluntary kin. *Journal of Social and Personal Relationships*, 27, 388–407. doi: 10.1177/0265407510361615.

Clark, S. C. (2002). Communicating across the work/home border. *Community, Work, & Family*, 5(1), 23–47. doi: 1080/13668800020006802.

Cohen, P. (2014, September 14). Family diversity is the new normal for America's children: A briefing paper prepared for the Council on Contemporary Families.

Coontz, S. (2000). *The way we never were: American families and the nostalgia trap*. New York: Basic Books.

DePaulo, B. (2006). *Singled out: How singles are stereotyped, stigmatized, and ignored and still live happily ever after*. New York: St. Martin's Press.

Dixon, J. (2011). *Ambiguity, uncertainty, and othering: A queer phenomenology of the organizational socialization of sexuality* (Unpublished doctoral dissertation). University of Missouri, Columbia, MO.

Dixon, J. & Dougherty, D. S. (2014). A language convergence/meaning divergence analysis exploring how LGBTQ and single employees manage traditional family expectations in the workplace. *Journal of Applied Communication Research*, 42(1), 1–19. doi: 10.1080/00909882.2013.847275.

Dixon, J. & Liberman, C. J. (2015). Shedding light on dark structures constraining work/family balance: A structurational approach. In E. Gilchrist & S. Long (Eds.), *Contexts of the dark side of communication*. New York: Peter Lang.

Dougherty, D. S., Kramer, M. W., & Klatzke, S. R. (2008). Language convergence, meaning divergence: A meaning centered communication theory. *Communication Monographs*, 76(1), 20–46. doi: 10.1080/03637750802378799.

Dovidio, J. F. & Gaertner, S. L. (2004). Aversive racism. *Advances in Experimental Social Psychology*, 36(1), 1–52. doi: 10.1016/S0065-2601(04)36001-6.

Drew, E. & Murtagh, E. M. (2005). Work/life balance: Senior management champions or laggards? *Women in Management Review, 20*(4), 262–278. doi: 10.1108/09649420510599089.

Fairhurst, G. T. & Putnam, L. (2004). Organizations as discursive constructions. *Communication Theory, 14*(1), 5–26. doi: 10.1111/j.1468-2885.2004.tb00301.x.

Farley-Lucas, B. S. (2000). Communicating the (in)visibility of motherhood: Family talk and the ties to motherhood with/in the workplace. *Electronic Journal of Communication, 10*(3–4), 3–20. Retrieved from www.cios.org/www/ejcrec2.htm (accessed March 31, 2017).

Floyd, K., Mikkelson, A. C., & Judd, J. (2006). Defining the family through relationships. In L. H. Turner and R. West (Eds.), *The family communication sourcebook* (pp. 21–39). Thousand Oaks, CA: Sage.

Galvin, K. M. (2004). The family of the future: What do we face? In A. L. Vangelisti (Ed.), *Handbook of family communication* (pp. 675–697). Mahwah, NJ: Lawrence Erlbaum.

Galvin, K. M. (2006). Diversity's impact on defining the family: Discourse dependence and identity. In L. H. Turner & R. West (Eds.), *The family communication sourcebook* (pp. 3–20). Thousand Oaks, CA: Sage.

Galvin, K. M. (2014). Blood, law, and discourse: Constructing and managing family identity. In L. A. Baxter (Ed.), *Remaking "family" communicatively* (pp. 17–32). New York: Peter Lang.

Gerson, K. (2010). *The unfinished revolution: Coming of age in a new era of gender, work, and family.* New York: Oxford University Press.

Haas, S. M. & Whitton, S. W. (2015). The significance of living together and importance of marriage in same-sex couples. *Journal of Homosexuality, 62*(9), 1241–1263. doi.org/10.1080/00918369.2015.1037137.

Kirby, E. L. (2000). Should I do as you say or do as you do? Mixed messages about work and family. *Electronic Journal of Communication, 10*(3–4). Retrieved from www.cios.org/EJCPUBLIC/010/3/010313.html (accessed February 12, 2017).

Koch, A. R. & Binnewies, C. (2015). Setting a good example: Managers as work-life-friendly role models within the context of boundary management. *Journal of Occupational Health Psychology, 20*(1), 82–92. doi: 10.1037/a0037890.

Kurdek, L. A. (2004). Are gay and lesbian cohabiting couples *really* different from heterosexual couples? *Journal of Marriage and Family, 66*(4), 880–900. doi: 10.1111/j.0022-2445.2004.00060.x.

Medved, C. E. (2004). The everyday accomplishment of work and family: Exploring practical actions in daily routines. *Communication Studies, 55*(1), 128–145. doi: 10.1080/10510970409388609.

O'Neill, J. W., Harrison, M. M., Cleveland, J., Almeida, D., Stawski, R., & Crouter, A. C. (2009). Work-family climate, organizational commitment, and turnover: Multilevel contagion effects of leaders. *Journal of Vocational Behavior, 74*(1), 18–29. doi: 10.1016/j.jvb.2008.10.004.

PBS (2014, September 11). Single? So are the majority of U.S. adults. *PBS Newshour.* Retrieved from www.pbs.org/newshour/rundown/single-youre-not-alone/ (accessed April 10, 2016).

Powell, G. N. & Mainiero, L. A. (1999). Managerial decision making regarding alternative work arrangements. *Journal of Occupational and Organizational Psychology, 72*(1), 41–56. doi: 10.1348/096317999166482.

Raw Story. (2015, April 12). Brit Hume: Americans don't want Hillary Clinton's "weird marriage." Retrieved from www.youtube.com/watch?v=ZZU5WUW4 Vnc (accessed July 20, 2015).

Shapiro, H. (1988). *White violence and Black response: From Reconstruction to Montgomery.* Amherst: University of Massachusetts Press.

Soliz, J., Ribarsky, E., Harrigan, M. M., & Tye-Williams, S. (2010). Perceptions of communication with gay and lesbian family members. *Communication Quarterly*, 58(1), 77–95. doi: 10.1080/01463370903538622.

Tracy, S. J. & Rivera, K. D. (2010). Endorsing equity and applauding stay-at-home moms: How male voices on work-life reveal aversive sexism and flickers of transformation. *Management Communication Quarterly*, 24(1), 3–43. doi: 10.1177/0893318909352248.

Trost, J. (1990). Do we mean the same by the concept of family. *Communication Research*, 17(4), 431–443. doi: 10.1177/009365090017004002.

Turner, L. H. & West, R. L. (2013). *Perspectives on family communication* (4th ed.). Boston, MA: McGraw-Hill.

Turner, L. H. & West, R. L. (2014). The challenge of defining "family." In L. H. Turner & R. L. West (Eds.), *The Sage handbook of family communication* (pp. 10–25). Thousand Oaks, CA: Sage.

U.S. Census Bureau (2014). Fertility: Historical time series tables. Retrieved from www.census.gov/hhes/fertility/data/cps/historical.html (accessed July 10, 2016).

Wayne, J. H., Musisca, N., Fleeson, W. (2002). Considering the role of personality in the work-family experience. *Journal of Vocational Behavior*, 64(1), 108–130. doi: 10.1016/S0001-8791(03)00035-6.

Weick, K. (1979). *The social psychology of organizing* (2nd ed.). New York: McGraw-Hill.

Whitchurch, G. G. & Dickson, F. C. (1999). Family communication. In M. B. Sussman, S. K. Steinmetz, & G. W. Peterson (Eds.), *Handbook of marriage and family* (2nd ed.; pp. 687–704). New York: Springer.

White, J. M. & Klein, D. M. (2014). *Family theories* (4th ed.). Thousand Oaks, CA: Sage.

Wilkie, C. (2017, January 30). U.S. diplomats draft a "dissent memo" objecting to Trump's Muslim ban. *The Huffington Post.* Retrieved from www.huffington post.com/entry/us-diplomats-dissent-memo-trump_us_588f5901e4b08a 14f7e70b8e (accessed January 30, 2017).

Zarroli, J. (2017, January 5). Trump relatives' potential White House roles could test anti-nepotism law. *NPR.* Retrieved from www.npr.org/2017/01/ 05/508382236/trump-relatives-potential-white-house-roles-could-test-anti-nepotism-law (accessed March 31, 2017).

2 Ambiguous Expectations & Precarious Prospects

Just as family is a tricky concept to encapsulate, describing the experience of paid work in any reliable way is just as challenging. Work can be liberating, humiliating, validating, demanding, consuming... perhaps, for many, all the above. Work can be an orderly reprieve from an otherwise disorderly existence; work can be a soul-crushing detractor of one's quality of life. In addition to invoking a variety of feelings, work (or the lack thereof) is often a central feature of personal identity: When someone asks, "what do you do?," she's likely not inquiring of what errands you regularly run or your personal hygiene regimen. The centrality of work is probably never so salient as when one is out of work and fending off the stigma of chronic unemployment (Gist, 2016; Oberholzer-Gee, 2008). Among those fortunate enough to find work, some live for it—touting the highly recognizable title of "workaholic," while others see work as a designated set of hours in which they must suspend their existences in order to finance the lives they otherwise lead. Of course, these are two extremes. Work might even take the form of a calling, a designation that "situates work as the meaningful pursuit of a noble, transcendent goal" (Berkelaar & Buzzanell, 2015). Whatever our opinions might be of work, for those of us who rely on a wage, it dictates (or at the very least influences) how we distribute our time and attention.

Of course, a look at one's own work history will illustrate that not all work is the same. When I was eight, I walked a Dachshund named Remmington Steel for a quarter per stroll; at 22, I assistant-managed a regional office responsible for delivering the telephone book. A handful of other jobs helped finance the education that allowed me to become a college professor. Several participants I spoke with took me through their work histories, and explained the logistics of working two or more jobs at once. With some, it was particularly interesting to hear the distinction between jobs and callings. For example, Allison, 37-year-old dancer, choreographer, and teacher explained:

> This is a really new thing for me to be putting a punctuation mark on my work, and I think a lot of it also has to do with the fact that ... like, teaching dance is a job to me, and it's a job that I'm

invested in quite deeply, but it is also a job. Whereas being a dancer and being a choreographer and making my creative work, like that has always felt like more of a calling. So then I never thought about creating boundaries on that work.

Like many others, Allison juggles two sources of income, one of which carries a much greater significance to her and is a more engrained part of her identity. By remarking that she punctuates her work as a teacher—suggesting there are times in her week when she is a teacher and times when she isn't—Allison creates a point of contrast in which being a dancer and choreographer is a part of her identity that she carries all the time. Another participant, Paul, at 34, works as a bartender to ensure reliable income while pursuing his dream of selling his own line of clothing. Similar to Allison, Paul's two jobs served two very different purposes in his life. The former takes away from the latter, as Paul remarked, "a day job makes it really hard to balance my creative work," but was necessary to stay financially afloat. Several participants worked two or three jobs—each of which contributing to making ends meet. And some, like Allison and Paul, worked multiple jobs to provide financial stability while (to use a popular phrase among millennials) pursuing their "passions."

Because occupations vary widely, work is often categorized by the color of one's collar. As Mumby (2012) summarizes, "white-collar workers work with ideas and generate organizational knowledge; blue-collar workers do the work of actually making things; pink-collar workers provide the auxiliary support that greases the wheels of corporate enterprise." (p. 198). White-collar work is often associated with professionalism and doing brainwork, whereas, blue-collar work is more closely associated with the use of the body. Pink-collar work describes roles historically performed by women (hence the pink collar), and are generally thought to have lesser prospects for advancement than other "collar" work.

In addition to the varying types of work, it is interesting to consider how we negotiate the notion of being good workers. Though many of us resemble mechanical engineer, Fredrick Taylor's (1934) assumption that workers are motivated primarily by money, much of what motivates us to be dedicated employees goes beyond a paycheck. Douglas McGregor (1960) acknowledged this by delineating between two theories of management: Whereas Theory X affirms the idea that workers dislike work and are only motivated by wages, Theory Y, in part, acknowledges that workers experience motivation through achievement, itself. McGregor (1960) felt that influence, rather than coercion, was the superior management strategy. This assumption seems to have endured. In a study asking 200,000 employees from more than 500 organizations what motivates them to go the extra mile and "give 110%" at work,

money ranked #7 behind responses such as "camaraderie, peer motivation" (#1) and "feeling encouraged and recognized" (#3; Lipman, 2014).
Of course, the different types of work we balance motivate us differently. As will be discussed later in this chapter, we may pour ourselves
into work to maintain a personal brand of being *that person* who gets
things done. Branding ourselves as go-getters and successfully securing
brand recognition may take an immeasurable amount of our time and
be required to maintain employment. But for whatever might motivate
us to do work—camaraderie, money, self-actualization, etc.—it is more
important, for the understanding of work–family balance, to consider
what work demands of us.

Culture

A helpful way of thinking about the experience of work is to consider
the workplace as *being* a culture. Pacanowsky and O'Donnell-Trujillo's
(1982) foundational work on organizational culture emphasizes that
the purpose of examining culture is to "understand how organizational
life is accomplished communicatively" (p. 121). Just as we communicate
family identity into being, as argued in the previous chapter, we construct the broader workplace culture in much the same way. Culture is
conveyed through routines, policies, and procedures as well as through
everyday interactions, email exchanges, and stories that make their way
into institutional memory (Keyton, 2014). Despite the omnipresence of
workplace culture, we often can't see the proverbial forest for the trees.
   Many times we don't see the finer points of workplace culture until
we are presented with a basis for comparison (e.g., working two jobs).
Organization members generally don't talk explicitly about the culture
of where they work, but instead reinforce or disrupt culture through
communication (Keyton, 2014). One example of communicating workplace culture is by dressing in a certain way—perhaps "button down"
as opposed to "business casual." One's dress may reinforce culture by
following suit with what others are wearing, or it may disrupt culture
by subtly or explicitly violating spoken or unspoken standards. Another
example is placing a family photo on one's desk. Whether the photo
reinforces or disrupts an aspect of workplace culture depends on the
culture as it currently exists. Of course, the photo's cultural compliance
may depend largely on who, specifically, is in the photo.
   Importantly, the creation and maintenance of culture is far more
complex than a grouping of stakeholders who contribute evenly to the
workplace reality. Oftentimes, we can't simply communicate the change
we wish to see in the workplace. This can be due to power hierarchies
and/or a limited vision of cultural possibilities. Put another way, just
as communication shapes culture, we must also take into account the
ability of culture to shape communication, or for the two to be mutually

constitutive (Bisel, Messersmith, Keyton, 2014). Workplace members in positions of authority may limit communication; furthermore, the parameters of the existing culture may limit the changes we see as possible. For example, if Joel, from this book's opening vignette, worked in an office from Monday through Friday for the first ten of his working years, and he was surrounded by comic strip cutouts of Garfield professing his dislike for Mondays, and co-workers talking about counting days until the weekend, it's entirely plausible that Joel wouldn't question the necessity of the five-day work week. Similarly, if organizational leaders believed in the importance of five days of "face time," they likely would avoid broaching the feasibility of telecommuting.

In addition to being limited by power structures and by our own difficulty with seeing outside of cultural norms, culture can be contradictory and contrived. Martin (1992) distinguishes among three perspectives of organizational culture: The *integration perspective* assumes a single, overarching culture that stretches over the entirety of the workplace. Usually integrated culture is dictated, formally, through mission statements and company-wide email messages. The *differentiated perspective* accounts for various subcultures, within an organization, that don't resemble one another. Disparities in cultural norms between different divisions of the organization, different work shifts, etc., illustrate the differentiated perspective. Differentiated culture emerged several times in the interview data as participants explained taking time off from work as being acceptable to one division of the organization, but not another. Eliza, a 34-year-old sales representative, explains: "Within my sales group, when we know someone has something going on with their family, we help each other out a lot. It's beyond our sales group, management, is less sympathetic." Here, culture differentiates across management and employees. Though this was the most typical cultural disparity, the reverse, in which management is sympathetic to employees taking time off, but co-workers are skeptical, was also occasionally the case. Another example of the differentiated nature of culture can be found in the work of Kirby and Krone (2002), which highlights reasons why people would elect to not take time off of work, even if it is afforded to them by workplace policy. The policy, itself, would suggest a culture that is understanding of people's non-work obligations. However, interpersonal communication between co-workers and/or management may—either explicitly or implicitly—discourage taking time away, leaving us to wonder if taking the granted time away is unwise.

Both the integrated and differentiated perspectives assume a steadfast cultural landscape that spans across the organization (in the case of integrated culture), or at least across organizational divisions (in the case of the differentiated perspective). But what accounts for the culture that is always in flux? The *fragmented perspective* accounts for the capacity of culture to be ambiguous (Martin, 1992). Whereas the differentiated perspective accounts for differing cultural sensibilities across different areas within the organization, the fragmented perspective considers contradictory messages that come from a single source. For example, management may tout an "open door policy" for employees to voice concerns and yet employees occasionally feel that the metaphorical door is shut and locked. Another example would be a workplace that expresses a commitment to diversity, but consistently hires new employees that reinforce a homogenous group.

Finally, it is important to consider the capacity of culture to be contrived (Ross, 2003). In any given workplace, we might find a performance of culture that isn't genuinely felt by the actual performers. The performance of the "Wal-Mart cheer" (Ehrenreich, 2011, p. 178) comes to mind as a timeless example. Wal-Mart employees likely aren't filled with glee whenever they join in; and yet, a meeting full of chanters suggests a happy (or, at very least, willfully compliant) workplace culture. Another example is the attendance of workplace-sponsored social events. Workers may not feel comfortable attending the events, perhaps feeling the pressure to bring a "plus one," thus outing one's sexual orientation, relationship status, etc. (Dixon, 2013). Rather than simply not going, and thereby helping to construct a culture of ill-attended social functions, the employee may feel pressured to attend to demonstrate devotion to the workplace. A particularly humorous example of a contrived workplace culture comes from Ross's (2003) study of the now-defunct tech company Razorfish. One employee shared the experience of being asked to function as one of several ringers, tasked to instigate pseudo-spontaneous office fun, such as "spontaneously" cutting pictures out of magazines and gluing them to the wall. I suppose this was intended to make employees feel creative, weird, avante- garde (and productive?).

Understanding what is expected of us in the workplace requires an understanding of workplace culture. Though all organization members create culture, it is far from a seamless and democratic co-creation. As this chapter will illustrate, a brief look at the history of managerial styles in the U.S. reveals our arrival at workplace cultures that are largely fragmented. This chapter will argue that the norms and expectations of workplaces are difficult to navigate, not necessarily because of an ushering in of a new era of workplace cultures (although that is a part of it), but because old and new ideals co-exist in many workplace environments despite their largely contradictory expectations of organization members. For example, telecommuting fosters a workplace culture that blurs boundaries of what it means to be "at work," however being physically present (putting in "face time") remains a highly valued notion in many workplaces (Bailyn, 2006). This presents ambiguity as workers allowed to work from home are left to wonder whether the time away will inadvertently convey a lack of interest in work. To illustrate the contradictory nature of workplace culture, this chapter will provide a brief examination of the history of workplace management in the United States, and focus on the implications of technology, and work teams. Though most of this chapter considers the cultural expectations of workplaces on employees—therefore holding the assumption that all paid work connotes steady and reliable employment—this chapter will also examine the rise and implications of precarious work. Finally, the ambiguous expectations and precarious prospects of work are considered in relation to affirming and advocating for diverse family needs.

Workplace Standards and Expectations

Work, in the United States, began with farming and the establishment of cottage industries.[1] Though a thick description of agrarian culture is outside the purpose of this chapter, it is intriguing to consider how the Industrial Revolution stole workers away from their properties and into larger cities where factories were being built. Semblances of the systems of management developed at the very beginning of *going* to work are still found in today's workplace.

Modernist Work

The Industrial Revolution brought about entrepreneurial innovation and factory labor, as well as questions of how workers should be managed. In 1911, mechanical engineer, Fredrick Taylor, wrote a book prescribing the scientific method for workplace efficiency (that was even intended to extend into the household). Concern for efficiency might best be remembered through Henry Ford, who emerged in U.S. history as an emblem of the Modern Age of what it means to work. Perhaps best known for the implementation of an assembly line, by the end of 1913, the Ford factory churned out a Model T every 10 seconds (Snow, 2013). Efficiency experts, following Taylor's lead, assumed workers to be purely self-interested and with limited needs (Ross, 2003). But Ford's workers found the production line largely demoralizing. Tasks were so simplified that it was often felt they could be completed by a small child (Snow, 2013). Additionally, the monotony of the job weighed heavily on workers. As it has been explained, "[t]he man who places a part does not fasten it—the part may not be fully in place until after several operations later. The man who puts on a nut does not tighten it" (Snow, 2013, p. 206). Coping with the general discontentment, Ford managers had to hire 963 workers to ensure that 100 would stick around (Snow, 2013).

As indicated at the beginning of this chapter, employees are motivated through means that extend beyond—and in many instances replace—a decent wage. This notion was highlighted as a byproduct of the Hawthorne studies, conducted in 1924–1932, in which workers in an electrical factory outside Chicago were more productive when lights were made brighter as well as when they were made dimmer. The take-home message was that workers worked harder when they felt interest was being shown to them and their quality of life (Mumby, 2012). Since then, management specialists have built a science of manipulating workplace cultures through means of signaling care for the welfare of the employee, including providing opportunities that are free of nepotism and other forms of unjust favoritism.

One particularly recognizable administrative system to come from the lineage of Fordist or Modernist workplace ideals is bureaucracy—system of rules, hierarchies, and record-keeping intended to support the functioning of large and complex organizations. (If you've ever signed up for college courses, set foot in a Department of Motor Vehicles, or hurried through the paperwork at an urgent care facility, you have experienced the tedium of bureaucracy.) A glowing improvement on its feudalist predecessor, bureaucracy was theoretically intended to support consistency and fairness within the workplace: if you are allowed three days of sick leave per year, the availability of this benefit is at least somewhat reliable. However, bureaucracy has a reputation for being paradoxically counterproductive. For example, a professional consultant may miss out on cultivating new clients because the quarterly report is past due. Similarly, the time and energy that goes into conducting college assessments may take away from the individual attention promised to students that could, depending on its area of focus, give the assessment more positive results. Processes, such as reports and protocols, that restrain employees from doing their jobs to the best of their abilities leaves workplace members experiencing what sociologist Max Weber and Hans Heinrich Gerth (1958) termed the "iron cage" of bureaucracy.

Though the average 21st-century nine-to-five job isn't quite as tedious as turning a nut 90 degrees clockwise all day long, expectations of workers that began as a cultural norm of the Ford Motor Company can now be found in the jobs we go to and aspire for. Informing the exploration of work expectations in relation to work–family balance, many of these modernist influences focus on the time employees are expected to dedicate to work, and the space they are expected to occupy. For example, the modernist workspace requires a distinct physical space in which work is completed. Depicted using the metaphor of a container (Deetz, 2001), the modernist workplace is comprised of physical boundaries. Phrases such as "leave your personal issues at the door" aptly depict modernist workplace culture. Modernist notions also have a lasting influence on our notion of work and time. The modernist workplace includes distinct working hours. It might even be open to flextime arrangements in which an employee leaves work everyday at 4:00 p.m., but arrives at 7:00 a.m., to make up the time. As companies grow, these expectations are exacted through bureaucratic features such as clocking in, completing reports that account for time spent, etc.

Much of what we think of as work gives primacy to efficiency, and functions through disciplined notions of time and space. Though it is of no surprise that most of my participants went to work at a specified location and worked for designated hours, their depictions of work obligations were rarely limited to what occurs in the time spent in the container. For example, despite being required to clock in and out, Samantha, 34-year-old clinical social worker, explains how work obligations seep outside the designated work hours. She explains,

> We have patients who come in and it's the last appointment of the day and they're either suicidal or homicidal, and we have to decide if we're going to send them to the hospital or not, there've definitely been times where I needed to be somewhere, and I have to cancel because of a crisis.

In addition to patients who need her time and attention outside of her scheduled working hours, Samantha also must manage the emotions from work that inevitably permeate her non-work life. She explained, that with practice, she had developed the ability to compartmentalize work-related emotions. Yet the necessity for this skillset speaks to the limitations of modernist notions of time- and space-bound work. Indeed, the modernist work environment, while influential, does not aptly describe how most people experience work. Workplace obligations may be blurred by the emergence of postmodernist work.

Postmodernist Work

Postmodernist work has implications both for what it means to complete work tasks, specifically, as well as what it means to be employed, more generally. The latter will be discussed later in this chapter. In contrast to its predecessor, postmodernist work can be thought of as an unclenching of time and space: Working does not require being physically "at work" and can be completed (deadlines not withstanding) at a pace dictated by the employee. A postmodernist workplace might be described using the metaphor of a performance (Deetz, 2001) in that the workplace is anywhere in which work is enacted.

Amid postmodernist/post-Fordist characteristics is a blurring of work life and non-work life. As Mumby (2012) explains "[m]any distinctions between work and other aspects of our lives have been subtly and not-so-subtly eroded by the post-Fordist work environment" (p. 187). Examples of this integration include on-site gyms, daycare centers, and medical facilities. Featuring free nap pods and professional massages on one's birthday, the offices of Google have become an almost belabored example of the postmodernist integration of work and play (Stewart, 2013). Zappos has a ball pool in the human resources department of their Las Vegas headquarters (Noguchi, 2015)—perhaps curtailing workplace burnout by contriving a workplace culture that promotes childlike fun. But is this integration a benefit for workers or a muddling of worker expectation? ("Both" is a viable answer.)

Productivity-based notions of work seem ideal for working adults seeking to integrate work and family obligations (e.g., working on a project from home while intermittently checking in on an elderly parent). However, even when presented with the opportunity to integrate work and family obligations, lingering modernist sensibilities make this a risky choice in many organizations. Specifically, many workplaces conflate productivity with commitment, which results in "transform[ing] an instrumental, contractual relationship into an open-ended moral bond" (Bailyn, 2006, p. 70). So, even when invited to work from home (a postmodernist opportunity), there is no guarantee that the time away from the workplace won't signal a lack of productivity (a modernist assumption). Workplace uses of technology as well as the trend toward teamwork serve as rich contexts for considering uncertain, (post)modernist, workplace expectations.

Technology

It has become almost cliché to remark on the integration of technology into our everyday lives. However, in proper postmodernist fashion, technology has changed when and where we do work. Many of these changes are perceived to be for the better. In Golden's (2013) study of how information and communication technologies mediate work–family balance, she explains that "[e]mployees framed the movement of work across the work-life boundary as not only unproblematic but as enhancing their control over the conditions work [sic], making the completion of tasks 'easier,' more 'convenient,' and 'efficient'" (p. 111). Certainly many feel the affordances of technology in relation to time management. Email, alone, has cut back on the necessity of in-person meetings. However, amid the feelings of ease, convenience, and efficiency exist ambiguity regarding work expectations. For example, to what extent does having the technologically facilitated opportunity to work outside of designated work hours obligate one to do so?

Understanding work expectations in relation to the accelerated integration of technology into our work lives may best be understood by turning, once again, to Bailyn's argument that workplaces tend to conflate productivity and commitment. Productivity can be easily demonstrated: you are given a task, and you complete it in a timely manner. Commitment, on the other hand, is more difficult to demonstrate. Instead of allowing productivity to speak for itself, we often feel compelled to show commitment as well. For example, one might elect not to put an "away" message on his email when he goes on vacation, to avoid being identified as "away" from his work obligations. Perhaps the best example for consideration is telecommuting. Telecommuting "occurs when workers rely on technology to transfer finished products from locations away from company headquarters ..." (Hylmö & Buzzanell, 2002). Many studies about telecommuting include employees contending with assumed or actual skepticism as to whether telecommuters are actually working. As one participant in Gregg's (2011) study of work–life integration explained,

> I think that if I'm working from home, unless I reply instantly, they'll think I'm baking a chocolate cake, or at the coffee shop or something. So I find myself replying really quickly, partly because ... I'm conscious that if I don't, then it may be perceived that I am slacking off somehow.
>
> (p. 42)

Here, this participant astutely encapsulates the uncertainty of postmodernist work as goaded by modernist notions of being present, "at work," at designated, expected times.

In addition to performing commitment by making one's self unequivocally available through technological means, demonstrating workplace commitment also comes in the form of one's online presence and branding acumen. Whether work-related or personal, technology can be used to store identities. Sometimes these stored identities serve to perform workplace commitment. Will the employee who uses Facebook to record work accomplishments be measured against the employee who uses it to document leisure time? Unless one's privacy settings are manipulated accordingly, there is really no way of knowing where the communication of work commitment begins or ends.

As we may be left guessing the extent to which work expectations extend to our online identities, technology also prompts a remarking of the boundary line between work and non-work activities. As actress and producer Rashida Jones commented in the July 2015, issue of *Wired*,

> [t]he tricky part is that everything is located in the same little place: Work, pleasure, distraction, misbehaving, responding, wasting time, buying, selling, dreaming, focusing ... all options live together, and I can float from one to another with no effort.
>
> (p. 70)

Jones touches on the mixed blessing of having everything together: it's convenient, but it also fails to draw boundaries on when the work ends. Bailyn (2006) uses the term *absorptiveness* to describe the effect of the subtotal of emotional, cognitive involvements in the workplace. We may cope with this feeling of always being there (i.e., at work) by refining schemas of what it means to work and acceptable work boundaries. For example, one of Gregg's (2011) participants felt that attending to work email didn't count as work. Similarly, when I was a graduate student, it was inevitable that I take my work home with me. For a time, I had the self-imposed rule that I would never take my work to bed with me. This changed when I began receiving email on my cellphone. As odd as it feels to admit, I would wake up in the night, check my email, and, if the question could be answered with brevity (e.g., "it is on the syllabus"), reply. Countless other examples exist of rethinking work and pushing boundaries of where work may occur because the ability to perform commitment to one's work (and, perhaps, the expectation) is immediate.

As Kirby et al. (2013) explain, "[t]echnologies can be both exploitative and empowering—exploitative in 'intruding' across 'boundaries' of home and work yet empowering in allowing workers to increased control over where and when they do their work" (p. 383). The modernist pull to "clock in" (even if only figuratively) as a means of demonstrating commitment has us performing work through the postmodernist affordance of technology in some almost deleterious ways—for example, feeling that little to no delay in replying to work email is acceptable. Another source of ambiguity regarding workplace expectations is the growing popularity of teamwork.

Teamwork

As mentioned above, postmodernist workspaces are characterized, in part, by the rules and values of a workplace being defined by groups, rather than a single authority figure. This can be seen in the flattening of the hierarchy at Zappos.com, in which CEO Tony Hsieh announced that the company would take the form of a *holacracy* in which employees run ideas and problems by group members or "circles," instead of any sort of managerial figure (Noguchi, 2015). At first blush, this would seem like an ideal structure for navigating work–family balance: Rather than appealing to a boss, one simply approaches one's peers. However, research suggests that group-based power tends to circle back to the bureaucratic authoritative model it sought to eliminate.

This phenomenon has been articulated by the influential work of James Barker (1993). Barker's (1993) ethnographic examination of an organization's[2] transition from bureaucratic to self-managing teams resulted in the emergence of a phenomenon known as *concertive control*. Through concertive control, rules and values become manifest through the collaborative interactions of organization members. Therefore, rather than attempting to appease a single authority figure, employees must appease a group of equals. The problematic side of concertive control became exceptionally clear when teams gained new team members: Rather than re-constructing rules and values, the older members sought to socialize new members to the rules and values as they currently occurred. What was once a loose system of rules became tightly unequivocal. A prominent example to appear in Barker's research was the team's response to lateness. As Barker (1993) explained:

> A team member who came in five minutes or more late would be charged with an "occurrence" and considered to be absent for the whole day. If a worker accumulated four occurrences a month, the team facilitator would place a written warning in that person's company file. A person who came in less than five minutes late received a "tardy," and seven tardies equaled one occurrence.
>
> (p. 430)

There was a chart, publicly displayed, which served to keep track of everyone's punctuality-related infractions. It bears emphasizing that the conceptualization of "occurrences" developed as a result of teamwork among equals, within a workplace culture prescribed as an alternative to bureaucracy.

Barker concludes that concertive control, exercised through team-based management, creates a paradox in which the bars of bureaucracy's aforementioned iron cage are invisible yet stronger than ever. The implications for work–family balance are considerable. In Barker's report, he relayed a story of a co-worker who made arrangements with her group members to bend the rules because one of her children was sick. Some time later, she was joking in celebration of having an "occurrence" removed (apparently they get erased with punctual behavior, over time), saying that now that her occurrence is gone, she can get another one. The next day, she had to stay home with her sick child. The group was unsympathetic.

More recent discussions of teamwork also present reason for skepticism. Gregg (2011) describes teamwork as "mythically egalitarian," asserting that "the team becomes hegemonic in the office culture due to its effectiveness in erasing the power hierarchies and differential entitlements that clearly remain in large organizations" (p. 74). Concertive control emerged in my interview data largely in the form of awareness of who is taking time away from work and speculation as to whether the stated reason might differ from the actual one. As Ben, a 45-year-old college professor stated, "if you're attentive, you'll hear every reason why somebody's gone." That is to say, when someone takes time away from work, co-workers take time to speculate why. Though, in this example, work colleagues don't decide whether someone can take time away from work, they can, however, invoke team-like concertive control by creating a culture of awareness and speculation.[3] Rather than eliminating the iron cage of bureaucracy, the concertive control of teamwork may simply add fortifications. Thus far, this chapter has explored the precarity of work expectations with the assumption that work, in and of itself, is guaranteed. However, a prominent characteristic of postmodernism is the precarious nature of work itself (Mumby, 2012).

Precarious Work

As I began to interview organization members for this project, I quickly noticed that, more often than not, participants were in jobs that they described as either temporary or with limited guarantee of future employment. Candace, a 46-year-old public school teacher, spoke of hoping to be assigned a class for the fall (the interview took place less than a month prior to the start of the new school year). She shared with me one instance in which she was given a teaching assignment the day before the start of the semester. Another participant, a 61-year-old cab driver named Julio, explained that making a profit depended on the ability to pick up enough fares to cover the cost of gas and car rental. Of course, it makes sense that the employment of independent contractors hinges on the ability to contract work. However, I was surprised by the sheer variety of occupations that can work under this structure. But perhaps my feeling of surprise was ill-founded: Whereas the modernist companies sought to cultivate life-long employees, in a postmodernist workplace, people are far less likely to go to work for a single company and stay with said company until retirement. In some cases, people immerse themselves in a given profession, grow tired of it, and go on to something else. In her working years, my mother was a pilot and, some years later, an accountant. In other instances, people change jobs because their work is task or project-bound rather than institution-bound (hence the population of independent contractors). And in other cases, people change jobs because they have no choice.

This status of an uncertain work future has been recognized as its own genre of employment. The precariat, "applies to workers in all segments of the workforce who find themselves in extremely precarious economic environments and are constantly under threat of losing their jobs, which are often 'outsourced' to other companies in other countries" (Mumby, 2012, p. 182). Furthermore, precarity is described as a decline in attachment to employers, increased long-term unemployment, growth in perceived job insecurity, growth in non-standard work arrangements and contingent work. Precarious work has always existed, but only since the 1970s has it crystallized as an important concern (Kalleberg, 2009).

Precarious work often means ambiguity regarding work identity and the extent to which the organization, with which someone is loosely affiliated, will accommodate basic needs that full-time workers take for granted. Consider Uber drivers: In a 2015 article in *The New Yorker*, titled "Gigs with Benefits," James Surowiecki considers whether Uber drivers are Uber employees or independent contractors. According to Surowiecki, Uber sets the prices, monitors performance (via passenger ratings), and can terminate employment. Uber also takes 20 percent of the total earnings. There are no Uber supervisors (Ubervisors?) to tell employees when to drive or for how long. Terms such as "flexpoitation" and "dispensability in exchange for flexibility" (Ross, 2008) mark the inherent disadvantage of precarious work. Of course, the price of flexibility is a lack of benefits and guaranteed company support (e.g., in the event a driver is sued). Surowiecki seeks to remedy the precarious nature of Uber, calling for "a third legal category of workers, who would be subject to certain regulations, and whose employers would be responsible for some costs (like, say, reimbursement of expenses and workers' compensation) but not others (like Social Security and Medicare Taxes)" (p. 31).

Precarity can also be found in many sectors of what Florida (2012) terms the Creative Class. The difference between the Creative Class and other classes are what its members are paid to do: "Members of the Working Class and the Service Class are primarily paid to do routine, mostly physical work, whereas those in the Creative Class are paid to use their minds—the full scope of their cognitive and social skills" (p. 9). Creative work is precarious insofar as one's work relies on one's capacity to be creative, and so, creative workplaces establish cultures with fostering creativity in mind. "Schedules, rules, and dress codes have become more flexible to cater to how the creative process works" (Florida, 2012, p. 7). While places like Google offer benefits, lifting the seasoned employee out of the "precarious" designation, many Creatives working independently in jobs, such as video production and fiction writing, rely unequivocally on their own creativity. The autonomy required of the creative class has been labeled "no-collar" work (Ross, 2008).

The creative class, producing "no-collar" work can seem like a sexy, untethered, frontier in which creative impulses are the vehicle of one's worklife. (Florida [2012] tells a story of a young man going from working at PricewaterhouseCoopers to arranging flowers for a living.) However, this autonomy comes at a price: the burden of constantly proving responsibility. Opportunities to obtain and maintain one's job skills to keep up with changing job requirements are also precarious. Many workers are hard pressed to identify ways of remaining employable in fast-changing economic environments in which skills quickly become obsolete (Kalleberg, 2009). As Ross (2003) explains, "[w]hereas persons of leisure had once enjoyed the highest social status, now it [is] prestigious to be too busy" (p. 44). Just as one's future employment is precarious, so is any notion of how much no-collar work is enough.

Work–Family Balance

This chapter has considered the ambiguity of workplace culture, styles of management, and the roles that technology and teamwork lend to the reality of what it means to work. The precarity of work lends to the landscape in that we often don't have the luxury of voicing our concerns when we feel work expectations have become unacceptable. Though work–family balance has been mentioned, here and there, throughout this chapter, this final section draws additional connections between what it means to navigate work expectations while striving to affirm and advocate for family needs.

Affirming and advocating for family needs may disrupt workplace culture, especially if one's family doesn't match commonly recognized structures. Interviews, overall, indicated that employees feel more comfortable talking about family at work if someone else with a similar structure has paved the way. For example, several lesbian, gay, and bisexual participants rationalized their ability to talk about their partners, based on whether there were other LGB people in their workplace. This makes sense as the previous employee (or whomever had the burden of being the first) set the cultural change in motion. Of course workplace leaders, as well as our own limitations of what we see as culturally possible, can limit the prospect of cultural change. Just like Joel who never thought to question the five-day workweek, it may not occur to us that affirming and advocating for family is possible. Many participants, especially those belonging to a family of choice, spoke of keeping the topic of their families away from workplace conversation without indicating that a cultural shift was possible.[4]

The culture of affirming and advocating for family needs may depend on the collar of one's occupation. Work–family balance research focuses largely on white-collar workplaces (see Bochantin & Cowan, 2016; Cowan & Bochantin, 2011 as notable exceptions). Within blue-collar work, leeway in regard to work–family balance can, sometimes, depend on skill level. Highly skilled blue-collar workers, such as construction workers may have more agency in negotiating work hours, whereas unskilled laborers, such as janitors, may abide by more stringent expectations (Bochantin & Cowan, 2016). Some assumptions about social class would have us believe that blue-collar work environments, and by extension the people inhabiting them, lack the communication skills to affirm and advocate for family. In her psychology blog, Grasher (2014) explains that in traversing from a blue-collar household to a white-collar professional, she had to learn the art of small talk. Similarly, Lubrano (2004) dramatizes blue-collar communication norms as being at either one extreme (stoic) or another (emotion-filled). The supposed lack of discursive nuance would suggest that blue-collar cultures are a den of stand-offs and impasses. But actually, Bochantin and Cowan (2016) found that blue-collar workers employ a number of proactive strategies in making requests to help balance work and family, including making factual appeals and approaching a request with honesty.[5] These tactics were similar if not identical to common tactics used by white-collar workers (Medved, 2004). This suggests that, though communication codes may vary by collar, the tactics for affirming and advocating for family within these cultures are largely the same.

Though workplace cultures do vary from one organization to the next, navigating workplace cultures gains complexity in that they are rarely the predictably integrated set of opportunities and customs that mission statements and policies would have us believe. Fragmented cultures within workplaces can render affirmation and advocacy tricky, because it's difficult to predict how communication about family will be received. Even an aspect of culture that is assumed to be steadfastly integrated—such as the benefits afforded by the Family and Medical Leave Act (FMLA)—can more aptly serve as an example of differentiated culture resulting from confusing paperwork and unanswered requests for help in understanding the policy. Culture is also differentiated when a policy affords certain benefits but communication within the organization says otherwise. Eliza provided an excellent example of this disparity that came to light on account of her husband being out of town, for work, the majority of the time:

> My company is a larger company so we have a lot of health benefit packages and we have a lot of personal days that we can take. However, being in sales and having customers, it's challenging to … [pause] There's an understanding that it needs to be serious to have a personal day. So to say, "my husband is coming into town and I want to see him" wouldn't qualify, to the managers, as a high priority.

Here, we see a differentiated culture in that even though Eliza is allowed, through an allotment of personal days, to take time off to see her husband when he is in town, managers don't believe this is a viable reason to be away. Affirming and advocating for a family dynamic in which she only occasionally sees her spouse runs counter to the cultural "understanding" Eliza describes.

Cultural fragmentation can be instigated by any number of factors. Perhaps a co-worker was found fraudulent in her reasons for taking time away from an overall trusting workplace culture, causing a temporary cultural shift that now includes vigilance and skepticism. In addition to the possibility of a fragmented culture, the potential for culture to be contrived can complicate the ability to bring the topic of diverse family structures into the workplace. Many participants discussed workplace cultures in which the supposed integrated valuing of diversity didn't extend to daily cultural enactments. For example, diversity programs are at times only in place as rhetorical devices or as means for protecting the company from litigation (Dobbins, 2009). Participants shared stories of accepting jobs, in part, because of indications that the organization has a commitment to a diverse workforce, only to find this "commitment" to be empty.

The often-ambiguous workplace cultural sensibilities of affirming and advocating for family needs are further complicated by the mixed messages of modernist and postmodernist work expectations. The modernist workplace expects work and family to exist in two segmented spheres. We might be allowed a framed picture, but overall, affirmation of family is thought unprofessional, and perhaps even inefficient. The postmodernist workplace, in contrast, allows for integration of family. Technology can be used to affirm and advocate for our families in non-obtrusive ways. For example, several participants discussed not coming out of the closet at work but rather allowing the information to be available on a Facebook page. We might also indirectly introduce our family members to our colleagues by virtue of posting pictures and updates that serve to humanize them. However, technology can also encroach on what was once unequivocally work-free space. Natalie, 32-year-old customer service representative, explained the experience of taking time off to care for her ailing mother:

> It wasn't that I didn't have the paid time off to cover it because, I did, but there was a lot of guilt tripping that happened. Even at that time I was basically on call because I had the company laptop and I could work from the hospital or from my mom's house.

Even though Natalie used time off that was afforded to her, she was still available to her company, bringing the company laptop to the hospital where her mother was staying. Interestingly, even though Natalie was available to work from a remote location (a postmodernist norm), she was nonetheless "guilted" for being physically away from the workplace (a modernist expectation). And though Natalie was not part of a work team, it was her co-workers who were resentful of her time away. In addition to the competing demands of (post)modernist expectations, employees also must factor in the often precarious nature of work itself.

The precarity of work has many implications for one's ability to affirm and advocate for family needs. Whereas modernist workplaces include a sense of commitment on the part of the employer, precarious work—by definition—comes with no guarantees. We may not have the luxury to take a stand for our diverse family accommodation needs, but at the same time, moving on to the next gig is all part of the profession. Adam, a 30-year-old software developer, explained,

A: About two years ago, I was doing a lot of independent contracting a lot of 6-month, 4-month ... I did a job that was 6 weeks and this happened right at the time that [my mother's] health started to decline and I was taking a lot of time off and because it was a contract job, there was no PTO [paid time off] or anything ... They actually didn't want to deal with it at all and let me go because of all the time I was taking off to take care of her. And it wasn't even that unreasonable.

J: So there wasn't any policy you could rely on?

A: No, as a contract worker, I was dime a dozen.

In Adam's situation, he had no recourse for being fired. The only solace was in the fact that finding other contracts was a regular part of his job.

With regard to "no-collar" work, the ability to dictate one's own hours may be helpful in tending to family needs. However, the uncertainty regarding how much work is enough can lead workers to put work before family, with no real certainty that this is necessary. Also, the social support afforded to full-time workers may be missing in the life of the precariat, no-collar worker. Finally, it is important to consider the emotional strain of not having job security. Nourishing one's family needs (e.g., beginning a college fund, building a 401k, etc.) is difficult without the support of organizational affiliation.

Of course, precarious work might serve as a safe haven for adults whose family lives are patently stigmatized. For example, in an interview with a transgender construction worker, who was living in the rural Midwest, he explained to me that independent contractor gigs were ideal for him, because people did what they were commissioned to do and rarely asked questions. Though the solution of hiding one's personal identity through the transient nature of precarious work is counter-intuitive to the purpose of this book, Bill's experience does speak to the capacity of precarious work to liberate employees from potentially damaging workplace cultures.

Conclusion

"As the composition of the paid workforce continues to change, men and women are rearranging what used to be a rigid distribution of wage, work, and family responsibilities in traditional families" (Kirby et al., 2003, pp. 1–2). How responsibilities should be arranged to ensure work–family balance is fraught with ambiguity. Work was an encompassing aspect of my participants' lives, sometimes even precluding the experience of family life. As Allison explained,

> Performances are when performances are and we would be traveling all over the world, you know, and you can't jump home, you know, from your tour to Berlin to do something. But it was really, like, I missed some of like my best friends' weddings. My grandfather died, you know, I missed my grandmother's funeral. [I missed] a lot of things that had been significant markers in my life. I was at work.

Allison discussed missing out on "significant markers" in her life on account of her work as a dancer. Some participants found their dedication to work to have a point of diminishing returns. As Paul pithily remarked, "sometimes you just have to be a person," meaning sometimes family and personal needs have to come before work.

The present chapter added complexity to the prospect of affirming and advocating diverse family needs by illustrating the various workplace cultures within which communication about family may or may not be welcomed. The modernist notions of work occurring in distinct segments of time and space mingle with postmodernist notions that work can be done anytime and anywhere. Working adults attempting to balance work and family are often left uncertain of how much dedication to the workplace is enough. Cultural emblems such as the use of technology and the formation of supposedly egalitarian work teams can further muddle expectation. The precarious nature of work may liberate us from the notion that the harder we work the better people we are. But, at the same time, precarity can render us unable to take risks in affirming and advocating for our work–family balance needs.

Amid ambiguous expectations and precarious prospects, working adults belonging to diverse family structures face unique constraints in balancing their work and family obligations. The next four chapters explore family structure as an element of diversity and propose ways of shifting constraints to opportunities.

Notes

1 A cottage industry is a system of production in which goods are manufactured exclusively out of one's home (Merriam-Webster, 2016).
2 The organization under study manufactured circuit boards for the telecommunication industry.
3 This isn't to suggest that speculation is inherently ill-founded. If someone has been found to be dipping into a pool of sick leave that is shared by everyone, it makes sense that speculation with regard to future leaves would result.
4 Given that family of choice is the "poster child" for discourse dependence (see Chapter 6; Braithwaite & DiVerniero, 2014, p. 175), it is likely that very few workplaces are cultures that embrace family of choice conceptually, let alone as worthy of work–family balance accommodation.
5 Participants also demonstrated reactionary tactics, such as ultimatums. White-collar practices, such as evasion, were also reported (Medved, 2004).

References

Bailyn, L. (2006). *Breaking the mold: Redesigning work for productive and satisfying lives* (2nd ed.). Ithaca, NY: Cornell University Press.
Barker, J. R. (1993). Tightening the iron cage: Concertive control in self-managing teams. *Administrative Science Quarterly, 38*(3), 408–437. doi: 10.2307/2393374.

Berkelaar, B. L. & Buzzanell, P. M. (2015). Bait and switch or double-edged sword? The (sometimes) failed promises of calling. *Human Relations*, 68(1), 157–178. doi: 10.1177/0018726714526265.

Bisel, R. S., Messersmith, A. S., Keyton, J. (2010). Understanding organizational culture and communication through a gyroscope metaphor. *Journal of Management Education*, 34(3), 342–366. doi: 10.1177/1052562909340879.

Bochantin, J. E. & Cowan, R. L. (2016). Acting and reacting work/life accommodation and blue-collar workers. *International Journal of Business Communication*, 53(3), 306–325. doi: 10.1177/2329488414525457.

Braithwaite, D. O. & DiVerniero, R. (2014). "He became like my other son": Discursively constructing voluntary kin. In L. A. Baxter (Eds.), *Remaking "family" communicatively* (pp. 175–192). New York: Peter Lang.

Cowan, R. L. & Bochantin, J. E. (2011). Blue-collar employees' work/life metaphors: Tough similarities, imbalance, separation, and opposition. *Qualitative Research Reports in Communication*, 12(1), 19–26. doi: 10.1080/17459435. 2011.601521.

Deetz, S. (2001). Conceptual foundations. In F. M. Jablin and L. L. Putnam (Eds.), *The new handbook of organizational communication* (pp. 47–77). Thousand Oaks, CA: Sage.

Dixon, J. (2013). Uneasy recreation: Workplace social events as problematic sites for communicating sexual orientation. *Florida Communication Journal*, 41, 63–38.

Dobbins, F. (2009). *Inventing equal opportunity*. Princeton, NJ: Princeton University Press.

Ehrenreich, B. (2011). *Nickeled and dimed: On (not) getting by in America*. New York: Henry Holt. (Original work published 2001).

Florida, R. (2012). *The rise of the creative class. Revised.* New York: Basic Books.

Gist, A. (2016). Challenging assumptions underlying the metamorphosis phase: Ethnographic analysis of metamorphosis within an unemployment organization. *Qualitative Research Reports in Communication*, 17(1), 15–26. doi: 10. 1080/17459435.2015.1088891.

Golden, A. G. (2013). The structuration of information and communication technologies and work-life interrelationships: Shared organizational and family rules and resources and implications for work in a high-technology organization. *Communication Monographs*, 80(1), 101–123. doi: 10.1080/ 03637751.2012.739702.

Grasher, E. (2014). Blue collar roots vs. white collar reality. *Psych Central*. Retrieved from http://psychcentral.com/blog/archives/2014/10/18/blue-collar-roots-vs-white-collar-reality/ (accessed August 3, 2016).

Gregg, M. (2011). *Work's intimacy*. Malden, MA: Polity.

Hylmö, A. & Buzzanell, P. (2002). Telecommuting as viewed through cultural lenses: An empirical investigation of the discourses of utopia, identity, and mystery. *Communication Monographs*, 69(4), 329–356. doi: 10.1080/0363 7750216547.

Jones, R. (2015). All work & all play with Rashida Jones. *Wired*. Retrieved from www.wired.com/video/2015/06/wired-issue-preview-june-2015-all-work-all-play-with-rashida-jones/ (accessed July 20, 2015).

Kalleberg, A. L. (2009). Precarious work, insecure workers: Employment relations in transition. *American Sociological Review, 74*(1), 1–22. doi: 10.1177/000312240907400101.

Keyton, J. (2014). Communication, organizational culture, and organizational climate. In B. Schneider & K. M. Barbara (Eds.), *The Oxford handbook of organizational climate and culture* (pp. 118–135). New York: Oxford University Press.

Kirby, E. L. & Krone K. J. (2002). The policy exists but you can't really use it: Communication and the structuration of work/life policies. *Journal of Applied Communication Research, 30*, 50–77. doi: 10.1080/00909880216577.

Kirby, E. L., Golden, A. G., Medved, C. E., Jorgenson, J., & Buzzanell, P. M. (2003). An organizational communication challenge to the discourse of work and family research: From problematics to empowerment. *Communication Yearbook, 27*, 1–43.

Kirby, E. L., Wielend, S. M. B., & McBride, C. M. (2013). Work-life conflict. In J. G. Oetzel & S. Ting-Toomey (Eds.), *The Sage handbook of conflict communication: Integrating theory, research, and practice* (pp. 377–402). Thousand Oaks, CA: Sage.

Lipman, V. (2014, November 4). New study answers: What motivates employees to "go the extra mile?" *Forbes*, Retrieved from www.forbes.com/sites/victorlipman/2014/11/04/what-motivates-employees-to-go-the-extra-mile-study-offers-surprising-answer/3/#2d7e31c75e8b (accessed July 20, 2015).

Lubrano, A. (2004). *Limbo: Blue-collar roots, white-collar dreams.* Hoboken, NJ: John Wiley.

Martin, J. (1992). *Cultures in organizations: Three perspectives.* New York: Oxford University Press.

McGregor, D. (1960). *The human side of enterprise.* New York: McGraw-Hill.

Medved, C. E. (2004). The everyday accomplishment of work and family: Exploring practical actions in daily routines. *Communication Studies, 55*(1), 128–145. doi: 10.1080/10510970409388609.

Merriam-Webster (2016). *Merriam-Webster learners dictionary.* Retrieved from www.merriam-webster.com/dictionary/cottage%20industry (accessed July 20, 2015).

Mumby, D. K. (2012). *Organizational communication: A critical approach.* Thousand Oaks, CA: Sage.

Noguchi, Y. (2015, July 21). Zappos: A workplace where no one and everyone is the boss. *National Public Radio.* Retrieved from www.npr.org/2015/07/21/421148128/zappos-a-workplace-where-no-one-and-everyone-is-the-boss (accessed August 1, 2015).

Oberholzer-Gee, F. (2008). Nonemployment stigma as relational herding: A field experiment. *Journal of Economic Behavior & Organization, 65*(1), 30–40. doi: 10.1016/j.jebo.2004.05.008.

Pacanowsky, M. E. & O'Donnell-Trujillo, N. (1982). Communication and organizational cultures. *Western Journal of Speech Communication, 46*(2), 115–130. doi: 10.1080/10570318209374072.

Ross, A. (2003). *No-collar: The humane workplace and its hidden costs.* New York: Basic Books.

Ross, A. (2008). The new geography of work: Power to the precarious? *Theory, Culture & Society, 25*(7–8). doi: 10.1177/0263276408097795.

Snow, R. (2013). *I invented the modern age: The rise of Henry Ford.* New York: Scribner.

Stewart, J. B. (2013, March 15). Looking for a lesson in Google's perks. *New York Times.* Retrieved from www.nytimes.com/2013/03/16/business/at-google-a-place-to-work-and-play.html?_r=0 (accessed July 20, 2015).

Surowiecki, J. (2015, July 6 & 13). Gigs with benefits. *The New Yorker.* Retrieved from www.newyorker.com/magazine/2015/07/06/gigs-with-benefits (accessed March 31, 2017).

Taylor, F. W. (1934). *The principles of scientific management.* New York, NY: Harper. (Original work published 1911).

Weber, M. & Gerth, H. H. (1958). *From Max Weber: Essays in sociology.* New York: Oxford University Press.

3 Balancing a Lingering Compulsion

Every once in a while, Lisa brings her two kids to work. They usually play with toys and make little fuss. Though some workplaces would consider this unprofessional, Leslie assumes that Lisa is given some leeway among her colleagues because she is a single mom with limited support from the children's father. Even though she has no children of her own, it makes Leslie happy to be in a place that is understanding of employees' personal responsibilities.

Leslie's attitude shifts as she recalls the conflict between Maria and Jeremy in which Maria wanted time off to attend a school play and Jeremy needed the same afternoon free to pick up his sister from the airport. Leslie remembers Maria's concerns of missing out on seeing her children grow up. Jeremy relented, booked a car service for his sister, and worked the shift.

***

In a powerful moment in season four of the Netflix series, *House of Cards* (Willimon, 2016), the first lady of the United States, Clair Underwood, is casually conversing with Hannah Conway, the wife of the mayor of New York. The Conways are staying in the White House as the Underwoods' guests, amid an overseas hostage situation that the president and governor work to amend. The Conways have with them their two young children. It is clear, almost humorous, that having children in the White House is jarring to the first lady. Within a casual conversation, Hannah asks Clair if she regrets not having children. Though Clair is unflustered by the question, she clearly finds it unexpected. Hannah apologizes, saying "I'm sorry, that's too personal." Clair then flatly inquires, "Do you regret having them?"

The question is further punctuated by an abrupt ending to the scene. The exchange between Hannah and Clair begins in a typical fashion. Here we have two women, capable of bonding through the mutual experience of being the wives of politicians, but with a fissure between them over the topic of children. Hannah's question borders on invasive because, to many, no pleasant rationale can be made to account for being childless. Clair's question is scathing because it is virtually unthinkable.

Granted, there are likely long nights or financial setbacks that leave new moms and dads wondering, "what was I thinking?" but these times of frustration likely don't extend to long-standing regret.

As apparent in the scene with two fictional first ladies, talk of children is a common social script in U.S. society. Interestingly, despite the prominence of spouses and children as topics of conversation, a large segment of the population has only one or neither. Fifty-two percent of the adult population is single and 47.6 percent of women between the ages of 16 and 44 do not have children (Bureau of Labor Statistics, 2014; Daly, 2014). With the increasing number of single and/or childfree (henceforth "Sa/oCf") adults comes an increase in Sa/oCf members of the workforce (Steuber, 2014). Despite the prevalence of Sa/oCf adults, there exists a lingering compulsion: a narrative trajectory that favors coupling and parenting. Whether one marries and has children, or not, the traditional "spouses and child[ren]" structure is the yardstick against which families are measured. Many are confronted by the lingering compulsion in subtle (and occasionally not so subtle) ways: friends fixing up friends on blind dates; mothers and aunts expressing concerns about ticking clocks and impending infertility. One's immersion in, or deviation from, the traditional family structure is a highly personal aspect of one's life. Yet the compulsory narrative extends to the workplace and, for many, stands in the way of work–family balance.

When considering the prevalence of Sa/oCf adults juxtaposed with the lingering compulsion toward coupling and childrearing, one can see the potential for a harmful conflation of acceptance and equality. An employee may be Sa/oCf without feeling marginalized but, as this chapter's opening vignette illustrates, when resources are scarce, accommodation often goes to the employee who has followed the expected familial course. But a vignette carries little weight in demonstrating a need for organizational justice for Sa/oCf adults. This chapter explores the lingering compulsion toward marriage and parenting, considers how this compulsion extends to the attempt at balancing work and family, and proposes the employment of an existing framework (Casper et al., 2007) to locate opportunities for affirming and advocating for the needs of Sa/oCf working adults.

The Lingering Compulsion

The lingering compulsion toward marriage is emboldened by stereotypes of what *kinds* of people get married, versus those who stay single.[1] For example, DePaulo (2006) discusses the myth that marriage "transforms the immature single person into a mature spouse" (p. 13). Older singles who have had plenty of time to find a lasting relationship and somehow managed to miss the mark are considered the "most infantile singles of them all" (DePaulo, 2006, p. 113). Other stereotypes position married people as friendlier, more attractive, more generous, and more reliable (Morris et al., 2008; Casper & DePaulo, 2012), while singles were seen as lonely, shy, insecure, flirtatious and unhappy (Casper & DePaulo, 2012; DePaulo, 2011).

Perhaps the most scathing stereotype of singles is that they are undesirable and that there is something inherently wrong with them that prompts this undesirability (Morris, 2005). When asked to scale the assumed happiness of singles and married people on a scale of 1–9, married people received a 7.9 while singles received a 3.9 (Morris et al., 2008). In actuality, the only condition in which married people are happier than single people is when they are measured specifically against singles who were previously married (Morris et al., 2008). Interestingly, this assumption that married adults are happier than singles holds true even when said singles are depicted as having many close friends, or achieving professional, financial, and altruistic success (Morris, 2005). Amid these less than complimentary attributions, single adults were also assumed to be more career-oriented—a stereotype that holds serious implications for work–family balance, as explained later in this chapter.

Research has considered attributions of marriage at the intersection of gender (e.g., the working married man versus the working married woman; Jordan & Zitek, 2012) and context for single status (e.g., widowed vs. never married; DePaulo, 2006), but consideration of age highlights the pervasive quality of singlism. Morris et al. (2008) found that singles of all ages are viewed more negatively than coupled individuals, and while older singles are viewed more negatively than younger singles, college-age singles are viewed more negatively than their coupled counterparts. These attributions suggest a dominant perspective that becoming coupled (and married when age-appropriate) is the key to happiness and the unquestionable life trajectory.

In addition to the attribution of generally positive stereotypes, marriage carries with it privilege unrealized by unwed couples (e.g., social security benefits), including achieving a highly recognized milestone in adulthood. The internet is full of "confessions" of wedding days that weren't the best day of the bride or groom's (but primarily the bride's) lives (e.g. Weddingbee, n.d.), suggesting that it generally is and is supposed to be. The amount of money spent on weddings also suggests a certain transcendent life event is taking place. Domestic Partnership is a sort of "half married" or "marriage-light" set up in which some rights may be granted (e.g., health insurance benefits) but others are not (e.g., worker's compensation death benefits).[2] Unwed, cohabitating couples toe the discursive line insofar as they are pursuing a committed, assumed monogamous relationship and, perhaps, rehearsing for the married life to which they aspire.

A cohabitating couple with no intention of ever getting married may have trouble communicating this decision. Coontz (2006) explains that,

> fifty years ago, if a couple decided to live together outside of marriage, they were choosing an unconventional course that pigeon-holed them into a tiny and suspect segment of the population. Their lives would be much less stable than those who followed accepted rules.
>
> (p. 296)

Though unwed cohabitation is broadly accepted in the US, and has increased by 900 percent in these last 50 years (Kuperberg, 2014a), pockets of disapproval of those of us "living in sin" nonetheless exist (e.g., Stanley, 2014), and may have a dominant presence in a given workplace. Part of this disapproval may come from assumptions that cohabitating couples are inherently unstable. It's long been a dominant, and puzzling, bit of public knowledge that cohabitating couples are more likely to separate than couples that moved in together upon marriage. This, however, isn't true. In fact, the greater determinant of relational longevity/success is the age at which couples move in together—the older one is, the greater the likelihood of cohabited success (Kuperberg, 2014b). Discrimination against cohabitating couples may present something of a confirmation bias for those who feel that unwed cohabitation is a disreputable relationship status: In an intriguing comparison between satisfaction levels of unmarried and married cohabitating couples in Italy, Pirani and Vignoli (2016) found that the "cohabitation gap" or the reported decrease in satisfaction for unwed cohabitants, weakened as communities developed more accepting attitudes of unwed cohabitation.

Likewise, thoroughly single individuals may face problems establishing themselves as grounded, mature, etc. Questions such as *are you seeing anyone?* and *are you planning to marry?* suggest that the person's life is likely in flux and that they are in need of an outlet to explain themselves or to solicit help in finding a spouse. This invasiveness, to be sure, rarely goes in the other direction (imagine asking a married co-worker, *Are you happy in your marriage or was it all a giant mistake?*).

The lingering compulsion toward marriage also suggests a linearity that simply does not exist for many working adults. "Happily ever after" (or even "functionally ever after") is often disrupted by relational disillusionments such as separation, divorce, or the (untimely) death of a partner. For many, this means constructing an identity and advocating for work–family balance needs from the standpoint of being re-single.

Divorce has always been available in the United States, initially tolerable only in the cases of adultery or desertion (Cherlin, 2009). In the 1800s, Indiana and later the Dakotas and Arkansas liberalized their divorce laws, rendering each state a veritable "divorce mill" (Cherlin, 2009, p. 227). Even in these states, divorce was largely perceived as "not a right, only a remedy for a wrong" (Hartog, 2000, p. 84). This changed with the "no-fault" divorce, which began in California in 1969 (Cherlin, 2009). The last quarter of the 20th century brought about more of an emphasis on the individual and on personal growth. Cherlin (2009) explains that by this point in American history, someone who is unhappy in marriage is virtually, if not explicitly, expected to divorce.

But there are at least three reasons to speculate that the acceptance of divorce is on the decline: First, the divorce rate is actually lower than the oft-cited 50 percent (Luscombe, 2010). The 50 percent myth may endure because, as Luscombe (2010) explains, "it's something of a political Swiss Army Knife, handy for a number of agendas. Social conservatives use it to call for more marriage-friendly policies, while liberals find it handy to press for funding for programs that help single moms" (n.d.). About 70 percent of marriages that took place in the 1990s reached their 15-year anniversary, up from the 60 percent of those who married in the 1980s (Paul, 2011; Wong, 2014). People wed in the 2000s are even more likely to reach the 15-year mark (Wong, 2014). It's worth considering whether the lowering divorce rates result in reduced social support for those who are divorced or going through a divorce, due to a possible dearth of fellow divorcees in one's social circle. Second, seeing as divorce was at an all-time high in the 1980s (Paul, 2011) children of divorce may approach marriage with elevated caution. Consider the saying that begins, "fool me once, shame on you ...," the *once* occurring in childhood. Finally, maintaining a marriage is thought to be part of a list of things one does as a stereotypically well-adjusted person (akin to recycling, eating local, exercising, etc.; Paul, 2011). Whereas divorce was at one time shunned for being ungodly, perhaps it is now stigmatized for being imperfect.

But how is social support for the divorced individual conveyed in the workplace? Can the depiction of the responsible and successful employee withstand divorce? There isn't a lot of research about how divorce impacts work (however, there is research on the impact of work on divorce; McKinnish, 2007). Working adults who are divorced may maintain their marital respectability in the workplace because they *attempted to* settle down. Conversely, divorce may be seen as a mark of failure. One may fail to comply with the lingering compulsion toward marriage but may receive partial credit for being a parent.

What to Expect When People Expect You to be Expecting

Having children rounds out the creation of the traditional family. The lingering compulsion is propelled by *pronatalism*, or "a value which encourages reproduction and exalts the role of parenthood" (Jamison et al., 1979, p. 266). Pronatalist leanings can be found in scholarly and popular resources that position personhood (and, more specifically, womanhood) to inevitably include having, or at least wanting, a child. Hewlett (2007) warns of the "creeping non choice" in which biological realities render having children less and less possible as time goes on. She advises that women must plan strategically to ensure that the viable childbearing years don't slip away. Though Hewlett (2007) does acknowledge that not all women have children, far less is stated about the experiences of those who don't want children. Pronatalist leanings are also evident in research indicating that childless couples are viewed more favorably if they are thought to be so because of medical complications that are beyond their control (Steuber, 2014). This makes sense within the pronatalist lens as those who are childfree due to biomedical reasons may conform to the assumed narrative of experiencing a tragedy forcing them to deviate from the compulsory trajectory. Attributions of childfree adults have also been examined in the workplace, with single parents considered more mature than singles without children (Eby et al., 2004).

In addition to viewing pronatalism by virtue of attributions afforded to childfree adults (LaMastro, 2001), the expectation that everyone has (or, at the very least, wants) children is evident in everyday conversations. Research on self-disclosure and infertility shed light on the invasiveness of inquiries about having children. McQuillan et al. (2012) use the term *childlessness concerns* to capture the difficulty of participating in family gatherings due to unmet expectations to have children. In a study of how women respond to intrusive questions about childbearing and infertility, Bute (2009) explains that,

> [w]omen described conversations in which people asked them direct questions about their plans to have children; inquired as to whether they were currently pregnant; or asked pointed questions as to whether a woman received 'help' in achieving pregnancy, who was to blame for the infertility problem, why a woman chose not to pursue a particular treatment, or whether the woman had considered adoption.
>
> (pp. 756–757)

These questions might be especially biting given that adults who are childless due to biomedical reasons are more likely to experience childlessness concerns (McQuillan et al., 2012). Though participants' accounts didn't occur exclusively in the workplace, Bute illustrates how having children can be a taken for granted topic of discussion. Such a topic necessitates coping strategies for those who have resisted the lingering compulsion.

Communicating childlessness by choice (CBC) is often met with pity or disappointment (Durham, 2008), prompting strategies for discussing the topic. These include passing (e.g., pretending to want children), identity substitution (e.g., claiming to be infertile), condemning the condemners (e.g., perpetuating negative opinions of people with [especially large numbers of] children), and self-fulfillment (e.g., noting the benefits of childlessness; Park, 2002). An especially pointed example of condemning the condemners is offered in a study of privacy management among CBC adults. Specifically, a 30-year-old woman recounts a reunion with friends in which having children becomes the topic of conversation:

> First it was casual, "When you gonna start a family?" And then I just decided at that point in my life to just be upfront with people and said, "We're not. I'm going to die childless." And that's when I started getting a hard time about it. Friends argued with me, not in a joking way, or they're shocked, or they can't believe it, and why would I choose that point of life. There they were, not enjoying themselves at this reunion because their children were running around and screaming and throwing their food. I'm sorry, but their parents were having a miserable time. Moreover, while some of us could stay late and talk and reminisce over a beer as late as we wanted, and, if they wanted to … they couldn't because they had to go home with their children! Right? So, we just fired back and said, "Hey, look around. You guys are having a piss poor time at this reunion. You're not enjoying yourself with us because your kids are driving you fucking crazy … and so I'm just not seeing happiness there."
>
> (Durham, 2008, pp. 141–142)

Much of what makes this participant's account so provocative is that it runs counter to common social scripts and yet rings true as a highly plausible set of circumstances.

As with childfree married couples, single parents have achieved a portion of the life experiences expected of them. And just as research suggests that widows are viewed more favorably than adults who have never been married, parents who are single as a result of divorce are viewed more favorably than singles who have become parents (Usdansky, 2009). Though over a quarter of children born in the last 5 years were welcomed to the world by unwed cohabiting parents (Shah, 2015), moral regard for single-by-choice parents is ambiguous at best. As previously mentioned, cohabiting couples are sometimes assumed to lack stability, which is considered critical for the healthy upbringing of children (Wilcox, 2011). Similar to the couple who is childfree due to biomedical reasons, parents who are single-via-divorce may receive partial credit for at least attempting the spouses and child(ren) model.

A final point of consideration brings us to working adults who are both single and childfree. The aforementioned stereotype of being career-oriented would leave us to assume that singles at the very least have branding power on the job market. After all, if someone is assumed to be career-oriented, based on their voluntarily communicated relationship status, wouldn't they be in a prime position to argue for their commitment to the job? But a laboratory experiment testing perceptions of single parents and single and childfree adults found single parents were more likely than childfree singles to get the job that did not require relocation, and were more likely to receive a merit stipend (Eby et al., 2004). As will be explained later in this chapter, it is possible that job offers and merit stipends—such as those used as variables in Eby et al.'s (2004) study—are products of (perceived) need-based allocations of workplace resources. Although it is interesting to consider how different attributions may be made to different people based on their level of adherence to an expected life course, and the invasive communication regarding one's deviation from the expected trajectory, of greater importance to the consideration of work–family balance is the consideration of how resources are granted or withheld depending on one's ability to affirm their family structure and advocate for their work–family balance needs.

Affirming and Advocating for the Single/Childfree Family at Work

Clearly, there are many family forms that deviate from the lingering compulsion. Some form familiar narratives, such as stepfamilies, that require little discursive dependence (Galvin, 2006; see Chapter 1). Others, such as those who are childfree by choice, require consistent affirmation and advocacy in order to be seen as deserving of work–family balance accommodation.

Casper et al. (2007) developed a scale measuring five dimensions of singles-friendly[3] workplace culture: *social inclusion, equal respect for non-work life, equal work opportunities, equal access to benefits,* and *equal work expectations.* They define singles-friendly culture as

> the shared assumptions, beliefs, and values regarding the extent to which an organization supports the integration of work and non-work that is *unrelated to family,* and the degree to which equity is perceived in the support an organization provides for employees' non-work roles, irrespective of family status.
> (emphasis maintained from original text; p. 480)

I agree with this definition but acknowledge that the "non-work" obligations could have to do with family that deviate from the family structures that have been negotiated within the workplace. Casper et al.'s (2007) five dimensions are used as a heuristic guide for exploring how Sa/oCf adults represent and advocate for their work–family balance needs. Specifically, the dimension of social inclusion is useful for considering issues of affirmation. The remaining characteristics provide a framework for considering self-advocacy.

Affirming Single and Childfree Families through Social Inclusion

The ability to affirm one's family (needs) at work depends on whether the workplace culture offers social inclusion. Casper et al. (2007) define social inclusion as, "the degree to which there are similar social expectations and opportunities for single employees and those with families" (p. 480). Opportunities include viable instances to affirm one's family structure. As Chapter 1 established, we affirm our families in our everyday conversations at work. Topics of spouse-finding and child-raising may be part of a conceptual archetype of a life well lived. Mentioning a stepchild, parent, or uncle humanizes that person, giving one's work–family balance narrative a sense of fidelity to co-workers and managers. Recalling that some families are more discourse dependent than others, some families are more reliant on communication at work than others. And yet, it isn't a simple matter of talking about family members until they become important to co-workers.

Considering the vignette at the beginning of this chapter, Jeremy likely didn't have to do extensive discursive work to humanize his sister—80 percent of the population has a sibling (Lyon, 2009). Despite their prevalence, adult siblings who invest time and energy to look out for one another require a great deal more discursive maintenance than a mother investing time and energy to care for her children. On one hand, this makes sense on a logical level: Children are in much (perhaps much, much, much) greater need of care than adult siblings, or any adult family relationship. But consider the vignette: Is watching a play necessarily childcare, or have we simply placed unequivocally positive attributions on diversions from work that involve children? Turning, now, to my conversations with single and childfree working adults, three dominant themes emerged: (a) the prevalence of communication about children (and, to a lesser degree, spouses), (b) the cultural awareness and discursive participation in co-workers' having and raising children, and (c) uncomfortable questions broached to childfree organization members.

Several of my research participants discussed difficulty in cultivating social situations at work, because of the pervasive talk about children. Some participants shared that they avoid talk about family, sometimes going so far as to leave the room when talk of children begins. In many cases, single and childfree participants weren't repulsed or offended by talk of spouses and children, but were disillusioned by the frequency with which the topic came up. Jamie, a 36-year-old veterinary technician, listed "[b]abysitting and birthday parties and school starting, and who learned to use the potty this week," as some of the topics discussed at work that she finds difficult to ease into as someone who doesn't have children. Several participants discussed trying to engage in talk about children in an attempt to connect with co-workers. As Jackie, a

35-year-old information technologies specialist confides, "I want to have good relationships with my co-workers, I ask them about their kids and sometimes I'm legitimately interested in what their kids have going on, but I mean they're all kind of doing the same thing." For Jackie, fostering good relationships requires talk about children. Though many participants felt that they didn't have anything to contribute to conversations about kids, several, like Jackie, attempted to be a part of the conversation, nonetheless. These attempts often occur as one-way interactions, as childfree co-workers had nothing to contribute that was perceived as having equal value. Talk about children, in and of itself, serves as social support because it affirms co-workers' home lives and gives narrative fidelity to their work–family balance needs.

In addition to one's ability to merely participate in conversation about children, social inclusion occurs through the participation in care and regard for co-workers with children. A particularly illuminating perspective came from Samantha, a 34-year-old clinical social worker, who, at the time of the interview, was expecting a child:

> I think that people are, at work, probably the most excited. They've been wanting this for me for a while and they know I've been wanting this for a while and they just are all giving their personal recommendations and watching what I eat, like monitoring me and when they watch me going outside, they look to make sure I'm watching before I cross the street. They're very protective, in a way, and I'm very surprised by how much ... how protective they are.

The overwhelming care and regard given to Samantha is likely an exaggeration of that experienced by the typical employee who is expecting a baby. Samantha counts herself lucky to be in such a caring work environment. This climate of care was also conveyed in how participants described their co-workers. Chris, a 43-year-old administrative assistant shared,

> One of my co-workers was actually getting ready to have her first child in June, so, we definitely ... that [topic] comes up more and more, because she's been trying for years and years and years and years and she's finally having one, so kids come up a lot.

Having an expectant mother in the workplace no-doubt heightens the amount of conversation about children. But Chris's knowledge that his co-worker had "been trying for years and years..." speaks to the culture of regard and discursive inclusion in the workplace. This common culture of social support extended to communicating about children by way of comparing child-raising experiences with other co-workers and also calling on co-workers for advice. As Debbie, a 35-year-old college professor explained, "I'm dating someone who now has kids, so that's been kind of a challenge in and of itself ... I'll text message other women in my department, 'oh my God, how do you deal with this situation?'" In Debbie's situation, she wouldn't characterize her boyfriend's child as *her child*, and yet the narrative of caring for children allows her to be a recipient of the care and regard typically shown to parents. Many participants, both with and without children, expressed gratitude for being a part of a workplace in which families are discussed. One common theme, however, highlighted instances in which attempts at including childfree co-workers in conversations about kids ran afoul.

Experiencing difficulty in integrating one's self (and family discourse) into workplace conversation and becoming the recipient of support and regard isn't nearly as taxing as being invited into the conversation in uncomfortable ways: Confirming trends found in existing studies (Bute, 2009; Dixon & Dougherty, 2014), many working adults I interviewed voiced frustration at being asked inappropriate and demeaning questions. Allison, a 37-year-old dancer, choreographer, and professor explains,

> I feel like, 'cuz as a woman in my late 30s, the amount of people that ask me, like, "when am I going to have a kid?", and "why am I not procreating?" it's like, constant, and I'm like, "oh my God, this is such a personal decision." And, actually, it is a decision that people make, like it's not an imperative, it's not required. And, like, and also, "fuck you" because what if I really did want to have a kid and I couldn't, then you would be pushing a really painful button.

Allison not only illustrates the obtrusiveness of her co-workers asking her if she plans to have kids, she also considers the pain caused by posing such a question to someone who wants to have children, but is unable. Like Allison, many female participants without children explained being included in talk about children in unwanted, awkward, and even painful ways. These interactions sometimes occur in highly gendered communication networks (Durham, 2008; Dixon, 2015) in which talk of children was assumed to be appropriate conversation among groups of women. When asked what people talk about at work when they aren't talking about work, all genders brought up traditional family, although women may find themselves in "mom's club" conversations more than men find themselves in a "dad's club" equivalent. However, a few men also shared experiences of being included in talk about kids. Gary, a 37-year-old college professor and administrator, explains:

> They don't ask why [my wife and I] don't want to have children, they ask why we don't have children. They ask, "how did you get 7 years into your career, you're in your late 30s and you're married, you've been

married for almost 5 years and you don't have children." They don't position it as a want thing; they approach it from a position of time.

As Gary mentions, his co-workers don't acknowledge the possibility that he and his wife might not want children. Instead, in alignment with the lingering compulsion, they assume that his being married, having a job, and being of a certain, biologically feasible age means that having kids is the indubitable next step. Invasive questions about having children can have an affect opposite from the one intended: rather than including Sa/oCf co-workers in the conversation, questions about getting married and having children often create uncomfortable moments.

Importantly, the purpose of this chapter is to condemn workplaces that cultivate supportive work environments for employees with traditional families. Many childfree participants made clear that they are not anti-child, nor do they wish to see any affordances currently given to working parents taken away. Instead, they expressed a desire to expand the workplace conversation to additional relatable topics, such as family situations that don't involve spouses and children. Family representation through social inclusion is merely a foundation—a starting point for cultivating perceptions of Sa/oCf working adults as being worthy recipients of (potentially scarce) work–family balance accommodations. After the foundation of family discourses is set—through the stewardship of social inclusion—advocacy is needed to build work–family balance equity.

Advocacy

Equal Respect for Non-Work Life

Advocating for the work–family balance needs of Sa/oCf families means positioning need as equal for all employees. Equal respect for non-work life is "the degree to which similar value is placed on non-work roles of all employees" (Casper et al., 2007, p. 482). Though situations occur that render one person temporarily more deserving of accommodation than others (e.g., death of a family member), equal respect for non-work life guards against biases that position one employee's personal life as more important—and more deserving of regard—than another's.

In her exceptionally influential book, *Lean In* (2013), Sheryl Sandberg relays a story of a woman on a panel titled *Women in Consulting* that she attended while in business school. Similar to research findings (Dixon & Dougherty, 2014), the childfree panelist said that she was left to pick up the slack while her co-workers with children took time off. She said,

> My co-workers should understand that I need to go to a party tonight— and this is just as legitimate as their kids' soccer game—because

going to a party is the only way I might meet someone and start a family so I can have a soccer game to go to one day!

(p. 132)

Sandberg's story leaves us with an illustration of a workplace culture in which time spent with children is more important than time spent finding a partner with whom to eventually have children. But even the panelist's interests have a pronatalist bend. Equal respect for non-work life means honoring co-workers' non-work experiences regardless of the nature of the experiences. The consultant should have had equal access to free time, even if her intentions had nothing to do with eventually starting a traditional family.

Several participants felt that double standards existed in which Sa/oCf employees were expected to be available and flexibly work around the needs of their traditionally familied colleagues. Inequalities with respect to non-work life became especially clear to participants when they experienced a new aspect of work–family balance, such as dealing with a personal health issue, or making the commitment to earn a college degree. Kelly, a 31-year-old director of college admissions, took me through her experience of becoming aware of work–family balance inequalities in her workplace:

> I have had some recent health issues, just in the past four months, and I know if it was someone's child, it would be, "take time, go, absolutely." For me, it was like "you can't do this at another time of the day? You can't see the doctor at 7[p.m.]?" I take vacation time but it's seen as I should be doing doctor's visits and MRIs and CAT scans on my own time. But when people who have children have serious illnesses, it's "absolutely, no questions asked, totally fine."

Kelly feels that she is expected to make doctor's appointments that work around her regular work hours. Though Kelly wasn't vying for time away to attend to a family issue, she was attempting to navigate serious personal health needs against what she felt was a double standard that favors employees with children. For Oscar, a 31-year-old case manager for a state agency, the lack of equal respect for non-work life was made clear when he decided to go back to school, in addition to working full time. Oscar describes how he requested a more flexible work schedule that would allow him time to go to the campus tutoring center, which was only open for a limited number of hours each week. He explained, "[my supervisor]'ll try to put up lots of little road blocks, but, you know, if she needs to leave 20 min early to go pick up her kids, it's not a big deal." Similar to Kelly, Oscar finds that his non-work life is deemed unworthy of accommodation. These experiences resemble high school and college attendance policies in that non-work obligations that do not fit the traditional family archetype are deemed unexcused.

Equal consideration for non-work life includes acknowledging that single and childfree adults would seldom describe themselves as being "without families." Single adults often position being a family member as their primary life role (Casper et al. in press, as cited by Casper & DePaulo, 2012). Additionally, the aforementioned stereotype that singles and childfree are career-oriented may result in single employees lacking the time to cultivate relationships (traditional or otherwise) while married and childrearing counterparts are allotted such time.

Advocating for equal respect for non-work life is tricky in at least two ways: First, honoring everyone's personal life should not mean reducing maternity/paternity, bereavement, or sick leave opportunities so as to ensure equal accommodation for all. A childfree employee working extra hours to cover for a co-worker who is on paternity leave is not, in itself, an injustice. The injustice occurs when the "what goes around comes around" (Kirby & Krone, 2002) assumption never comes full circle because the needs of those who are childfree are not considered equally worthy of accommodation. Second, while social inclusion should provide a space for representing one's family needs, violations of privacy should not be required. Inequality lingers if employees have to campaign for accommodation in ways that others do not. If at all possible, organizations should allow equal time off for all. In instances where one's needs exceed what might be available for all, proper measures should be taken to ensure the employees picking up the slack are sufficiently compensated and never narratively relegated to the role of unchecked support.

Equal Work Opportunities

Whereas equal respect for non-work life represents the equal validity of every employee's time away from work, *equal work opportunities* "exist when opportunities (e.g., promotions, assignments), are provided without respect to family status" (Casper et al., 2007, p. 481). Casper et al. (2007) distinguish among a need-based system in which work opportunities are given, based on perceived financial necessity; an equality-based system in which everyone is given equal opportunity to work; and an equity-based system in which opportunities are based on employee contributions, such as skills or effort. Work opportunities, such as those that come with a stipend or heighten the possibility for promotion, often go to employees who are perceived to have the most need. For example, an employee's status as a new father[4] might clench his candidacy for a work project that brings in extra money. This aligns with Eby et al.'s (2004) findings that single parents are more likely to receive merit stipends than childfree singles.

Some participants brought up instances in which promotion inevitably went to "the guy with kids." However, I was surprised that this issue didn't come up more frequently. One possible reason for this is workplace gatekeepers becoming more conscientious of discrimination against employees without traditional families. Another, less optimistic, possibility is that job opportunities are going to employees with spouses and children, without other employees knowing that the opportunity was available in the first place.

The need-based system should not be eliminated in order to ensure that everyone has equal access to work opportunities. Instead, diverse narratives of need should be accepted, including those put forth by single and childfree employees. As with advocating for one's non-work life, Sa/oCf adults should make their financial needs known, whenever possible. More importantly, managers and other gatekeepers of workplace resources should be receptive and reflective of the possible needs of all employees.

Equal Access to Benefits

Equal access to benefits refers to "the degree to which similar ability exists for single employees and those with families to use benefits" (Casper et al., 2007, p. 481). Benefits may be conceptualized as formal policy or informal workplace culture. Formal family benefits are known to raise productivity, lower turnover, and attract new employees (Dobbin, 2009). Yet, several exist that benefit parents but not childfree working adults (e.g., on-site childcare), prompting the need for equitable accommodation (e.g., vouchers for elder care[5]). Additionally, formal policies may exist that employees—of any family structure—feel reluctant to use. Problems such as lack of managerial support, fear of poor performance evaluations, fear of ostracism from co-workers, and lack of programs' ability to actually meet the employee's needs points to the potential weaknesses of formal policy (Kirby & Krone, 2002; Batt & Valcour, 2003; Dobbin, 2009).

Perhaps the most pervasive inequality in formal benefit allocation, in the US, is social security. Two employees can work the same job, for the same number of years. Imagine one employee is married and the other is not. Were both employees to die in an accident (or were both to coincidentally take ill), the spouse of the married employee would be entitled to benefits, whereas the family of the single employee would not receive benefits—even if she or he had a cohabitating partner of many years (Casper & DePaulo, 2012). Similarly, with health insurance, married people and (in some instances) those with domestic partners can add a partner/spouse to their insurance. There is no otherwise +1 option for those with siblings, cousins, etc., in need of insurance. Finally, the Family Medical Leave Act (FMLA), under certain circumstances,[6] allows employees up to 12 weeks of unpaid time away from work to care for ailing children, spouses, or parents, but does not cover instances of caring for siblings, friends, or extended family (US Department of Labor). Another way to look at the limitations of FMLA is to consider that if a single person were to become ill, nobody except a parent could use FMLA to care for the person.

The lack of structural support can have consequences on less formal workplace norms. As Wood and Dow (2010) explain,

> basic parental leave policies do not specify what, if anything, working parents are entitled to for all the parenting activities beyond births, adoptions, and medical emergencies. As a result, informal social systems evolve to deal with what is not managed by the formal, institutional system.
>
> (p. 215)

They coin the concept of the "informal parenting support system." This support system adversely impacts Sa/oCf employees who "feel strong normative pressure to honor the parenting choices of colleagues but do not expect equivalent honoring of other commitments outside of work" (Wood & Dow, 2010, p. 209). Indications of the informal parenting support system can be found in the regard that Samantha experienced when she became pregnant. The system is informal in that it isn't dictated by a policy, it is largely involuntary in that workers are rarely consulted about their willingness to participate, and the system is invisible in that people rarely call attention to it. Co-workers may yield to the needs of parents out of fear of being labeled anti-child or anti-family (Wood & Dow, 2010).

Participants consistently voiced the need for a "cafeteria style" approach to receiving benefits. In such a model, a childfree employee might elect to utilize flex time in order to take college classes, but turn down (for obvious reasons) the opportunity to put a biological child on their insurance plan. Participants also wished for a more liberal understanding, on the policy-level, of what counts as acceptable time away from work.

Affirmative changes in work–family balance policy are possible (see Chapter 4 for information about the utility of FMLA for LGBT employees). Sa/oCf adults should use spaces of social inclusion to advocate for their accommodation needs. This is easier said than done: Highly pronatalist organizational cultures may find the idea of non-parenting accommodation laughable, especially in instances of scarce resources. Additionally, excessive advocacy, especially among junior employees, may be interpreted in lapses in organizational commitment or excessive distraction from work. The best course of action may be to make one's family needs subtly familiar, all the while advocating for accommodations that would benefit a large number of people who represent a diversity of family forms.

Equal Work Expectations

Equal work expectations refer to the degree to which there are similar work obligations for all employees, without regard to non-work life (Casper et al., 2007). Single and childfree working adults experience unequal work expectations when they are assigned largely undesirable work times (e.g., holidays and weekends) and tasks (e.g., aspects of the job that may be considered dangerous). Interestingly, unequal work expectations are the byproduct of the inequalities addressed in several of the other dimensions: Employees who experience a lack of social inclusion, a lack of respect for non-work life, or a lack of accommodating work–family balance policies will likely experience elevated work expectations.

Sa/oCf participants definitely felt that they had to pick up the slack, and work undesirable hours, to accommodate the needs of co-workers with spouses and children. Jackie, the 35-year-old IT specialist, explains:

> So people talk about their kids all the time and [are] getting preferential treatment. I mean, everybody's leaving work who have kids and it's frustrating for us [co-workers without children] because we end up working off hours and weekends and things like that because we're the ones who don't have kids.

The norm that childfree employees at Jackie's workplace work "off hours and weekends" suggests a cultural enactment of the stereotype that Sa/oCf employees are workaholics. Jackie's choice of words—that Sa/oCf employees "end up" working at undesirable times suggests that this unfair distribution of labor is something that happens on a case-by-case basis, and therefore, a systemic pattern isn't readily visible, as it would be, for example, on a dedicated work schedule.

There is absolutely nothing wrong with covering a weekend shift for a co-worker who needs to take his child to a birthday party, or cover for a colleague who has a wedding anniversary coming up. The problem lies in the unspoken assumption that those events are more important than the (family) lives of single and childfree colleagues. As mentioned above, a popular stereotype of single adults is that they must be married to their work (DePaulo, 2006). While this could be nice branding for employees seeking promotion, it also lends to organizational injustice.

Conclusion

A lingering compulsion drives narratives that give primacy to the life trajectory of getting married and having children. With the large number of single and childfree working adults, it is likely that the stereotypes such as being selfish or immature don't extend explicitly to the workplace. Despite almost certainly being accepted as equals within the workplace, Sa/oCf adults likely do not receive equal work–family balance accommodation.

Affirmation of one's family (needs) is a prerequisite to advocacy. Familiarizing one's family with co-workers serves to legitimize and humanize them. Additionally, affirmation through social inclusion serves to dispel negative and/or inaccurate assumptions about one's family structure. However, the propensity of talk about children (and spouses), and the level of support, regard, and even communicated participation in the lives of co-workers with children, leave Sa/oCf working adults out of the conversation. This situation is made worse when attempts to integrate Sa/oCf co-workers into conversation results in awkward or harmful situations, leaving Sa/oCf working adults all the farther from social inclusion.

Advocating for work–family balance needs is tricky because one runs the risk of appearing uncommitted or of seeking to devalue others' accommodation needs. Nonetheless, some practical options are available: Wood and Dow (2010) offer four criteria that might be used when considering whether to accommodate a co-worker: (1) Is it an emergency? (2) Is the situation rare or regular? (3) Could affecting the workplace have been avoided? (4) Can (dis)agreement about accommodation be conceptually separated from judgment regarding parenting style? Employing these criteria could help remove pronatalist bias, while creating new narratives that honor the family lives of single and childfree working adults as equally worthy of regard.

Notes

1 The fact that singlehood is becoming more common may only strengthen the belief that marriage is the superior status (Koropeckyj-Cox, 2005), because it requires a set of qualities or skills to become married.
2 Examples yielded from the City of New York Office of the City Clerk, Marriage Bureau.
3 Though the five dimensions are specifically in reference to singles, I'm applying them, here, to childfree (but perhaps not single) adults as well.
4 As briefly discussed in Chapter 5, this work advantage is afforded to fathers, in particular (Hodges & Budig, 2010).
5 Some literature advocates for a dating service in place of childcare. It's not a horrible idea in that it honors the goals of those seeking to be in a relationship. It does, however, abide by the lingering compulsion that a single employee must wish to remedy the situation.
6 Employees are entitled to FMLA if they have worked for an employer for 12 months, have worked at least 1,250 h over the previous 12 months, and work at a location or territory of the U.S. where at least 50 employees work within 75 miles.

References

Batt, R. & Valcour, P. M. (2003). Human resources practices as predictors of work-family outcomes and employee turnover. *Industrial Relations: A Journal of Economy and Society*, 42(2), 189–220. doi: 10.1111/1468-232X.00287.

Bureau of Labor Statistics (2014). Monthly labor review. Retrieved from www.bls.gov/opub/mlr/2014/home.htm (accessed July 20, 2015).

Bute, J. J. (2009). "Nobody thinks twice about asking:" Women with a fertility problem and requests for information. *Health Communication, 24*(8), 752–763. doi: 10.1080/10410230903265920.

Casper, W. J. & DePaulo, B. (2012). A new layer to inclusion: Creating singles-friendly work environments. In N. P. Reilly, M. J. Sirgy, & C. A. Gorman (Eds.), *Work and quality of life* (pp. 217–234). New York: Springer.

Casper, W. J., Roberto, K., & Buss, C. (in press). We have lives and families too! Balance between work and nonwork for single adults without dependent children. In Research in careers (Vol. III). Greenwich, CT: Information Age Press.

Casper, W. J., Weltman, D., & Kwesiga, E. (2007). Beyond family-friendly: The construct and measurement of singles-friendly work culture. *Journal of Vocational Behavior, 70*(3), 478–501. doi: 10.1016/j.jvb.2007.01.001.

Cherlin, A. J. (2009). The origins of the ambivalent acceptance of divorce. *Journal of Marriage and Family, 71*(2), 226–229. doi: 10.1111/j.1741-3737.2009.00593.x.

Coontz, S. (2006) *Marriage, a history: From obedience to intimacy or how love conquered marriage.* New York: Viking Penguin.

Daly, N. (2014, September 11). Single? So are the majority of U.S. adults. *PBS Newshour.* Retrieved from www.pbs.org/newshour/rundown/single-youre-not-alone/ (accessed April 10, 2016).

DePaulo, B. (2006). *Singled out: How singles are stereotyped, stigmatized, and ignored and still live happily ever after.* New York: St. Martin's Press.

DePaulo, B. (2011). Living single: Lightening up those dark, dopey myths. In W. R. Cupach & B. H. Spitzberg (Eds.), *The dark side of close relationships II* (pp. 409–439). New York: Routledge.

Dixon, J. (2015). *Family*arizing: Work/life balance for single, childfree, and chosen family. *Electronic Journal of Communication, 25*(1–2). Retrieved from www.cios.org/getfile/025107_EJC (accessed March 23, 2017).

Dixon, J. & Dougherty, D. S. (2014). A language convergence/meaning divergence analysis exploring how LGBTQ and single employees manage traditional family expectations in the workplace. *Journal of Applied Communication Research, 42*(1), 1–19. doi: 10.1080/00909882.2013.847275.

Dobbin, F. (2009). *Inventing equal opportunity.* Princeton, NJ: Princeton University Press.

Durham, W. T. (2008). The rules-based process of revealing/concealing the family planning decisions of voluntary child-free couples: A communication privacy management perspective. *Communication Studies, 59*(2), 132–147. doi: 10.1080/10510970802062451.

Eby, L. T., Allen, T. D., Noble, C. L., & Lockwood, A. L. (2004). Perceptions of singles and single parents: A laboratory experiment. *Journal of Applied Social Psychology, 34*(7), 1329–1352. doi: 10.1111/j.1559-1816.2004.tb02009.x.

Galvin, K. M. (2006). Diversity's impact on defining the family: Discourse dependence and identity. In L. H. Turner & R. West (Eds.), *The family communication sourcebook* (pp. 3–20). Thousand Oaks, CA: Sage.

Hartog, H. (2000). *Man and wife in America: A history.* Cambridge, MA: Harvard University Press.

Hewlett, S. A. (2007). *Off-ramps and on-ramps: Keeping talented women on the road to success.* Boston, MA: Harvard Business School Press.

Hodges, M. J. & Budig, M. J. (2010). Who gets the daddy bonus? Organizational hegemonic masculinity and the impact of fatherhood on earnings. *Gender & Society, 24*(6), 717–745. doi: 10.1177/0891243210386729.

Jamison, P. H., Franzini, L. R., & Kaplan, R. M. (1979). Some assumed characteristics of voluntarily childfree women and men. *Psychology of Women Quarterly, 4*(2), 266–273. doi: 10.1111/j.1471-6402.1979.tb00714.x.

Jordan, A. H. & Zitek, E. M. (2012). Marital status bias in perceptions of employees. *Basic and Applied Social Psychology, 34*(5), 474–481. doi: 10.1080/01973533.2012.711687.

Kirby, E. L. & Krone, K. J. (2002). The policy exists but you can't really use it: Communication and the structuration of work/life policies. *Journal of Applied Communication Research, 30*(1), 50–77. doi: 10.1080/00909880216577.

Koropeckyj-Cox, T. (2005). Singles, society, and science: Sociological perspectives. *Psychological Inquiry, 16, 2*(3), 91–97.

Kuperberg, A. (2014a). Does premarital cohabitation raise your risk of divorce? *Council on Contemporary Families.* Retrieved from https://contemporary families.org/cohabitation-divorce-brief-report/ (accessed April 10, 2016).

Kuperberg, A. (2014b). Age at coresidence, premarital cohabitation, and marriage dissolution: 1985–2009. *Journal of Marriage and Family, 76*(2), 352–369. doi: 10.1111/jomf.12092.

LaMastro, V. (2001). Childless by choice?: Attributions and attitudes concerning family size. *Social Behavior and Personality, 29*(3), 231–244. doi: 10.2224/sbp.2001.29.3.231.

Luscombe, B. (2010, May 24). Are marriage statistics divorced from reality? *Time Magazine.* Retrieved from http://content.time.com/time/magazine/article/0,9171,1989124,00.html (accessed April 10, 2016).

Lyon, L. (2009, June 31). 7 ways your siblings have shaped you. *U.S. News & World Report.* Retrieved from http://health.usnews.com/health-news/family-health/articles/2009/07/31/7-ways-your-siblings-may-have-shaped-you (July 20, 2015).

McKinnish, T. G. (2007). Sexually integrated workplaces and divorce: Another form of on-the-job search. *Journal of Human Resources, 42*(2), 331–352. doi: 10.3368/jhr.XLII.2.331.

McQuillan, J., Greil, A. L., Shreffler, K. M., Wonch-Hill, P. A., Gentzler, K. C., & Hathcoat, J. D. (2012). Does the reason matter? Variations in childlessness concerns among US women. *Journal of Marriage and Family, 74*(5), 1166–1181. doi: 10.1111/j.1741-3737.2012.01015.x.

Morris, W. L. (2005). *The effect of stigma awareness on the self-esteem of singles* (Unpublished doctoral dissertation). Department of Psychology, University of Virginia.

Morris, W. L., DePaulo, B. M., Hertel, J., & Taylor, L. C. (2008). Singlism—another problem that has no name: Prejudice, stereotypes, and discrimination against singles. In M. A. Morrison & T. G. Morrison (Eds.), *The psychology of modern prejudice* (pp. 165–194). New York: Nova.

Park, K. (2002). Stigma management among the voluntarily childless. *Sociological Perspectives, 45,* 21–45. doi: 10.1525/sop.2002.45.1.21.

Paul, P. (2011, June 17). How divorce lost its groove. *The New York Times*. Retrieved from www.nytimes.com/2011/06/19/fashion/how-divorce-lost-its-cachet.html (accessed April 10, 2016).

Pirani, E. & Vignoli, D. (2016). Changes in the satisfaction of cohabitors relative to spouses over time. *Journal of Marriage and Family*, 78(3), 598–609. doi: 10.1111/jomf.12287.

Sandberg, S. (2013). *Lean in: Women, work, and the will to lead*. New York: Alfred A. Knopf.

Shah, N. (2015, March 10). U.S. Sees rise in unmarried parents: Sociologists fret that more children risk losing out on economic benefits of living in married households. *The Wall Street Journal*. Retrieved from www.wsj.com/articles/cohabiting-parents-at-record-high-1426010894 (April 15, 2016).

Stanley, S. M. (2014, July 29). The hidden risk of cohabitation: If you can't be bothered to change your phone plan... *Psychology Today*. Retrieved from www.psychologytoday.com/blog/sliding-vs-deciding/201407/the-hidden-risk-cohabitation (accessed April 15, 2016).

Steuber, K. R. (2014). Life without kids: In (voluntary) childless families. In L. A. Baxter (Ed.), *Remaking "family" communicatively* (pp. 121–136). New York: Peter Lang.

U.S. Department of Labor (n.d.). FMLA (Family & Medical Leave). Retrieved from www.dol.gov/general/topic/benefits-leave/fmla (accessed April 15, 2016).

Usdansky, M. L. (2009). A weak embrace: Popular and scholarly depictions of single-parent families, 1900–1998. *Journal of Marriage and Family*, 71(2), 209–225. doi: 10.1111/j.1741-3737.2009.00592.x.

Weddingbee (n.d.). Concession: My wedding day was not the happiest day of my life. Retrieved from http://boards.weddingbee.com/topic/confession-my-wedding-day-was-not-the-happiest-day-of-my-life/ (accessed April 10, 2016).

Wilcox, W. B. (2011). Suffer the little children: Cohabitation and the abuse of America's children. *Public Discourse, 4*(22). Retrieved from http://ccgaction.org/uploaded_files/FedStudy-ChildAbuseandNeglect-Marriage%20breakdown.pdf (accessed April 15, 2016).

Willimon, B. (2016). Chapter 51. In D. Fincher et al.'s *House of Cards*. US: Netflix.

Wong, B. (2014, December 2). The truth about the divorce rate is surprisingly optimistic. *The Huffington Post*. Retrieved from www.huffingtonpost.com/2014/12/02/divorce-rate-declining-_n_6256956.html (accessed April 10, 2016).

Wood, J. T. & Dow, B. J. (2010). The invisible politics of "choice" in the workplace: Naming the informal parenting support system. In S. Hayden & L. O'Brien Hallstein (Eds.), *Contemplating maternity in an era of choice: Explorations into discourses of reproduction* (pp. 203–225). New York: Lexington.

4   Balancing LGBTQ Identities

Thanks to the Supreme Court ruling a few years ago, Jeremy and Vlad have upgraded their domestic partnership to marriage. Both were relieved to learn that getting married was the economically viable option as Vlad was previously on Jeremy's health insurance as a domestic partner, and was incurring some pretty steep fees that aren't charged to married dependents. Their dog, Parker, was even a part of the ceremony, led down the isle with wedding bands tied to his collar. Everyone from work came to the wedding, affirming Jeremy's belief that his co-workers were also friends and allies.

At work, Jeremy counts himself lucky that he can show pictures and talk about his family, just like everyone else. He knows he shouldn't have to feel *lucky* to do these simple things but stories from friends in other workplaces leave him feeling appreciative of his work environment. Occasionally, Lisa will go overboard in her support, declaring that all the good men in the world are gay; or, Nora will offer to set him up with her gay friend, even though she knows he is in a monogamous relationship with Vlad. But Jeremy accepts Lisa's compliment, in the light humor in which it is intended, and thanks Nora for looking out for him. Unfortunately, the accepting workplace climate is compromised when clients come in with comments of their own.

On one particular day, a client happened to catch a glimpse of Jeremy and Vlad's wedding photo, and began asking a series of questions including, *Who is the man in the relationship?* and *Do you have kids? Are they gay, too?* Leslie intervened and tended to the client's reason for stopping by, and everyone within earshot apologized for the client's behavior. But, Jeremy couldn't help but feel embarrassed. That evening, as he left his cubicle, Jeremy packed his wedding picture in his satchel and took it home.

***

"The last thing we need is another label." This response, from a thought-leading undergraduate student in my interpersonal communication course, received a cascade of nods from her classmates. The question that I had posed was whether *LGBTQ families* was a necessary term or, conversely, whether families that happen to include one or more LGBTQ members should simply be referred to as *families*, without the nod to sexual orientation or gender identity. On the one hand, I see my student's point: to employ the label of *LGBTQ family* would be to suggest that there is something inherently different, perhaps lesser, than families that have the luxury of simply being called *families*. On the other hand, to relinquish the LGBTQ label presents the risk of obscuring the obstacles that families with one or more LGBTQ individuals face. Though Jeremy is happily married to Vlad and they are building a life together that is, in many ways, indistinguishable from Trent and his wife Pam, Maria and her husband Edwin, etc., communication about his family—perhaps in the form of a wedding picture—can prompt unwelcomed responses that neither Trent nor Maria face.

The distinguishable experiences for LGBTQ adults in the workplace extend to work–family balance. LGBTQ adults experience largely the same work–family balance obstacles as their straight and cisgender counterparts. Some research even indicates that gay and lesbian couples better maintain relationship health that is often jeopardized by strains in attempting work–family balance (Kurdek, 2004). This relational preservation occurs, in part, by rejecting traditional gender roles that add complexity to balancing work and family (Goldberg, Downing, and Moyer, 2012; Goldberg, 2013). So if research would suggest equitable if not superior approaches to work–family balance, why the need to consider it? Why toss a label on LGBTQ working adults and risk othering a population that has been othered enough? The answer can be found in considering the need to balance identities, in addition to obligations.

The previous chapter explored how being single and/or childfree resisted the compulsory traditional family ideology. Sa/oCf adults have the burden of contending with the idea that co-workers with spouses and children are more worthy of accommodation. LGBTQ organization members need to carefully build family identity. In short, where Sa/oCf families may be seen as inferior, families with one or more LGBTQ adults may be seen as inferior and also inappropriate—even in a time when supporters for LGBTQ rights have seen several victories. Obstacles in balancing LGBTQ identity occur in at least three forms: First, sexual orientation and gender identity point to one's sexuality. To talk about family is to signal sexuality in ways that may or may not be conspicuous in a given workplace culture. Second, LGBTQ working adults often must decide whether to disclose their sexual orientation and/or gender identity, knowing that to do so could mean familiarizing their families to their co-workers, while also being aware of the risk to reputation and occupation. Third, both the sexualizing aspect of sexual orientation and gender identity and the uncertainties about whether and how to disclose are rendered more difficult to navigate due to the ambiguous and contradictory nature of workplace cultures and policies (e.g., a workplace that has a non-discrimination policy, but allows discrimination to flourish). This chapter will explore the barriers in affirming and advocating for work–family balance needs amid the added element of balancing LGBTQ identity. Specifically, workplace cultures of sexuality, decisions regarding disclosure, and contradictions on workplace policy and culture are considered.

Workplace Cultures of Sexuality

Where, in the workplace, does sexuality belong? Workspaces can display a range of explicit sexuality, from the raunchy porn shop on the side of the highway to the upscale intimate apparel boutique. Recalling from Chapter 3 that postmodern companies sell brands, rather than products, part of a brand can be the allure of sexual freedom or prowess. Employees, by extension, may be expected to exude the sexuality that the brand promises (the shirtless models at Abercrombie and Fitch, circa 1996–2015, makes for an almost too-perfect example [Frizell, 2015; Schlossberg, 2016]). But, of course, not all workplaces expect a performance of sexuality.

As elaborated in Chapter 3, workplaces can be a confusing and contradictory blend of modern and postmodern ideals. The same company that expects a somewhat playful performance of personal (sexual) identity may also expect employees to enact (un)spoken characteristics of what it means to be professional. Max Weber's (1943) extensive study of bureaucracy—which is an overarching tenant of the modern workplace—highlights the process of "eliminating from official business love, hatred, and all purely personal, irrational, and emotional elements" (p. 219). To be professional is to have control of one's self. So just as it is unprofessional to engage in sexual flirting, it is also unprofessional to cry, burst with uproarious laughter, or walk around with a ketchup stain on your shirt. In many workplaces, and especially white-collar work cultures, professionalism is a rhetorical tool to indicate that the company and its stakeholders are in control and capable of following basic cultural codes that separate the public sphere from the private (Brewis & Sinclair, 2000). Additionally, workplaces may encourage a professional environment in order to cultivate a safe space—a space that, for example, discourages sexual harassment. Though a workplace's culture of sexuality is different than a person's sexual orientation or gender identity, the two can potentially be at odds.

One way that sexual orientation and gender identity can clash with workplace culture is that LGBTQ relationships tend to be sexualized—not necessarily by the LGBTQ employee, but by others in the workplace. In *The Corporate Closet*, James Woods (1993) claims that whereas a straight couple is seen as a social construction, a gay (or lesbian) couple is seen as a sexual construction.[1] In many spaces, to signal sexual orientation or gender identity is to signal sexuality, even though neither are direct indicators of sexual behavior. Though the legalization of gay marriage has no doubt afforded LGBTQ social regard where none previously existed, LGBTQ working adults are still highly sexualized through a phenomenon known as hypervisibility.

Hypervisibility occurs when an aspect of someone's identity is emphasized by other people in a way that often invites scrutiny (Dixon & Dougherty, 2014). Hypervisibility toward LGBTQ adults in the workplace often occurs in the form of asking invasive and inappropriate questions, such as the ones asked of Jeremy in the opening vignette. Many LGBTQ participants shared experiences in which they were asked exceptionally invasive questions such as "Who is the man and who is the woman in your relationship?" and "How does sex work for you?" Without a doubt, these questions are a form of sexual harassment. It is of no surprise that employees struggling with harassment of this nature fear for their job security (Rostosky & Riggle, 2002), feel cut off, separated, ostracized, or barred from co-workers (Skidmore, 2004), become subjected to verbal disrespect and disparagement (Eliason et al., 2011), and, unsurprisingly, experience decreased job satisfaction (Waldo, 1999).

Hypervisibility is not always explicitly sexual. Oscar, a 31-year-old case manager for a state agency, shared an experience of coming out to a group of his co-workers:

> Immediately one co-worker, she was like, "oh my God! You're gay?? Oh my God, I need to set you up with my brother! Oh, but he lives in Austin and he has a boyfriend." And I'm like, "Okay, do you just really want to say that you're cool with me being gay, because you could have just said that."

As Oscar conveyed the words and inflections, it was clear that he felt an (albeit accepting) overreaction on the part of his co-worker. Of course seeking to set him up with her brother may be a nod to the lingering compulsion, discussed in the previous chapter, but more to the present point is that the co-worker expressed her acceptance in the form of trying to cultivate a private relationship (with someone who lived hundreds of miles away and was already in a relationship). Further instigating the hypervisibility of sexuality, Oscar's account demonstrates the stereotype that gay men are promiscuous (Lipp, 2016). Of course, gay men aren't the only ones who have experienced this stereotype.

Bisexuals, in particular, may find that attributions made toward their sexuality run counter to workplace cultures of professionalism. Participants explained being wary of discussing bisexual identity in the workplace due to the stereotypes of bisexuals being fickle, promiscuous, or gays or lesbians who are afraid to come out of the closet (Hayfield, 2016). Lynn, a 41-year-old Post-Doctoral Fellow and instructor of

Sociology, sums up what she gathers to be stereotypes of bisexuality in the workplace:

> Bisexual people still face the same sorts of crap [in the workplace] ... where the assumptions are that you're either too wish-washy; you're really gay and that you're afraid to give up your privilege. Or that you're so hyper-sexual that you've gotta fuck everything. A lot of bisexuals are perceived as being undiscerning.

Lynn's depiction of navigating bisexual identity in the workplace points to a scrutiny about the legitimacy of one's stated sexual orientation ("that you're really gay") and sexual practices ("that you've gotta fuck everything"). Similar to Woods' (1993) distinction between gay and straight couples, Monro (2015) argues that while gay and lesbian identity has been somewhat domesticated, bisexuality is still seen as a blatant affront to the rational and professional workplace.[2] Also considered an affront to many workplaces is perceived violations of gender identity.

More people claim to have seen a ghost than to know a transgender person (Michelson, 2015). Despite the visibility of being transgender cast by celebrities such as LaVerne Cox, Eddie Izzard, and Caitlin Jenner, the majority of Americans lack a language for talking constructively about transgender experiences. This lack of understanding about what it means to be transgender may heighten the hypervisibility of transgender working adults. In addition to there being fewer out transgender people in the workplace, compared to gays or lesbians, transgender issues continue to be sublimated by lesbian and gay concerns within the "LGBT" umbrella (Minter, 2006; Schilt, 2010). Just as workplaces have varying expectations regarding sexual identity, they also have either implicit or explicit rules about gender presentation. In American society, where sexuality and gender are often confused with one another, what is perceived to be a deviant presentation of gender (such as wearing clothes generally attributed to those of the "opposite" sex) is also considered to be a statement of sexuality (that wearing said clothing is an indication of sexual perversion, rather than gender identity). The unfortunate assumption that gender non-conformity is bound to sexual perversion can be seen in legislation or "bathroom bills" requiring transgender individuals to use public restrooms that correspond to the biological sex specified on their birth certificates (Goodwyn, 2017). Though some proponents of the laws claim that they serve to protect women from straight, cisgender men, seeking to enter ladies' rooms under a gender disguise, the likelihood of such a sequence of events is virtually nil (Tannehill, 2016), plus it is already illegal to harass someone in the restroom, regardless of gender identity.

Though sexual identity has become an, at least partially, accepted aspect of the postmodern workplace, semblances of the rational/professional model from the modern era remain. The hypervisibility of being LGBTQ may draw out assumptions of sexual or gender identity that run counter to the workplace culture of sexuality. This perceived sexual deviance from workplace culture can weigh heavily on a working adult's decision to disclose sexual orientation or gender identity.

The Workplace Closet

Originally, "coming out" meant revealing one's self as a gay person to the gay community. Orne (2016) compares the custom to the "coming out" of debutantes at a ball. It was later that "coming out" became a metaphor for coming out of the closet.[3] The closet metaphor is reflective of the dominant cultures—workplace and otherwise—that we are immersed in. Adams (2011) explains that the closet highlights a culture in which we are all assumed heterosexual until otherwise communicated. A study by HRC (2014) indicates that 53 percent of LGBTQ working adults are closeted in the workplace. This statistic suggests that the literature published in the 1990s and early 2000s about strategies for coping with being gay or lesbian[4] in intolerant work environments may still reflect the experiences of the majority of LGBTQ working adults. As an example of these tactics, Spradlin (1998) explores the intricacies of passing as straight, utilizing six alliterative strategies: *distancing*—removing one's self from conversations in which personal information is exchanged; *dissociating*—separating one's self from gay or lesbian stereotypes; *dodging*—avoiding topics such as gay rights; *distracting*—using "heterosexual identity messages" (p. 601), *denial*—refusing to grant the truth about one's sexual orientation, and *deceiving*—intentionally constructing dishonest messages. Even in workplaces that do not beckon a significant amount of self-disclosure, one can imagine the emotional labor and vigilance required to hide one's sexual orientation and/or gender identity. So why do it?

Very few of my research participants reported being in the closet.[5] In most instances, the closet was reserved for LGBTQs who (a) worked in stereotypically masculine work environments, (b) worked in highly professional (participants frequently used the phrase "button down") workplaces where sexuality of any sort is considered inappropriate for conversation, and (c) when individuals were in the process of determining their sexual orientation or gender identity. Those few participants who characterized themselves as closeted did so with the explanation that sexuality, of any kind, wasn't tolerated at work. Other participants explained that they chose to remain closeted out of concern that the hypervisibility of being gay would overshadow other aspects of their identity—including, for some, their work performance. There is an assumption that millennials bypass the phenomenon of coming out because they see sexual identity as public and not indicative of a minority status (Orne, 2016). However, Rachel Feintzeig (2014), of the *Wall Street Journal,* points to a trend in which LGBTQ young adults are completely out during their college years, but then return to the closet upon joining the workforce. Reasons for this regression center on anxiously avoiding risk to career (Feintzeig, 2014): These young adults are keenly aware that company policy (where present) does not always translate to an elimination of bias or a quelling of hypervisibility. An element of ageism may also be a factor. When traditionally aged college graduates enter the workplace for the first time, it is their first experience working alongside people who are significantly older than they are. In these situations, young adults may be less likely to discuss sexual orientation or gender identity due to a pervasive stereotype that older co-workers are less likely to tolerate the discussion of sexual topics in general (Dixon, 2013). Despite this unfortunate trend of reentering the closet upon coming to work, my participants far more frequently discussed going through the process of deciding to come out.

Amid the dismally high number of closeted working adults in the U.S., coming out of the closet has been a (risky) possibility for decades. Even in the early 1990s, Woods (1993) included integration or "the authentic expression of a man's sexuality" (p. 173) in his list of strategies for being a gay man in a hegemonically masculine work environment. Some of my research participants explained that they were unequivocally out at work, referring to the closet as "old school" or "a thing of the past." However, the vast majority of LGBTQs I spoke with explained that whether to be out or in was an ongoing decision to be made and remade based on changes within the workplace. Sometimes changes as simple as going from the night shift to the day shift meant recalibrating one's position in relation to the closet. Larger changes, like company acquisitions and changes in management, were like re-entering a new workplace all over again. Given the risks, including the possibility of termination, what are the antecedents for disclosure?

Given the frequent changes that can occur in the workplace, as well as the frequency with which we change jobs (Meister, 2012), LGBTQ adults face a lifetime of deciding whether to come out (King et al., 2008). Matty, a 26-year-old digital communications director, explained that upon taking a new position, he would have to come out again: "I'm going to have to go through that whole coming out ... process again with people. And I knew I would find people in the office that I would be more open with than others." As Matty intimates, there are always new decisions to make regarding communicating sexual orientation and gender identity. Families may also negotiate—as couples—the extent to which sexual orientation should be known by co-workers (Beals & Peplau, 2001). LGBTQ couples often must negotiate whether, or the extent to which, their relationships are communicated into the workplace.

In the most general sense, these conversations occur with the goal of avoiding stigma.

Studying the disclosure of "invisible stigma" in the workplace, Ragins (2008) provides three antecedents of revealing sensitive information about one's self: (a) Self-verification or the need for people to be seen as their true self; (b) anticipated consequences of disclosure, or the assurance that disclosure will not be met with threat to one's self or career; and (c) environmental factors, such as whether there are other LGBTQ employees. Employees often times must be mindful of who, specifically, to disclose to (Ragins, 2008). Though perhaps favorable to being completely closeted, the "disclosure disconnects" (Ragins, 2008) or "social gymnastics" (Frable, 1993) in confiding in some workplace members but not others can have its own stressors, such as the looming possibilities of being outed to the wrong people. Social gymnastics can gain complexity when a former acquaintance joins the workplace, or when paper trails from health insurance point to a gender transition (Schilt, 2010).

Still, despite the general complexity of deciding whether to be out of the closet, many reject the closet metaphor as establishing a false dichotomy and instead argue that there are varying degrees of outness (Chrobot-Mason et al., 2001; Deitch et al., 2004) as well as varying degrees in which one's sexuality or gender identity holds relevance. Participants discussed allowing subtle clues to exist, such as identifying as LGBTQ on social media and then allowing co-workers access to this information. Others expressed ambivalence—as if sexual orientation were as provocative as disclosing the month in which they were born. Kris, a 32-year-old human resources director, who is bisexual, explains,

> I don't even know whether I'm out at work. It doesn't usually come up. I sort of assume that people will look at me and think "this person is probably not straight." I assume that but, you know, who knows?

Other participants explained that sexual orientation and gender identity was something of a non-issue at their workplaces. Count Andy, a bisexual musician in New York, says "[i]t's not really open and it's not really closed, there's a bit of some sort of silence about it. We don't really talk about it much." Count Andy's ambivalence may be a result of the region of the U.S. where he works (in generally liberal New York City), as well as his profession as a musician. For many, the luxury of one's sexual orientation or gender identity to be an incidental piece of personal information in the workplace is either never realized, or comes after years of identity negotiation. With many participants, the level of relevance they afforded to sexual identity was determined, in part, by their age and for how long they had identified as LGBTQ. Chris, a 43-year-old administrative assistant, explains,

> I came out kind of late. I was 30, and then as time went on I got a lot more ... because there was a time when I couldn't tell anyone, it was a big, big secret, blah blah blah then, you know, once you decide to come out, it just becomes easier and easier and easier and then it gets to a point where, you know, I really don't care, you know, if anyone has an issue with it.

Like Chris, many decided whether to come out based on whether doing so seemed appropriate to them. Some participants expressed an absurdity in pointing out sexual orientation and/or gender identity. As one participant, a transman in Missouri, pithily stated "I see no need to host an ice cream social."

Coming out gains complexity when considering whether one is expected to come out. It is interesting to consider whether there is a double bind in that if you don't "come out," you are perceived as squelching a large part of your identity, and if you do come out, you are perceived as distinguishing yourself in an environment that either (a) does not invite topics of sexuality and gender identity, or (b) is considered to be inclusive in such a way that making it a point to disclose might be seen as antithetical to the supposedly accepting workplace culture. This double bind may be especially prevalent for bisexuals who happen to be coupled with someone of a gender different than their own. After all, if one is in a heterosexual relationship, one may have neither cause nor prompt to disclose bisexual identity.

Furthermore, coming out of the closet may require an ability/willingness to arrive at a set description of one's sexual orientation or gender identity. This may be paradoxical if one does not subscribe to a fixed identity. Fluid notions of bisexuality destabilize categories such as "heterosexual," and "homosexual" (Hayfield, 2016) in ways that might be difficult to explain in the workplace. For example, whereas *bi*sexuality suggests a dichotomy commiserate with the hetero-/homosexual, woman/man constructs, pansexuality—which implies that one's attractions aren't limited to (generally one of two) distinct and opposing categories—would be more likely to require explanation.

Transgender persons who choose to "go stealth" may have front row seats to lingering gender biases in that they have a basis for comparison that few if any cisgenders ever experience (Schilt, 2010). However, disclosure about gender identity has its own unique obstacles. First, it is possible, even amid celebrity representation and news coverage, that some organization members are still unaware of what it means to be transgender (Dixon, 2011). To come out would require also educating co-workers. Second, some workplaces may have a threshold of acceptance in which is it permissible to be gay, but it is not okay to be transgender. Finally, for those who join a workplace without having fully transitioned, the transition process is an overt indication of being transgender.

The uptick in closeted millennials in the workplace suggests that we are far from arriving at a place where all workplaces, across all occupations, are accepting of LGBTQ identities. Two central points of consideration in deciding whether and how to disclose sexual orientation or gender identity is workplace policy and climate.

Policy & Climate

The United States has seen a variety of wins and loses for the LGBTQ community. As of June 26, 2015, gay marriage is legal and recognized in all fifty states (de Vogue & Diamond, 2015) and as of June 30, 2016, transgender Americans can serve in the military (Terkel, 2016). Conversely, on June 12, 2016, 49 people were murdered at an Orlando gay bar (Ellis et al., 2016), and LGBTQ bullying remains an epidemic in American schools (Stomp Out Bullying, 2016). Furthermore, the election of Donald Trump as President of the United States and the subsequent repeal of the Affordable Care Act will result in transgender people facing discrimination in access to healthcare, and the appointment of conservative Supreme Court Judges will result in a roll back of marriage equality (Grinberg, 2016). LGBTQ rights, as a national issue, impacts how LGBTQ employees feel about being at work. As Jan, a 45-year-old film editor in New York, explains:

> As queer people, we're making pretty good gains in the last couple of years … When the world at large is doing well, it's less draining than when, say, before we were federally recognized, my wife and I. I find that that is a big turning point for me as far as how angry I got about things. And now it's like, well, okay, we have momentum, so my country sees me [laughs].

Just as legislation can improve how LGBTQ working adults feel about their sexual orientation and gender identities at work, national news stories and memes circulating on social media sites can lend to the visibility of LGBTQ issues. Discussion of anti-gay ballot initiatives occur in many workplaces.[6] For example, the highly controversial "bathroom bill" passed in North Carolina requires that individuals use public bathrooms and locker rooms that correspond with the biological sex reported on their birth certificate (Pearce, 2016). Though this has caused immeasurable harm to the transgender community of North Carolina (some even resorting to not using the restroom outside their homes; Pearce, 2016), it has also prompted discussion about transgender issues in workplaces nationwide. These discussions can reshape or reinforce workplace climates. In addition to LGBTQ issues that reach the national spotlight and therefore workplace conversations, policies related specifically to the workplace have an even greater impact on workplace culture.

There is currently no federal law prohibiting employment discrimination on the basis of sexual orientation or gender identity. The Employment Non-Discrimination Act (ENDA) is perhaps the most prominent marker, at the federal level, of attempts at protecting LGBTQ employees from discrimination, given that it has been proposed, been defeated, and stalled for the past 40 years (Gates, 2016).[7] ENDA would add gender identity and sexual orientation to the roster of protected classes, such as race, disability, and age for any workplace consisting of 15 or more employees (Gates, 2016). In 2014, President Barack Obama signed an executive order prohibiting discrimination based on sexual orientation and gender identity for federal contractors (Gates, 2013). According to the ACLU website (2016), 19 states have state-wide non-discrimination laws for sexual orientation and gender identity, and three states have non-discrimination laws for sexual orientation but not gender identity. Though sexual orientation and gender identity are not protected classes, there have been cases in which the EEOC has protected against such discrimination, citing Title VII of the Civil Rights Act of 1964 (EEOC, 2016; Gates, 2016). Protection might also be sought from the Civil Service Reform Act of 1978 (EEOC, 2016). When considering how LGBTQ employees will be treated in the workplace, many turn their attention to organization-level policy and policy use.

Workplace policy has the ability to communicate a company's position of LGBTQ workplace rights, foster a safe work environment, offer training and education of LGBTQ issues, and dictate terms and conditions of employment (Rumens, 2016). It stands to reason that people are more likely to come out when policies are in place (Riggle et al., 2009) and that policy lowers the likelihood of discrimination (Griffith & Hebl, 2002). It also makes sense that employees view the employment of non-discrimination policy as an admirable characteristic for a company to have (Dixon, 2015). However, it is important to understand reasons in which policy might not provide an unequivocally positive work environment. First, policies may not extend to the needs of transgender employees. As indicated above, patterns in the creation of non-discrimination policies show that policy regarding gender identity lags behind policy regarding sexual orientation. Therefore, it is entirely possible for a company to have the reputation of being "LGBTQ friendly," but not specifically accommodate transgender needs. For example, though a growing number of companies offer health insurance that covers gender transition (Herman, 2016), it would be a mistake to assume it is available.

Second, policies may be in place that are intended to bolster the image of the workplace, improve productivity, and attract desirable job candidates (Sheridan, 2009). The rhetorical perks of having a policy may breed instances in which companies have policies but lack the ability or willingness to enforce them. In some workplaces, policy is less about adherence to "the letter of the law" and more about how the policy is communicatively interpreted, or neglected as the case may be (Kirby & Krone, 2002; Dixon & Dougherty, 2014). This can result in false assurances that one is coming out in an accepting environment. Mixed messages between organizational policies and co-worker communication add to the difficulty in determining whether a workplace is genuinely LGBTQ-friendly (Compton, 2016).

Third, there are instances when discrimination occurs, but not in a way that adheres to the language of policy, and therefore goes unprotected. Deitch et al. (2004) distinguish between formal and informal discrimination, describing the latter as "negative actions directed toward 'LGBs' because of their sexual orientation that do not directly involve organizational policies or decisions" (p. 200). An example of informal discrimination (which is similar to aversive sexism discussed in Chapter 5) is when a manager fails to mentor an employee to the extent of other colleagues. As will be discussed below, this informal discrimination often extends to work–family balance needs.

Rather than relying solely on policy, LGBTQ employees rely upon multiple interpersonal communication messages as resources for determining how to manage sexual orientation and gender identity (Compton, 2016). Deitch et al. (2004) speculate that an informal workplace climate may be a better predictor of discrimination than formal policy. The power of the workplace climate was made clear in the interview data. Mo, a 25-year-old transman who worked at a grocery store, shared a story of receiving death threats in the store parking lot by a fellow employee. The co-worker was given a verbal warning, which, Mo explained, wasn't in compliance with a zero-tolerance policy regarding bullying. As one can imagine, these obstacles accentuate the contrast in how LGBTQ and non-LGBTQ people experience employment. Considering the capacity for LGBTQ identities and relationships to be sexualized, as well as the ambiguity regarding how sexual orientation and gender identity are to be performed in the workplace, this inequality may be poignantly felt within the realm of navigating work and family.

Balancing LGBTQ Identity

Varying and contradictory workplace policies and climates result in an additional dimension in negotiating work–family balance for LGBTQ employees—a dimension in which representing and advocating for work–family balance needs comes with extra guesswork. This guesswork is not limited to questions of whether a workplace is "LGBTQ-friendly" amid possible contradictions in policy and culture. Even if a workplace is welcoming of LGBTQ identity, this acceptance may not extend to regarding

LGBTQ families as equally worthy of work–family balance accommodation. Also, it is important to remember that LGBTQ employees are never finished coming out of the closet (Orne, 2016). Though there are no grand solutions for ensuring work–family balance equality in every workplace across the US, LGBTQ working adults can affirm their families by actively integrating them into workplace conversations, and advocate for work–family balance needs by pointing to the similarities and differences in the daily lived experience of balancing work and family.

Affirming Identity and Family

As discussed above, while some have the luxury of being ambivalent about their sexual orientation or gender identity in the workplace, many people remain closeted. Obviously, passing for straight is incommensurable with considerations of work–family balance, yet it is important not to dismiss the level of risk involved in coming out of the closet. Even something as simple as listing one's partner as an emergency contact cannot be done without calculation. Furthermore, the deconstruction of identity labels that come with identifying as queer or pansexual makes it difficult to establish a shared sense of identity (Hayfield, 2016). However, where possible, LGBTQs and allies can encourage a space for honoring family members, creating metaphorical scripts for discussing family and family-related needs, and making injustices known.

Many participants discussed wanting to find a balance in which their families are known and honored within the workplace without being pegged as LGBTQ to the exclusion of other identities. For example, Patricia, a 58-year-old retired social worker, who is a lesbian, stated about her relationship with her partner, "it's very important for me to have people honor our relationship, but I don't want to be identified as the *Lesbian Patricia* … I am so many more things than that." Other participants similarly talked about wanting to integrate their family lives into their workplace communication, but were leery of instigating hypervisibility. For some, affirming family by mentioning them is a tenuous process. When asked the hypothetical question of whether they would bring a significant other to a company-sponsored social event, like a company picnic, several immediately considered the risk factors of putting their families on display. These factors could include prompting uncomfortable questions or instigating gossip. For others, it is especially important to be able to talk about family to the same degree as straight co-workers. Kevin, a 36-year-old manager of a bar who is gay, elaborates on the double standard of representing family needs at work:

> Co-workers, if they have a fight with their spouse or they break up with their boyfriend or whatever; nobody flinches when they

come into work upset … You know what I mean? Or they come into a setting and they need to leave because: there were some people that I worked with that were going through a divorce and there was a carte blanche of "oh, I have court that day." And I'm not saying that's not important, but someone in a gay relationship going through an equally emotional […] rollercoaster, whether is was good or bad, they were falling in love, they met someone new, they were ready to adopt, maybe they're ready to move in together. I don't think our society creates an environment where you can be on equal footing with a heterosexual person or relationship in terms of expressing those experiences on the rollercoaster of life.

Kevin illustrates how, from his perspective, LGBTQs are unable to describe their experiences on "the rollercoaster of life" and have it be received with the same respect and legitimacy as their straight counterparts. This could be exacerbated by the ambiguous nature of many workplace climates in that it may be *possible* to discuss joys and concerns to the same degree at straight people, but the risk isn't worth it. Where possible, LGBTQ employees might do well to test the waters,[8] and allies should be careful to publicly and vocally respond to "rollercoaster of life" issues in the same way as if they were conveyed by a straight co-worker. Assuming one feels comfortable sharing life experiences at work, the next step would be to communicate issues that are unique to LGBTQs.

As stated above, this chapter contends that LGBTQ families and straight families are fundamentally the same with regard to work–family balance struggles. However, biases that occur outside of the workplace can result in obstacles that families consisting of only straight working adults don't likely face. Issues such as housing discrimination (Lauster & Easterbrook, 2011), and having children who face heterosexist bullying at school (Vinjamuri, 2016) occur outside of work, but nonetheless contribute to the obstacles that may or may not be permissible to talk about at work. Where they feel safe to do so, LGBTQ working adults can make their co-workers and managers aware of injustices outside the workplace that hinder work–family balance. Thus far, affirmation has been limited to talking about family, and family-related issues, at work. The next and final step in affirming family is bringing them along.

As previously mentioned, the prospect of bringing a spouse or other family member to work, as opposed to simply talking about them, illuminates the complexity of integrating family identity into the work environment (Dixon, 2013). Using the threat of hypervisibility as an overarching theme, participants found that they had to yield to dominant workplace expectation of opposite-sex coupling. Even in instances when employees where out of the closet, bringing a same-sex partner highlighted difference and prompted unwanted conversation. The reluctance to bring a partner to an event likely extends to reluctance to advocate for work–family balance needs.

Advocating for Identity and Family

In the beginning of this chapter, I argue that the difference in work–family balance for LGBTQ working adults exists largely in the added obstacle of (perhaps familiarizing and) integrating sexual orientation and gender identities—basically getting workplace colleagues past the idea that families with one or more LGBTQ adults are fundamentally different. LGBTQ and straight working adults experience many of the same work–family balance stressors (Huffman et al., 2015). For example, Bergman, Rubio, Green, and Padron (2010) studied 40 gay fathers who had become parents via surrogacy and found that most of the men worked fewer hours, got less sleep, and continued with work after the children went to bed. Had the study examined straight parents, the same results would likely have been yielded. Advocacy should begin with communicating the many shared experiences and needs related to work–family balance. In addition to pointing out commonalities, advocacy should occur, where appropriate, as teachable moments.

Advocacy can come in the form of rallying for work–family balance benefits that are more flexible and have a higher potential to benefit a greater number of people. Many participants, of all sexual orientations and gender identities, discussed needing family benefits that were not available to them. As Joy explains,

> I want to live in an educated world and I'm happy to pay [taxes] for other people's kids [to be educated]. [My wife] is a college professor and like most colleges, there is a tuition benefit that we are never going to use but I would sure love dental insurance, and it would cost a whole lot less to let me pick off a menu and say "here are the benefits that are available to me, here's one that I would really like" and take all that money for tuition that I'm never going to use and upholster[…] some of it to [*pause*] you know, I'd like to be able to get a crown done when I need a crown done.

In this excerpt, Joy points out that dental insurance would be less costly for her spouse's college than a tuition waiver, and would be of much greater use to her. Of course, Joy isn't being denied dental insurance because she's a lesbian, but rather dental insurance simply isn't included in the list of available benefits. The tuition waivers offered by the college are likely most frequently afforded to children of the employee of the college. Though an increasing number of LGBTQs have children, with approximately 22 percent of gay male couples and 33 percent of lesbian couples living with children under 18 (Lavender-Scott & Allen, 2016), straight couples are still far more likely to benefit from tuition waivers, especially at institutions where most students are of traditional college student age (Gates, 2013; Bureau of Labor Statistics, 2014). Advocating for a broader menu of benefits to choose from would be a step in the right direction for having diverse benefits that match a diverse workforce.

In addition to highlighting needs that can potentially be afforded at the organizational level, advocating for diverse work–family balance needs can extend to legislation. On the federal level, LGBTQs and straight co-workers are afforded the same amount of time off from work to tend to family issues. In the United States, The Family Medical Leave Act (FMLA) has expanded the definition of family to include same-sex spouses. As of 2010, same-sex couples are allowed to use FMLA to care for their children and for spouses who have become ill (US Department of Labor, 2016). Many working adults, of all sexual orientations and gender identities, are displeased with the lack of paid family leave in the United States (e.g., Rubin, 2016). LGBTQ work–family balance advocacy can occur in the form of pushing for resources, such as paid family leave, with the understanding that all families would be equally eligible.

Though strides can be made by advocating for work–family balance needs by highlighting that many lived experiences of balancing work and family are the same for LGBTQ and straight families alike, it is also important to make managers and colleagues aware of the unique obstacles that occur as a result of balancing LGBTQ identity. Of course, in workplaces that are unequivocally accepting, LGBTQs can simply ask for what they need (such as extra time to recover from gender affirmative surgery). For workplaces where no policy exists, or policy seems to contradict workplace climate, finding smaller, teachable moments may be the better option.

Returning to the study of workplace-sponsored family events, participants who choose to bring their partners to the events often found themselves using the event as a teachable moment by showing co-workers that they interact in the same way as their straight counterparts. LGBTQs may also choose to answer questions about what it's like to be an LGBTQ family. However, it is important not to create expectation that renders LGBTQ employees obligated to share private information about their lives. Also, as the opening vignette indicated, it is important that all questions asked of LGBTQ working adults are respectful and noninvasive. Teachable moments can be helpful to workplace environments, but no one is owed an explanation. They needn't even involve direct conversation: An employee could gradually communicate family into being, thereby showing family in a way that doesn't change from one sexual orientation to another.

Conclusion

As the title of this chapter may suggest, I have decided that I, at least partially, agree with my student—the LGBTQ family label shouldn't be necessary. However, the "social gymnastics" that often occur as LGBTQs navigate sexual orientation and gender identities with the cultures and policies of their respective workplaces, result in added obstacles in balancing work and family situations. Organizations and even occupations vary too broadly in their cultures of acceptance (Yoder & Mattheis, 2015). Deciding whether and how to disclose sexual orientation and gender identity is a critical prerequisite to affirming and advocating for work–family balance needs.

Notes

1 Woods creates a juxtaposition of the married [heterosexual] couple and the gay relationship between two unwed men.
2 Monro (2015) also argues that a cycle exists in that the silencing of bisexual identities in public spheres, such as the workplace, has resulted in a maintained mystery in what it means to be bisexual, which is used to bolster the sale of bisexual pornography, which perpetuates the stereotype of bisexuals as highly sexualized.
3 An examination of the etymology of the closet first takes us to the expression of having skeletons in the closet. The first written record of this expression has been traced to a periodical, *The Eclectic Review* (Adams, 1816), distributed in England, in which it is used as a metaphor for disease:

> Two great sources of distress, much aggravated by the uncertainty in which they are involved, are the danger of contagion and the apprehension of hereditary diseases ... The dread of being the cause of misery to posterity has prevailed over the most laudable attachment to a beloved object ... In these cases as in many other highly important questions, men seem afraid of inquiring after truth; cautions on cautions are multiplied to conceal the skeleton in the closet or to prevent its escape, til [*sic*] our very fears bring the object constantly before us, not in its real form but multiplied into every possible shape and magnified in all.
>
> (p. 468)

There appears to be no empirical evidence to suggest the expression references an actual practice of closeting skeletons (Idiom Origins, 2013). However, it has been suggested that the phrase gained prominence prior to the Anatomy Act of 1836. It is rumored that, during this time, tight restrictions on the use of corpses for medical purposes prompted doctors to conceal illegally held skeletons to be secretly brought out and used for teaching purposes. Whether a metaphor from the beginning or a homage to renegade physicians, having skeletons in one's closet presents a domestic imagery that gives an immediate and ever-present risk of discovery.
4 Though these strategies were written with gay men and/or lesbians in mind, they are applicable to bisexual and transgender working adults as well.
5 The disparity between my interview data and the HRC statistic points to a self selecting bias in which closeted LGBTQs elected not to participate in the study.

6 The Briggs Initiative of 1975, though never passed, would have required the firing of gay and lesbian teachers as well as teachers who were allies (Stone, 2016).
7 Some social justice advocacy organizations do not support ENDA because
of its high level of exemption for religious organizations (Gates, 2016).
8 I appreciate the element of risk involved in experimenting with what levels of affirmation may occur without consequences. In suggesting LGBTQ
working adults "test the water" of self-disclosure, I mean only within the
boundaries thought to preserve one's safety and wellbeing.

References

Adams, J. (1816). Adams' inquiry into the laws of different epidemic diseases. *The Eclectic Review*, *6*, 456–472.
Adams, T. E. (2011). *Narrating the closet: An autoethnography of same-sex attraction*. Walnut Creek, CA: Left Coast Press.
American Civil Liberties Union (2016). *Non-discrimination laws: State by state*. Retrieved from https://www.aclu.org/map/non-discrimination-laws-state-state-information-map (accessed March 23, 2017).
Beals, K. P. & Peplau, L. A. (2001). Social involvement, disclosure of sexual orientation, and the quality of lesbian relationships. *Psychology of Women Quarterly*, *25*(1), 10–19. doi: 10.1007/s12144-001-1014-3.
Bergman, K., Rubio, R. J., Green, R. J., & Padrón, E. (2010). Gay men who become fathers via surrogacy: The transition to parenthood. *Journal of GLBT Family Studies*, *6*(2), 111–141. doi: 10.1080/15504281003704942.
Brewis, J. & Sinclair, J. (2000). Exploring embodiment: Women, biology, and work. In J. Hassard, R. Holliday, & H. Willmott (Eds.), *Body and organization* (pp. 192–214). Thousand Oaks, CA: Sage.
Bureau of Labor Statistics (2014). Monthly labor review. Retrieved from www.bls.gov/opub/mlr/2014/home.htm (accessed March 23, 2017).
Chrobot-Mason, D., Button, S. B., & DiClementi, J. D. (2001). Sexual identity management strategies: An exploration of antecedents and consequences. *Sex Roles*, *45*, 321–336. doi: 10.1023%2FA%3A101435751.
Compton, C. A. (2016). Managing mixed messages: Sexual identity management in a changing US workplace. *Management Communication Quarterly*, *30*(4), 415–440. doi: 10.1177/0893318916641215.
de Vogue, A. & Diamond, J. (2015). Supreme court rules in favor of same-sex marriage nationwide. *CNN*. Retrieved from www.cnn.com/2015/06/26/politics/supreme-court-same-sex-marriage-ruling/ (accessed April 10, 2016).
Deitch, E. A., Butz, R. M., & Brief, A. P. (2004). Out of the closet and out of a job? The nature, import, and causes of sexual orientation discrimination in the workplace. In R. W. Griffin & A. M. O'Leary-Kelly (Eds.), *The dark side of organizational behavior* (pp. 187–234). San Francisco, CA: Jossey-Bass.
Dixon, J. (2011). *Ambiguity, uncertainty, and othering: A queer phenomenology of the organizational socialization of sexuality* (Unpublished doctoral dissertation). University of Missouri, Columbia, MO.
Dixon, J. (2013). Uneasy recreation: Workplace social events as problematic sites for communicating sexual orientation. *Florida Communication Journal*, *41*, 63–71.

Dixon, J. (2015). The workplace socialization of gender identity: A pheno-menological exploration of being transgender at work. In J. C. Capuzza & L. G. Spencer (Eds.), *Transgender communication studies: History, trends and trajectories* (pp. 19–32). Lanham, MD: Rowan & Littlefield, Inc.,

Dixon, J. & Dougherty, D. S. (2014). A language convergence/meaning di-vergence analysis exploring how LGBTQ and single employees manage traditional family expectations in the workplace. *Journal of Applied Communication Research, 42*(1), 1–19. doi: 10.1080/00909882.2013.847275.

Eliason, M. J., Dibble, S. L., & Robertson, P. A. (2011). Lesbian, gay, bisexual and transgender (LGBT) physicians' experiences in the workplace. *Journal of Homosexuality, 58*(10), 1355–1371. doi: 10.1080/00918369.2011.614902.

Ellis, R., Fantz, A., Karimi, F., & McLaughlin, E. C. (2016). Orlando shooting: 49 killed, shooter pledged ISIS allegiance. *CNN*. Retrieved from www.cnn.com/2016/06/12/us/orlando-nightclub-shooting/ (accessed June 15, 2016).

Feintzeig, R. (2014, May 6). Why gay workers decide to stay in the closet: Em-ployers are more supportive than ever, but some workers still worry about negative perceptions. *The Wall Street Journal*. Retrieved from www.wsj.com/articles/SB10001424052702304163604579531893392671188 (accessed April 10, 2017).

Frable, D. E. S. (1993). Being and feeling unique: Statistical deviance and psycho-logical marginality. *Journal of Personality, 61*(1), 85–110. doi: 10.1111/j.1467-6494.1993.tb00280.x.

Frizell, S. (2015, April 25). Abercrombie & Fitch is ditching its shirtless models. *Time*. Retrieved from time.com/3835521/abercrombie-fitch-shirtless-models/ (accessed April 15, 2016).

Gates, G. J. (2013). LGBT parenting in the United States. *The Williams In-stitute*. Retrieved from williamsinstitute.law.ucla.edu/wp-content/uploads/LGBT-Parenting.pdf (accessed March 23, 2017).

Gates, T. G. (2016). Employment non-discrimination act. In A. E. Goldberg (Ed.), *The SAGE handbook of LGBTQ studies* (Vol. 1, pp. 363–365). Thousand Oaks, CA: Sage.

Goldberg, A. E. (2013). "Doing" and "undoing" gender: The meaning and divi-sion of housework in same-sex couples. *Journal of Family Theory & Review, 5*(2), 85–104. doi: 10.1111/jftr.12009.

Goldberg, A. E., Downing, J. B., & Moyer, A. M. (2012). Why parenthood and why now? Gay men's motivations to pursue parenthood. *Family Relations, 61*(1), 157–174. doi: 10.1111/j.1741-3729.2011.00687.x.

Goodwyn, W. (2017, January 2). "Bathroom bill" fight brewing in Texas. *NPR Morning Edition*. Retrieved from www.npr.org/sections/thetwo-way/2017/01/02/507910587/bathroom-bill-fight-brewing-in-texas (accessed March 23, 2017).

Griffith, K. H. & Hebl, M. R. (2002). The disclosure dilemma for gay men and lesbians: "Coming out" at work. *Journal of Applied Psychology, 87*(6), 1191–1199. doi: 10.1037/0021-9010.87.6.1191.

Grinberg, E. (2016, December 5). What a Trump presidency could mean for LGBT Americans. *CNN*. Retrieved from www.cnn.com/2016/11/11/politics/trump-victory-lgbt-concerns/ (accessed March 23, 2017).

Hayfield, N. (2016). Bisexualities. In A. E. Goldberg (Ed.), *The SAGE hand-book of LGBTQ studies* (Vol. 1, pp. 127–131). Thousand Oaks, CA: Sage.

Herman, J. L. (2016). Health insurance coverage for transgender people, access to. In A. E. Goldberg (Ed.), *The SAGE handbook of LGBTQ studies* (Vol. 2, pp. 491–492). Thousand Oaks, CA: Sage.

HRC (2014). HRC study shows majority of LGBTQ workers closeted at the workplace. *Human Rights Campaign.* Retrieved from www.hrc.org/blog/hrc-study-shows-majority-of-lgbt-workers-closeted-on-the-job (accessed April 10, 2017).

Huffman, A. H., King, E. B., & Goldberg, A. E. (2016). Valuing lesbian and gay parenting in the workplace. In M. A. Paludi (Ed.), *Women, work, and family: How companies thrive with a 21st-century multicultural workforce* (pp. 173–189). Santa Barbara, CA: Praeger.

Idiom Origins (2013). Skeleton in your closet: Idiom Origin. *Idiom Origins.* Retrieved from http://idiomorigins.net/skeleton-in-your-closet/ (accessed April 10, 2016).

King, E. B., Reilly, C., & Hebl, M. (2008). The best of times, the worst of times: Exploring dual perspectives of "coming out" in the workplace. *Group & Organization Management, 33*(5), 566–601. doi: 10.1177/1059601108321834.

Kirby, E. L. & Krone, K. J. (2002). The policy exists but you can't really use it: Communication and the structuration of work/life policies. *Journal of Applied Communication Research, 30,* 50–77. doi: 10.1080/00909880216577.

Kurdek, L. A. (2004). Are gay and lesbian cohabiting couples really different from heterosexual married couples? *Journal of Marriage and Family, 66*(4), 880–900. doi: 10.1111/j.0022-2445.2004.00060.x.

Lauster, N. & Easterbrook, A. (2011). No room for new families? A field experiment measuring rental discrimination against same-sex couples and single parents. *Social Problems, 58*(3), 389–409. doi: 10.1525/sp.2011.58.3.389.

Lavender-Scott, E. S. & Allen, K. R. (2016). Parent relationship quality. In A. E. Goldberg (Ed.), *The SAGE handbook of LGBTQ studies* (Vol. 2, pp. 837–840). Thousand Oaks, CA: Sage.

Lipp, M. (2016, February 2). Myths and stereotypes that dehumanize gay men must be challenged: Start with these 10! *The Huffington Post.* Retrieved from www.huffingtonpost.com/murray-lipp/gay-men-myths-stereotypes_b_3463172.html (accessed April 10, 2016).

Meister, J. (2012, August 14). Job hopping is the "new normal" for millennials: Three ways to prevent a human resource nightmare. Retrieved from www.forbes.com/sites/jeannemeister/2012/08/14/job-hopping-is-the-new-normal-for-millennials-three-ways-to-prevent-a-human-resource-nightmare/#21d2774c5508 (accessed March 23, 2017).

Michelson, N. (2015). More Americans claim to have seen a ghost than have met a trans person. *The Huffington Post.* Retrieved from www.huffingtonpost.com/entry/more-americans-claim-to-have-seen-a-ghost-than-have-met-a-trans-person_us_5677fee5e4b014efe0d5ed62 (accessed July 20, 2015).

Minter, S. P. (2006). Do transsexuals [sic] dream of gay rights? Getting real about transgender inclusion. In P. Currah, R. Juang, & S. P. Minter (Eds.), *Transgender rights* (pp. 141–170). Minneapolis, MN: University of Minnesota Press.

Monro, S. (2015). *Bisexuality: Identities, politics, and theories.* London: Palgrave Macmillan.

Orne, J. (2016). Coming out, disclosure, and passing. In A. E. Goldberg (Ed.), *The SAGE handbook of LGBTQ studies* (pp. 246–250). Thousand Oaks, CA: Sage.

Pearce, M. (2016, June 4). What it's like to live under North Carolina's bathroom law if you're transgender. *Los Angeles Times*. Retrieved from www.latimes.com/nation/la-na-north-carolina-bathrooms-20160601-snap-story.html (accessed June 15, 2016).

Ragins, B. R. (2008). Disclosure disconnects: Antecedents and consequences of disclosing invisible stigmas across life domains. *Academy of Management Review 33*(1), 194–215.

Riggle, E. D., Rostosky, S. S., & Horne, S. G. (2009). Marriage amendments and lesbian, gay, and bisexual individuals in the 2006 election. *Sexuality Research & Social Policy*, 6(1), 80–89. doi: 10.1525/srsp.2009.6.1.80.

Rostosky, S. S. & Riggle, E. B. (2002). Out at work: The relation of actor and partner workplace policy and internalized homophobia to disclosure status. *Journal of Counseling Psychology, 49*(4), 411–419. doi: 10.1037/0022-0167.49.4.411.

Rubin, R. (2016, April 6). U.S. dead last among developed countries when it comes to paid maternity leave. *Forbes*. Retrieved from www.forbes.com/sites/ritarubin/2016/04/06/united-states-lags-behind-all-other-developed-countries-when-it-comes-to-paid-maternity-leave/#64ece8ee5ada (accessed March 23, 2017).

Rumens, N. (2016). Workplace policies. In A. E. Goldberg (Ed.), *The SAGE handbook of LGBTQ studies* (Vol. 3, pp. 1308–1310). Thousand Oaks, CA: Sage.

Schilt, K. (2010). *Just one of the guys? Transgender men and the persistence of gender inequality*. Chicago, IL: The University of Chicago Press.

Schlossberg, M. (2016, January 12). The bizarre history of Abercrombie & Fitch: And how the retailer is transforming yet again. *Business Insider*. Retrieved from www.businessinsider.com/abercrombie-fitch-crazy-history-2011-4/#abercrombie-was-the-place-to-go-for-hunters-in-the-early-1900s-1 (accessed June 15, 2016).

Sheridan, V. (2009). *The complete guide to transgender in the workplace*. Santa Barbara, CA: Praeger.

Skidmore, P. (2004). A legal perspective on sexuality and organization: A lesbian and gay case study. *Gender, Work & Organization*, 11(3), 229–253. doi: 10.1111/j.1468-0432.2004.00230.x.

Spradlin, A. L. (1998). The price of "passing": A lesbian perspective on authenticity in organizations. *Management Communication Quarterly, 11*(4), 598–605. doi: 10.1177/0893318998114006.

Stomp Out Bullying (2016). Anti-gay bullying. Stomp Out Bullying. Retrieved on July 26, 2016 from www.stompoutbullying.org/index.php/information-and-resources/about-bullying-and-cyberbullying/anti-gay-bullying/ (accessed July 26, 2016).

Stone, A. L. (2016). Antigay ballot initiatives (and LGBTQ activism). In A. E. Goldberg (Ed.), *The SAGE handbook of LGBTQ studies* (pp. 82–87). Thousand Oaks, CA: Sage.

Tannehill, B. (2016, November 28). Debunking bathroom myths. *The Huffington Post*. Retrieved from www.huffingtonpost.com/brynn-tannehill/debunking-bathroom-myths_b_8670438.html (accessed March 23, 2017).

Terkel, A. (2016). Transgender Americans can now fight and die for a country that doesn't protect them at home. *The Huffington Post*. Retrieved from www.huffingtonpost.com/entry/transgender-military-ban-discrimination_us_57758039e4b09b4c43bfab8a (accessed August 2, 2016).

The U.S. Equal Employment Opportunity Commission (2016). Facts about discrimination based on marital status, political affiliation, status as a parent, sexual orientation, or transgender (gender identity) status. Retrieved from www.eeoc.gov/federal/otherprotections.cfm (accessed March 23, 2017).

U.S. Department of Labor (2016). Fact sheet: The final rule to amend the definition of spouse in the Family and Medical Leave Act regulations. Retrieved from https://www.dol.gov/whd/fmla/spouse/factsheet.htm (accessed March 23, 2017).

Vinjamuri, M. (2016). "It's so important to talk and talk": How gay adoptive fathers respond to their children's encounters with heteronormativity. *Fatherhood, 13*(3), 245–270. doi: 10.3149/fth.1303.245.

Waldo, C. R. (1999). Working in a majority context: A structural model of heterosexism as minority stress in the workplace. *Journal of Counseling Psychology, 46*(2), 218–232. doi: 10.1037/0022-0167.46.2.218.

Weber, M. (1943). *From Max Weber: Essays in sociology*. In H. H. Gerth & C. Wright Mills (Eds. & Trans.) *Bureaucracy and law* (216–220). New York: Oxford University Press.

Woods, J. D. (1993). *The corporate closet: The professional lives of gay men in America*. New York: The Free Press.

Yoder, J. B. & Mattheis, A. (2016). Queer in STEM: Workplace experiences reported in a national survey of LGBTQA individuals in science, technology, engineering, and mathematics careers. *Journal of Homosexuality, 63*(1), 1–27. doi: 10.1080/00918369.2015.1078632.

5   Balancing Gendered Obligations

Leslie notices that Lisa has been coming to work looking even more tired than usual. Unsure if they are close enough for her to inquire about Lisa's appearance, Leslie simply asks Lisa if she's feeling okay. Lisa sighs and explains that her mother has become ill and that she's contemplating moving herself and her kids to the other side of town so that she could more easily provide care. Leslie asks if Lisa has siblings who could help ease the burden, to which Lisa explains that she has a brother who is adamant that Lisa is more skilled in caring for others, and therefore the right person for the job. Her brother also pointed out that if she and the kids move in with their mother, Lisa would no longer have to pay rent. He thinks he's graciously allowing her to take on this role, she explains.

Lisa shares her concern that her kids would have to change school districts and that she has no idea how she will balance raising two children, and caring for her mother, all the while putting a fair share of her energy into her job. Before Leslie can voice her sympathy, Joel and Maria enter the room. Joel is finishing up a story about taking his youngest daughter to a grown-up restaurant. At one point in the evening, she had lifted the bun off of her cheese burger, saw the lettuce and tomato, and shouted, "Daddy, there's a salad in my burger!" Everyone laughed as Joel finished the story, and Maria remarked how great it was that Joel helped out so much with his kids.

Though she made a point not to show it, Lisa was taken aback. Nobody ever praised her for the time she spent with her kids. Everyone in her family has taken for granted that she is the caregiver. Leslie could read the look on Lisa's face and quietly joined Lisa in her dismay. How is it that women are still relegated to caretaking roles? And how is it that men, Leslie embellished in her mind, get a parade in their honor if they participate in even a fraction of the burden?

***

Early notions of gender roles, in the workplace, depict a broad divergence between masculinity and femininity. Kanter (1977) describes four "role entrapments" assigned to "token women" (p. 981): *The Mother* – who listens to people's problems and takes on domestic chores; *The Seductress* – a prominent source of the male gaze, arousing sexual competition; *The Pet* – a mascot who encourages male prowess, who is expected to yield little, if any, substantive contributions; and *The Iron Maiden* – who resists the other roles, insisting on being an equal. The Iron Maiden is thought to be exceptionally if not excessively tough. Conversely, Brannon's (1976) "blueprint for manhood" includes *The Big Wheel* – being an admired and respected breadwinner; *No Sissy Stuff* – the avoidance of femininity and its emotional attributions; *The Sturdy Oak* – conveying unwavering toughness; and *Give 'Em Hell* – concerned with violence and adventure. Both sets of characteristics, published over 40 years ago, may seem laughable today. We may be hard pressed to even think of a female colleague who would take on the demeaning role of the seductress,[1] or a male co-worker who embraces the "Give Em Hell" motif. And yet, it's important to consider the extent to which expectations of gender—both in the workplace and elsewhere—maintain remnants of these blueprints/role traps.

You may find that this chapter takes a step back from the previous chapter, with regard to notions of gender. Whereas Chapter 4 assumes gender to be a fluid performance, this chapter will, for the most part, consider gender as distinct cohorts of feminine and masculine that are assumed to be inextricable from biological sex. The goal is not to ignore gender fluidity as it occurs in the workplace, but rather to consider how lingering dichotomous *perceptions* of gender influence work–family balance expectations. This chapter also considers family roles that violate traditional gender expectations, and how we can affirm and advocate for ourselves amid these gendered expectations.

There was a time when to talk about gender meant to talk almost exclusively about the experiences of women. This chapter will be somewhat guilty of this, in that it will start by considering how the integration of women resulted in a gendering of the workplace, creating an impetus for considering work–family balance in the first place. Despite the integration of women, the male career model (Hewlett, 2007)—consisting of long hours and an uninterrupted span of working years—has gone largely unquestioned. In addition to women working with an employment trajectory that wasn't ideal to the family role expectations that many women had, women also had to break through the stigma of employed women, in general.

Goldin (2006) discusses four phases of women's integration into the workplace,[2] noting that the first three phases are evolutionary and the final phase describes a "quiet revolution." Phase One depicts the independent female worker of the 1800s–1920s. This worker is young and unmarried (married women who worked were largely stigmatized[3]) and did dirty, dangerous work, such as laundresses who worked with harsh chemicals. Phase Two, which occurred during and immediately following World War II (1930–1950), found more acceptance for married women who worked. Women took on jobs such as pipefitters, mechanics, and welders, but were ushered out of these jobs when men returned from the war (Coontz, 2006). However, the emergence of new information technologies meant more demand for clerical work, no doubt designated women's work on account of the low prospect of advancement. Though still no match for the value of a working man, working women in offices were afforded a level of dignity denied to the factory workers in Phase One. In Phase Three, 1950s–1970s, working married women in the 35–44 age group increased to 46 percent. It was common, by this time, for women to seek a college education, however most saw college as an educational opportunity clouded by the expectation of finding a husband, thereby earning an "MRS" degree. Finally, Phase Four, the "quiet revolution" occurring from the 1970s to present day, depicts more of an investment in formal education for women, as well as the acceptability of creating a name for herself before (or perhaps instead of) changing her name upon marriage.

The most important implication of the quiet revolution, for the study of work–family balance, is the shift in identity. During Phase Four, the importance of career success and co-worker recognition could potentially be prioritized, despite the lingering compulsion (see Chapter 3). This was also a time in which women began marrying later, allowing time to develop a professional identity, with less of the burden of also nourishing a familial identity (Goldin, 2006), in the traditional sense. Though many women are still expected to prioritize family over work, the quiet revolution brought about the *possibility* that a woman could put work first.

So why, in a workforce where women's identities have been evolving since the 1800s, would a book about work–family balance need a chapter about how obstacles vary by gender?[4] First, for as absurd as the *Mother*-woman or the *Give Em Hell*-man may seem, workplaces and family structures still function in relation to these gendered roles. You can probably think of at least one or two people you work with who espouse gender-typical roles in the workplace; even if no one springs to mind, it is the deviation from these motifs that make the colleagues in your workplace appear gender progressive. We may wince at the woman who volunteers to serve coffee to everyone, or the man who unapologetically interrupts to get his point across, because these actions are reminiscent of historical workplace gender roles.

Second, gender politics are alive and well in the workplace (as well as in negotiations of labor within the household). The wage gap (Samuelson, 2016) and the dearth of women CEOs (Peck, 2015) are salient examples of gender politics regarding work. The continued need for sexual harassment legislation, and the frequency of sexual harassment cases also points to gendered power plays (Dougherty, 2006). But there is another power play that is far more subtle than the wage gap or sexual harassment: The positioning of women as caregivers—both at work and at home—and the primacy afforded to what has been referred to as the male model of success (Hewlett, 2007).

The Culture of Care

Different occupations and workplace cultures produce different gender norms. The role of the Mother is a persistent gender stereotype that creates work–family balance obstacles for women, especially for women who are actual mothers. Despite the "quiet revolution," it is still expected that women juggle childcare along with building a career, in ways that men generally do not. The U.S. Census (2011) reports that only 32 percent of fathers with wives in the workforce were a regular source of childcare. Though this number has likely risen since the time of data collection, women who work are still considered primary caretakers of children—a role that puts career mobility at risk (Ridgeway & Correll, 2004). This risk is the result of gendered work–family expectations: Whereas having children decreases time away from work for men (Goldin, 2006; Hodges & Budig, 2010) and increases perceptions of workplace competence (Cuddy et al., 2004), women who become mothers, are considered less committed, less competent, and less worthy of investment (Cuddy et al., 2004; Sabat et al., 2016). Though the work–family balance needs of mothers are often more highly regarded than others (see Chapter 3; Dixon & Dougherty, 2014), this perceived lack of commitment is a steep price to pay for work–family balance regard. Importantly, research suggests that women—childfree women and mothers alike—are assumed to put family before work, even when they don't (Hoobler et al., 2009). This leads us to the consideration of a double bind in which mothers who are dedicated to their work are deemed by their peers to be poor mothers, and women who prioritize motherhood are considered unworthy of respect as a dedicated worker.

The clash of motherhood and employee identities may be highlighted within the context of pregnancy. Hebl, King, Glick, Singletary, and Kazama (2007) astutely note that the visible pregnancy is the "epitome of the traditional female role"—a reality that prompts many pregnant women to think strategically about the extent to which pregnancy should be hidden in the workplace. Some women, upon disclosing pregnancy at work, feel that they must campaign for their ongoing commitment to the workplace and their intention to return to work after giving birth (Medved, 2016a). Of course the choice to downplay one's pregnancy may come at the cost of taking advantage of work–family balance opportunities.

Many women I interviewed spoke of the strain of balancing work with childcare responsibilities. A common thread throughout interviews with women was the prominence placed on being *the mom*.[5] Candace, a 46-year-old breadwinner with a husband and stepson, discusses the guilt she feels when work takes away from her role as mom:

> I had to always put my job first, which causes extreme guilt because even though I'm lucky, I have another parent helping me out, I have my husband, he's still [pause], he's not the mom, and I'm still the mom and for young kids, I think the mom is just the most important one a lot of the time.

Though Candace counts herself lucky to have her husband's help in caring for her stepson, she places emphasis on the role of being a mom. Like others, Candace positions the role of the mom in a way that suggests an unequivocal and irreplaceable presence in the life of a child. Emphasis on the importance of the mom role, as unhampered by career success, emerges in Buzzanell et al.'s (2005) study of how women frame being good working mothers, with themes such as arranging quality childcare and taking pleasure in the mothering role. The primacy placed on motherhood, be it derived from biological or cultural factors weighs heavily on work–family balance for working mothers.

The Mother role can also be detrimental to women who aren't mothers. A woman may decide not to have children, seeking instead to devote time and energy to career fulfillment. As Chapter 3 illustrated, many childfree women have unique work–family balance obstacles to contend with, despite not adding children to the balance. But the culture of care positions non-mothers in mothering roles. As Hewlett (2007) remarks, "if these women don't have two year olds, they do (or will) have serious elder-care and extended-family responsibilities" (p. 110). The experiences of my interview participants suggest that she's right.

In my interview protocol, I asked, *Who do you take care of and who takes care of you?* I was very surprised by the number of women who, upon hearing this question, were at a loss for where to begin. Women I interviewed experienced a pull to tend to family issues, even when those issues precluded childcare. Josephine, a 33-year-old guidance councilor who lives with her mother, father, and three nephews, gave the following explanation:

> I'm responsible for pretty much everything in the household—for finances and making sure that bills are paid on time, I manage my parents' money … my dad works as a full-time custodian, my mom's been staying home for the last few years, and she gets social security income, so between their two incomes and my two incomes, we pay the mortgage together … My mom doesn't drive, so I spend a lot of time taking her to doctor's appointments, I do the grocery shopping.

Josephine lists all of her responsibilities on top of balancing multiple counseling jobs. In addition to the litany of responsibilities participants listed, many also discussed the emotional toll of being pulled in different directions. Recall Natalie, from Chapter 2, a 32-year-old who works in customer service who was "guilted" for taking time to care for her mom, despite having a company laptop at the ready for when her workplace needed her. This pull in different directions compromises quality of life, in general, but also, more specifically, the opportunity to balance work and family in a way that allows quality engagement with both.

Finally, many women explained being treated, by family members, as though their time at work was less important. In addition to assuming the role of ongoing caregiver, women were pitted with surprise obligations. Joy, a 45-year-old film editor, was given the unexpected task of taking her father on vacation:

> Last month I took my dad to Miami because my mother doesn't travel, she doesn't travel well in a car, and there's just no way she's getting on an airplane and my parents are aging and my mom kind of pulled me aside and said "take him somewhere—anywhere." My father has wanderlust like you wouldn't believe and he hasn't had a lot of opportunity to travel. So, I made arrangements so that I could take the time off from work and spend a week with him in Miami. Because when your mom asks for something like that it's really impossible to just be like 'no, I'm super busy.'

In Joy's experience, saying "I'm super busy" was not a viable option. Later in the interview, it was clarified that Joy had a brother who was not approached about taking the trip to Miami. The gendered expectation of eldercare also emerged in a study examining how couples balance work and family at mid-life (this particular population was in their early 50s). For example, Maureen[6] stated,

> When my father was in the hospital ... I [used to] come home from work, stay with my son for a couple of hours ... and then go straight to the hospital and stay there overnight ... Well that was interfering with my family life ... but it was just what you had to do.
> (Emslie & Hunt, 2009, pp. 159–160)

Several accounts, in my research as well as in the literature, depict the culture of care as a set of obligations that are often competing, and routine (such as visiting an elderly parent every day after work) as well as unanticipated (such as being asked to take a parent on a trip).

My goal for this section is to illustrate the culture of care that positions women as natural or ideal caregivers, and that the pull to meet care expectations jeopardizes career success and work–family balance in ways men do not, as frequently, contend with. Importantly, this goal does not include demonizing men for not having similar experiences. Some of the men I interviewed spoke of caring for children and tending to eldercare needs. For example, Chris, a 43-year-old administrative assistant, shared:

> Two years ago, I lost my brother and I feel like, more than ever, I feel like I'm taking care of my mom, especially, because he was right there down the road from her and now, now, I'm all she has and I'm five hours away in Atlanta. And I feel like I've kind of taken on that "taking care of mom" role, even though she's perfectly fine, she's independent, I still just kind of fill that role.

Chris explains being a source of emotional support for his mom, following his brother's untimely death. Although he undoubtedly provides indispensable emotional care to his mother, his is a special circumstance in which he is his mother's remaining child. The majority of men, when asked *Who do you take care of?*, either simply said, "I take care of myself" or "I take care of my family, financially." Though men, more so than women, are expected to be the provider of their families (Tinsley et al., 2015) this pressure doesn't add to the complexity of work–family balance in the same way that caring for family does. In addition to physical tasks, such as housework, women also shoulder psychological burdens of keeping track of obligations, such as remembering doctor's appointments, children's birthday parties, etc.

Additionally, the wage gap may render favoring the husband's career a sensible option. After all, if a husband "happens" to make more than his wife, it makes sense that efforts would be made to cultivate the higher-earning career. Many men look back on the times their children were young as times in which they felt conflict between work and home life (Emslie & Hunt, 2009). This was mostly due to increased working hours required to put food on the table. As one participant in Emslie and Hunt's (2009) study notes, "[m]y wife and I were falling out, especially when he [his son] was younger, because I was never here, I was working" (p. 162). Similarly, in some of the interviews I conducted, the feminine culture of care was juxtaposed by the masculine culture of providing. Julio, a 61-year-old cab driver, discusses lingering feelings of guilt for the amount of time he spent working.

> In retrospect, if I could change a lot of things, I wouldn't change them. ... Given the choice, I choose to work ... but then again we're talking about years ago, maybe your wife wasn't working at the time, the kids are small, you need the money, it's a hustle, and you gatta make decisions just based on that, you know. I know it's not all about money, but when you need the money ... [*extended pause*].

Julio describes being torn between the need to work and the expectations to spend time with his family, and explains that he would change nothing. The money was needed to support his family. Though what Julio describes is a strain on work–family balance, this strain is less a pull to comply with a culture of care, but rather an expectation of general regard. In addition to navigating the culture of care, gendered work–family balance obstacles occur as a result of the male model of success.

The Male Model of Success

The barriers that many women experience occur as a result of work expectations that were established before women commonly joined the workforce. Hewlett (2007) describes the male career model as including a continuous employment history, an emphasis on full-time employment with abundant face time, and the expectation that one's career excels most in one's 30s. The model allows men to "shake off" most women who have children (Hewlett, 2007, p. 15). Hewlett believes the male model of success "doesn't mesh with the imperatives of women's lives" (p. 14)—a perspective that both affirms women as inherent caregivers, and calls for a change in workplace structure for those who are.

A gendered model of success that facilitates privilege to those who aren't ensconced in, or working against, the culture of care feeds an enduring perspective that the work of women is optional (see Tracy & Rivera, 2010). This is a stereotype that lingers from when men were the unequivocal breadwinners, and women occasionally took jobs to supplement their husband's income. The culture of care assumes that women will inevitably need to "off-ramp" from the male success model of work. Hewlett (2007) defines off-ramped women as "those who'd left demanding careers in order to take care of equally demanding personal obligations, such as young children or ailing parents" (p. 3). Similarly, Stone and Hernandez (2012) describe "opting out" as a lifestyle choice, a devotion to domesticity, distinguishable from taking a standard maternity leave. "Off ramping" or "opting out" may be inevitable for women who wish to take time to be at home. The problem with this exodus isn't that women value spending time at home, but rather that it is assumed by many that women *choose* domesticity over career.

Almost 30 years ago, Faludi (1991) pointed to an anti-feminist backlash in which the media exaggerated the number of women choosing to stay home, positioning the trend as a response to their foremothers who paved the way in the workforce. Their decision to "opt out" was depicted not as a reflection of constrictive gender roles creating impossible demands from work and family, but rather as a manifestation of a lifestyle preference that honors domesticity over paid work (Stone & Hernandez, 2012). Interestingly, women who "opt out" often employ the language of choice used in the media. Stone (2007) conducted a study of women who "opt out" and found their words do mirror the media's emphasis on choice. Despite using language that suggests individual agency in their departure from work, participants in Stone's study cited a push from the workplace in the form of denial of a flexible work arrangement after giving birth as the impetus for their "choice." Had the male model of success been altered—perhaps allowing flexible schedules or even telecommuting—many of these women would have likely made different "choices."

Women's ability to avoid "opting out" is often determined by those in leadership positions within the workplace. Supervisors have been found to perceive working mothers as less involved in the workplace and as having a less flexible schedule than working fathers (King, 2008). As discussed in Chapter 1, Tracy and Rivera (2010) conducted a study in which they spoke with 13 male managers, business owners, and CEOs, who were married and had children, about gender roles and work–family balance. The authors found that, "executives' preferred relationships with wives and children in the private sphere are closely connected to a generalized hesitancy about progressive work–life policy and women's participation in the public sphere" (Tracy & Rivera, 2010, p. 5). If executives espouse gender equality at work but simultaneously express preferences for the enactment of traditional gender roles "that discourage women's equal participation in organizational life," aversive sexism[7] may be at play (p. 8).

A perhaps additional issue with women leaving the workforce is the uncertainty of whether they will be able to come back in. Of the 93 percent of women who want to opt back in, only 74 percent are successful, diminishing some of the perceived agency in returning to work (Stone & Hernandez, 2012). Even when women are fortunate enough to "opt" back in, broken professional connections and an inability to be competitive with colleagues who did not take time off can haunt career ambitions and affirm misperceptions that women are less committed to work than their male counterparts.

Of course, amid the concerns that women with MBAs and other advanced degrees are leaving the workforce, far less has been written about what happens when women are pushed out of the workplace, but cannot afford to leave. Love, a 24-year-old member of the guest services industry, shared her story:

> There was a policy that we could take time off if we needed it. And my daughter was diagnosed with a developmental disability. So, there was FMLA and I was able to take a leave of absence. [I] took personal days because she needed more days than what FMLA allowed, ultimately [I] had to quit my job [at a social services agency] … They gave me an ultimatum: Am I going to put my daughter's needs on the back burner or am I going to branch out, and, you know, have

to navigate not having a job while having a, you know, a demanding [*pause*] a daughter with demanding needs … So I decided to stay home and I arrived at that because I feel like employment may come and go, and it was my priority to get my daughter in the best position she could be. And I'm very happy with my decision.

As she explains, Love was dealt an ultimatum: She could maintain her employment status or give her daughter the care she needed. Even Love framed her leaving work as a choice, however a strong argument could be made that she had no choice at all. Because of the male model of success, Love was not presented with the option of a work schedule that allowed her to attend to her daughter's needs.

The cultural assumption that women are the designated caregivers, coupled with the illusion that women are choosing to leave the work force out of some essentialistic preference for domesticity compromises women's ability to be seen as equally committed employees. Thus far, this chapter has considered women's caregiving roles and the supposed choice to assume those roles at the cost of a career. In addition to considering how women are pushed out of the workplace, it is also important to consider how they are pulled home by traditional gender norms within the family.

(Non-)Conforming Divisions of Labor

Though the purpose of this book is to explore the experience of work–family balance in the workplace, it is important to understand the pull toward family obligations created by gendered divisions of labor. In her exceptionally popular and influential book, *The Second Shift* (1989), Arlie Hochschild notes the inequality between women and men, in how people regard the breaking down of gender roles. She explains, "the image of the go-get'em woman has yet to be fully matched by the image of the let's-take-care-of-the-kids-together man" (Hochschild, 1989, p. 202). This is illustrated in the opening vignette of this chapter when Joel is praised for taking his daughter out to dinner, while Lisa stands by, noting to herself that no one compliments her for having dinner with her children. The reluctance of men to join in childcare with the same fervor that women join the workplace can be heard in everyday language, such as when fathers "babysit" their children (Coe, 2013), or when women describe urging their partners to do their fair share with the analogy of "pulling teeth" (Buzzanell et al., 2005, p. 271).

Of course, the negotiation of labor isn't a uniform standoff across all straight couples, everywhere. From her study, focusing on heterosexual married couples with children under six, Hochschild (1989) conceptualized traditional, egalitarian, and transitional marital roles. As one might guess, traditional women identify primarily with their responsibilities to the home, even if they work. Egalitarian women want to have equal power within the marriage. And transitional women want to identify with work roles as well as roles at home, but expect their husbands to maintain more or less exclusively work-related roles. Some couples seemed to be egalitarian on the surface but were traditional, (curiously, the opposite was true as well). Hochschild (1989) reports that of the 100 people (50 couples) she interviewed, of the wives, 12 percent were traditional, 40 percent were transitional, and 48 percent were egalitarian; of the husbands, 18 percent were traditional, 62 percent were transitional, and 20 percent were egalitarian.

The disparity in feelings about how family roles should be distributed suggest a strain on families as different family members have different ideas about the distribution of labor. Interestingly, Hochschild (1989) notes that several men defended their preference for traditional gender roles on upbringing—a classic "that's just how I was brought up" appeal to tradition. But Hochschild (1989) cunningly notes the selectivity in clinging to one's upbringing, explaining that one of her participants, Evan, "didn't do many other things he was brought up to do, like go to church, avoid using credit cards, or wait to have sex until marriage. In these areas of life he was his own man" (p. 215).

Differing ideas about the distribution of household chores still exist between husbands and wives. While there is more sharing of household chores than there used to be, equal contributions to chores and childcare is yet to be realized (Pew Research, 2007). Divisions of household labor widen further after having children. According to the Bureau of Labor Statistics (2012), 28.7 percent of full-time working mothers did housework on weekdays, compared to 12 percent of working fathers. Some contributions by men are recreational, and are perhaps considered (by said men) to be more helpful than they actually are. For example, Hochschild (1989) explains second shift fetishes that men would adopt. One man she interviewed boasted, "I make all the pies we eat" (p. 49). I doubt pie production, and other "chores" that are actually hobbies, lends much relief to a woman who works full time and is expected to do the majority of the housework.

Though the research collected for *The Second Shift* occurred in the 1980s, the book seems remarkably reflective of present-day divisions of labor. It would make sense that women feel a frustrating uphill battle: not only is the average American woman, in an opposite-sex relationship, having to negotiate down the amount of housework she does, she is doing this nearly twenty years into the 21st century. So when the battle is lost and she's washing the dishes when it is his turn, or cleaning the pan of the pie he so selflessly baked, there is an extra layer of humiliation … of it's almost 2020—why am I still in the kitchen?

Millennials are often stereotyped as being disinterested in housework, seeking instead lives in which chores are done for them, through service industries. There is even talk of the decline of the cereal industry on account of millennials not wanting to have a breakfast that requires washing a bowl (Ferdman, 2016). Despite what may seem like a genderless relinquishing of household responsibilities, Pew Research reports indicate that millennial moms are still doing more housework than their partners: In 2013, mothers with children under 18 spent an average of 14.2 hours per week on housework, whereas fathers spent only 8.6 hours (Parker, 2015). Although not everyone with a child under 18 is a millennial, the disparity in domestic workloads is telling.

It has been asserted that the new generation of couples has "no well-worn paths to follow" with regard to family structure and gender role enactment (Gerson, 2010, p. 7). Upon interviewing 120 young women and men between the ages of 18 and 32, Gerson (2010) reports that millennials see roles as less important than the context in which they are carried out. But it is possible that this is a description of a vague ideal, rather than a reflection of roles actually employed. After all— though some people thoroughly enjoy housework—one wouldn't count on such a "context" emerging in each cohabiting relationship across the lifespan.

Amid the pervasive reality that women do more housework than men, there is a common discourse of praise for women who accept excessive burden and make it look effortless. Looking specifically to identities created upon becoming a mother, in Buzzanell et al.'s previously mentioned study of 2005, women reframe the "good mother" image upon returning to work following maternity leave, taking pride in the ability to work through complex work–family balance challenges. They didn't seem to recognize that the accomplishment they felt was a result of shouldering obligations that rendered their relationships unequal. Though some women are drawn to the "have it all"[8] rhetoric, others recognize that this construct fosters gender inequality. After all, men can more or less count on never needing to choose between family or career. Buzzanell et al.'s (2005) research went on to illustrate how contributions from husbands did not come naturally—husbands had to be asked to help and women were sometimes faced with resistance—one participant referred to it as like a "scam" (p. 271) in which husbands pretend to lack the ability to do chores. This resistance among men at taking on equal work at home tarnishes some of the luster for women who "have it all."

Though most of this chapter focuses on straight, cisgender women and men, perhaps a genderless approach to thinking about the negotiation of domestic labor can be found in the lives of couples who are LGBTQ. Goldberg (2013) found that same-sex couples both "do" and "undo" gender through housework. Literature consistently suggests that same-sex couples divide housework more equally than opposite-sex couples; however, to suggest that gender is relinquished from the division of labor would be an over-simplification. In some instances, the person who worked fewer hours, or who worked from home, did the majority of the housework, and for many in Goldberg's (2013) study, the value of housework and management of the gendered attributions needed to be addressed. For example, if someone did the majority of the housework, that person might field questions regarding whether they are "the woman" in the relationship.[9] In addition to considering the role of gender in housework for couples who are LGBTQ, another illuminating point of focus is straight and cisgender families containing husbands and wives who have swapped roles.

Female Primary Breadwinners

The gendered obstacles of work–family balance can be illuminated further by considering variations to the male provider/female caregiver norm. Women who earn an income of any measure have far more decision-making power in their marriages, than those who don't (Coontz, 2006). With the ongoing struggle for equality in the distribution of household chores and childcare, it may be surprising to learn that four out of ten families with children have a female primary breadwinner (Medved, 2016a). Of course, the number of families containing female breadwinners is not matched with an ideology that separates gender from visions of labor. Even female breadwinners with unemployed or underemployed stay-at-home counterparts communicate in ways that reinforce traditional gender roles, sometimes positioning their labor distribution as the exception to the rule, and sometimes even the exception to the ideal (see Medved, 2016a; Meisenbach, 2010; Rosin, 2012).

Medved (2016a) examined how breadwinning mothers reinforce, resist, and challenge traditional notions of gender through the discursive positioning of identities and tasks. She found that gendered discourses of labor were at times reinforced, such as when participants explained being ideal breadwinners because of their proclivity to approach work with masculine traits (e.g., describing themselves as "aggressive," "competitive," or "driven"). But at the same time traditional notions of gender were resisted in that the participants espousing these traits were women. Importantly, participants in Medved's study found that they still had to push back against the idea that they should be primary caregivers (e.g., vetting questions about whether they feel guilty for coming back to work, and assuring co-workers that they plan to return to work following maternity leave). This notion that breadwinning expectant mothers must campaign their commitment to a career suggests the culture of care doesn't dissipate as women achieve career success.

In addition to both perpetuating and challenging gendered ideologies about paid and domestic labor, female breadwinners have the unique obstacle of negotiating non-work obligations in ways men do not. Meisenbach (2010) interviewed female breadwinners who described having control of the major household decisions, such as the way money is spent. Interestingly, some participants referred to themselves, light-heartedly, as "control freaks"—prompting one to ponder the gendered nature of such a label: Would a straight, cisgender, breadwinning man call himself a "control freak?" In Medved's (2016a) study, some participants shared that their husbands took responsibility for family finances, so as to retain some authority within the family structure. In this instance, entrusting the finances to the non-working spouse makes sense—with sharing the power comes sharing the burden. However, some female breadwinners experienced a pushback at home that resulted in extra work and a regression back to traditional gender roles. Despite having a larger decision-making role within the household, it is possible that breadwinning women may actually do more housework in a phenomenon termed "gender grievance neutralization" (Bittman et al., 2003). The female breadwinners in Meisenbach's (2010) study specified that the control they felt occurred to the exclusion of delegating household chores. The expectation that female breadwinners also engage in domestic labor accentuates a "pull" from work responsibilities that aren't felt by breadwinning men in traditional households.

The discourses men use to retain a semblance of authority in their households is also illuminating. Rosin (2012) asserts that stay-at-home men retain a language of being head of the household. When Rosin (2012) asked a stay-at-home husband if it made him feel like less of a man that his wife was providing for the family, he said, "I could have my wife stay at home and spend money, or I could have my wife out making some big money. Hmmm." The language of "having [his] wife" select one track or another points to the implied directorship that comes with trying to maintain the status of head of household. The need to maintain a semblance of power over the household is reminiscent of the work of Buzzanell and Turner (2003), who found that after a husband's job loss, the family engaged in discursive work to try to maintain a sense of normalcy. This need to maintain a regular routine in such situations may be just as much for the benefit of the other family members as it is for the husband/father. However, one of the reasons for this maintenance is to allow the former male breadwinner to maintain a sense of dignity that comes from being a successful provider.

In Medved's (2016a) aforementioned study of identity and task construction among breadwinning mothers, none of the participants positioned their husbands as negligent in their duties as fathers and husbands. In a different study, Medved (2016b) spoke with 45 stay-at-home dads, exploring how discourses reinforced, resisted, and (potentially) transformed masculinity. Participants in Medved's study maintain masculine identities by framing their role as protectors, including building/outside labor (e.g., cutting down trees) as an aspect of domestic labor, and sometimes not volunteering the identity of a stay-at-home dad upon meeting new people. Conversely, participants communicating care and empathy served to resist traditionally gendered roles. Research shows movement toward discourses that position caring and earning as gender neutral constructs (Medved, 2016b), even in instances when roles switch out of necessity (e.g., a man is a stay-at-home father as a result of being laid off from work [Chesley, 2011]). The notion that discourses, such as those Medved (2016b) examines, are the impetus for changing the (gendered) culture of care may be used as a point of departure for discourses that can change (gendered) barriers to work–family balance.

Work–Family Balance

Women in the workplace who are also wives and mothers are abiding by the traditional family structure commonly expected of them (see Chapter 3). Straight, cisgender women also avoid the hypervisibility and questioning often experienced by LGBTQ working adults (see Chapter 4). And yet, working wives and mothers experience unique work–family balance obstacles. Work–family balance literature, as well as my research, suggest that working wives and mothers experience (a) an expectation that family obligations are (or should be) a higher priority than work responsibilities, and (b) the assumption (communicated in workplace cultures) that immediate family is the extent of their caregiving obligations.

The wage gap is one way in which the devaluation of women in the workplace is communicated. Other devaluation may occur at the managerial and administrative levels. Tracy and Rivera (2010) found that, "executives discussed the qualities that make for 'good wives and mothers' as different and antithetical to the traits of 'good female employees'" (p. 24). Though it is possible for an employer to hold a personal belief all the while supporting a workplace policy or culture that contradicts said belief, aversive sexism is likely. It creates a curious and unfortunate paradox when the efforts of paid labor are viewed as misprioritized by the very stakeholder for which the efforts were made.

Utilizing the same ideology that women are supposed to prioritize domestic work, workplace members may also assume that women choose to work, whereas their male counterparts must work to support their families. This is, of course, patently untrue and also a nod to the lingering compulsion (see Chapter 3) as the only way most women could possibly afford to prioritize home life is with the financial support of a working spouse. Several participants discussed concerns about being able to provide, sufficiently, for their families. As Candace, a 46-year-old middle school teacher, stated, "most women, I think, put their families first and I feel like I have to put my job first or we're not going to have a decent place to live or food to eat." Candace's remark that "most women put their families first" suggests that she believes that she is, at least somewhat, alone in her need to prioritize work. This resonates with Medved's aforementioned research illuminating the lives of women who feel the need to hide their pregnancies, for example, so as to postpone reinforcing a stereotype. Even if a woman can afford to prioritize home over work, that doesn't mean it should be the purview of the workplace to decide that that's where her attentions should predominantly lie.

In addition to the devaluing of women at work, and the assumption that work is a choice, work–family balance obstacles occur when the time needed away from work is for someone other than a child. Many participants discussed caring for parents, grandparents, aunts, family of choice, etc. Providing further evidence of the notion of pronatalism, described in Chapter 3, participants explained that being away from work to provide eldercare did not garner the understanding attributed to caring for children. In some instances the compulsory focus on caring for children shows a need for a broader understanding of work–family balance and ethnicity. In the case of Adriana, who cares for her parents, sibling, and nephews, she explained that people in her workplace don't understand that caring for extended family is more common in Hispanic cultures.

Finally, there is the issue of social support. Given that only 57 percent of women participate in the workforce (US Department of Labor, 2016), it makes sense that they would be gender minorities in many workplaces, especially those that are stereotypically male professions. Women working among male colleagues, who belong to traditional family structures, may feel as though they cannot discuss stereotypically female topics, such as childcare, for fear of being considered unprofessional (Bailyn, 2006). If semblances of the Sturdy Oak still exist, one might feel disinclined to talk parenting with him.

Affirmation

When it comes to affirming and familiarizing one's family in the workplace, women experience a double bind. On the one hand, the premise of this book is that we communicate our families into being, and that regard for family in the workplace requires establishing a familiarity. On the other hand, work–family balance literature, as well as several of the women I interviewed for this project, caution against talking about family at work (Bailyn, 2006). The concern is that to talk about family at work risks perpetuating the stereotype that women prioritize family over work. Though many workplaces have pockets of conversation about children, workplaces composed primarily of male employees are less likely to offer these spaces. In such work environments, talk about taking time away from work for family was met with suspicion. Eliza, a 34-year-old wine sales representative from Texas, explains navigating time she spent away from work to care for her maternal grandmother:

E: Sometimes I would have to leave work a little early, or spend a few extra days out of town because she needed some help with some things, so I definitely made choices that affected work.
J: Were people sympathetic?
E: I was basically just very cautious of who I told, because I didn't want the perception placed on me that I was prioritizing this over my work, because I always got my work done and I never wanted to have that questioned.

Eliza used caution in communicating about taking time to care for her grandmother because she was concerned that talk about her work–family balance obstacles would betray her reputation as a reliable employee. Eliza later explained that she has to be extra careful about talking about family at work out of concern that she not separate herself from the "boy's club."

Though it is important that women use caution when communicating family into being, there are still opportunities to affirm one's work–family balance needs: (a) find little ways to deconstruct gendered representations as they predominantly exist and (b) frame family as an aspect of diversity. Ideally, time spent away from work to care for family would not be a deficit to one's career and would not be seen as a woman's obligation. Recalling the opening vignette, Joel was praised by co-workers for the time he spent with his daughter. Lisa, in contrast, didn't receive such praise. To call for men to represent their family structures at work, while silencing women out of fear of pitting them as natural caregivers is not the way to go. Women should discuss aspects of themselves that are unrelated to caregiving. Women who do feel that their role as a caregiver comes first should consider what it means for co-workers and managers to be aware of this. Would this add precarity to an already precarious work environment, or would candidly disclosing priorities lend to sympathy and understanding? Similarly, men who are caretakers should let this aspect of their lives be known in the workplace. Soak up the praise, but also recognize the work–family balance efforts of all genders.

In addition to deconstructing gendered assumptions of work–family balance, working adults should affirm family structures as rooted in diversity. Ethnicity presents one such opportunity. Adriana, for example, explained that her co-workers couldn't understand why she devoted the time to care for her nephew, as well as her parents and siblings. She attributed this dismay to misunderstandings regarding Hispanic culture. What may be dismissible to some as a "women's issue" within the culture of care may receive more regard when positioned as an aspect of cultural diversity.

Advocacy

Advocacy occurs in the ability to push back against the culture of care[10] and point to the flaw in the contention that "opting out" is an empowered choice that women are making. Workplace policy that deviates from the male model of success should be celebrated, promoted, and utilized as much as possible. Using policy requires an endorsement by senior management and assurance from the overall workplace culture that employees won't be seen as less than committed (Bailyn, 2006). Female employees may benefit from bosses who (a) have a spouse who works, or (b) envision their daughters and future daughters-in-law working (Tracy & Rivera, 2010). However, owing to the largely precarious landscape of paid labor, most women don't have the luxury of vetting potential bosses. Nonetheless, it may behoove both women and men to use, and encourage others to use, workplace policy that breaks down the notion that the male model of success is the only viable rubric for workplace commitment and success.

In addition to using, and encouraging the use of, work–family balance policy among both women and men, we should work to un-gender workplace commitment. Participants I spoke with conveyed a sense of futility regarding how men and women are valued in the workplace. Jackie, 35-year-old IT specialist, shares,

> I feel like there's this unspoken code among men, like this unwritten thing, that if a man is out of work, other men are going to work really hard to help him find a job because it's important because the man needs the job because it's this, he's the breadwinner, and there's not that [attribution], I think, for women.

This "code among men" that Jackie describes seems somewhat reminiscent of the "boy's club" described by Eliza (34-year-old wine sales representative in Texas) and in gender/organization literature (Wood, 2013). The "man code" that Jackie describes speaks to the notion that men are supposed to be at work and that measures should be taken to ensure they are. Women are possibly left out of this discourse because of a presumed split-commitment between home and work (in that order). Hewlett (2007) argues that women should have a "second shot at ambition" (pp. 137–138) and be welcomed back to work following taking extended time away. However, rather than being allowed to cope with the male model for career success, we should advocate for new ways to communicate workplace commitment (Bailyn, 2006). This could occur in the form of allowing flextime for all employees, or leaning toward more post-Fordist notions of being "at work" that, for example, relinquish the praiseworthiness of doing work *at work*. Advocating for flextime policies for all, as well as advocating for new ways of thinking about commitment, could go a long way in removing perceptions about gender from work–family balance.

Conclusion

Coontz (2006) astutely observes that "[w]e are all pioneers, picking our way through uncharted and unstable territory. The old rules are no longer reliable guides to work out modern gender roles" (pp. 282–283). Women have come a long way from the blatantly harmful workplaces of the 1800s and early 1920s. But the quiet revolution is not complete (Gerson, 2010). Although it is now within the realm of possibility for women to prioritize work over family, gendered obligations such as the culture of care and the structures of workplace commitment that favor the stereotypical male life trajectory (i.e., not needing to take time off from work to give birth) still render work–family balance a different experience for women and men.

Gendered ideologies that occur in the workplace—and are reflected in constructions of commitment and mobility that are untenable for women wishing to pursue a traditional family structure—extend into the home. Even with increasing numbers of breadwinning wives and stay-at-home husbands, women still experience difficulty brokering a fair distribution of domestic labor. Still, amid the barriers and brokering, "flickers of transformation" are occurring (Tracy & Rivera, 2010), and can be seen in transformative discourses about work–family balance (Medved, 2016a, 2016b), as well as new ways of looking at workplace commitment (Bailyn, 2006).

Notes

1 This isn't to say that being seductive, in and of itself, is demeaning, but rather the expectation that one's power lies exclusively within the purview of sexual desirability.
2 Goldin uses the term "economy" rather than "workplace," but the terms are interchangeable within their application of this chapter.
3 Coontz (2006) explains that, at this time, it was felt that women should stay at home because it was a sanctuary where they could be protected from the turmoil of all things economic and political.
4 Or, more accurately, why would it be necessary to write a chapter about work–family balance, biological sex, and the gender performance expected of said sex?
5 It would be interesting to consider perceptions of motherhood as they potentially vary across generations. Millennials, for example, reject the idea that motherhood requires "undiluted altruism" (Gerson, 2010, p. 146).
6 Pseudonyms are used in all quotes from Emslie and Hunt's (2009) study.
7 Tracy and Rivera employ the term aversive sexism as comparable to the term aversive racism, in which racism is enacted though the avoidance of

interaction with other racial groups. Aversive sexism describes a similar avoidance, but to people of other genders.

8 I'm referring, here, to the common trope of successfully having a family and a career. Supreme Court Justice Sonia Sotomayor (2013) defines "having it all" as having "career and family at no sacrifice to either," which she feels is "a myth we would do well to abandon" (p. 233).

9 Goldberg (2013) also brings up the point that gay men are more likely to be able to afford to pay a housekeeper and that housekeepers are predominantly women, therefore perpetuating traditionally gendered distributions of labor.

10 I do not intend to advocate for a devaluation of care, itself, but rather the expectation that women are inherently better suited for it.

References

Bailyn, L. (2006). *Breaking the mold: Redesigning work for productive and satisfying lives* (2nd ed.). Ithaca, NY: Cornell University Press.

Bittman, M., England, P., Sayer, L., Folbre, N., & Matheson, G. (2003). When does gender trump money? Bargaining and time in household work. *American Journal of Sociology, 109*, 186–214. doi: 10.1086/378341.

Brannon, R. (1976). The male sex role: And what it's done for us lately. In R. Brannon & D. Davids (Eds.), *The forty-nine percent majority* (pp. 1–40). Reading, MA: Addison-Wesley.

Bureau of Labor Statistics. (2012). How parents use time and money. Retrieved: www.bls.gov/opub/btn/volume-1/how-parents-use-time-money.htm (accessed January 23, 2017).

Buzzanell, P. M. & Turner, L. H. (2003). Emotion work revealed by job loss discourse: Backgrounding-foregrounding of feelings, construction of normalcy, and (re)instituting of traditional masculinities. *Journal of Applied Communication Research, 31*(1), 27–57. doi: 10.1080/00909880305375.

Buzzanell, P. M., Meisenbach, R., Remke, R., Liu, M., Bowers, V., & Conn, C. (2005). The good working mother: Managerial women's sensemaking and feelings about work–family issues. *Communication Studies, 56*(3), 261–285. doi: 10.1080/10510970500181389.

Chesley, N. (2011). Stay-at-home fathers and breadwinning mothers: Gender, couple dynamics, and social change. *Gender & Society, 25*(5), 642–664.

Coe, A. (2013, January 23). Dads caring for their kids: It's parenting, not babysitting. *The Atlantic*. Retrieved: www.theatlantic.com/sexes/archive/2013/01/dads-caring-for-their-kids-its-parenting-not-babysitting/267443/ (accessed January 23, 2017).

Coontz, S. (2006). *Marriage, a history: From obedience to intimacy or how love conquered marriage.* New York: Viking Penguin.

Cuddy, A. J., Fiske, S. T., & Glick, P. (2004). When professionals become mothers, warmth doesn't cut the ice. *Journal of Social Issues, 60*(4), 701–718. doi: 10.1111/j.0022-4537.2004.00381.x.

Dixon, J. & Dougherty, D. S. (2014). A language convergence/meaning divergence analysis exploring how LGBTQ and single employees manage traditional family expectations in the workplace. *Journal of Applied Communication Research, 42*(1), 1–19. doi: 10.1080/00909882.2013.847275.

Dougherty, D. S. (2006). Gendered discourses of power during discourse about sexual harassment. *Sex Roles, 54*(7), 495–507. doi: 10.1007/s11199-006-9012-4.

Emslie, C. & Hunt, K. (2009). "Live to work" or "work to live"? A qualitative study of gender and work–life balance among men and women in mid-life. *Gender, Work & Organization, 16*(1), 151–172. doi: 10.1111/j.1468-0432.2008.00434.x.

Faludi, S. (1991). *Backlash: The undeclared war on American women.* New York: New Rivers Press.

Ferdman, R. A. (2016, February 23). The baffling reason many millennials don't eat cereal. *The Washington Post.* Retrieved from www.washingtonpost.com/news/wonk/wp/2016/02/23/this-is-the-height-of-laziness/?utm_term=.e510bc7d5389 (accessed January 23, 2017).

Gerson, K. (2010). *The unfinished revolution: Coming of age in a new era of gender, work, and family.* New York: Oxford University Press.

Goldberg, A. E. (2013). "Doing" and "undoing" gender: The meaning and division of housework in same-sex couples. *Journal of Family Theory & Review, 5*(2), 85–104. doi: 10.1111/jftr.12009.

Goldin, C. (2006). The quiet revolution that transformed women's employment, education, and family. *The American Economic Review, 96*(2), 1–21. doi: 10.3386/w11953.

Hebl, M. R., King, E. B., Glick, P., Singletary, S. L., & Kazama, S. (2007). Hostile and benevolent reactions toward pregnant women: Complementary interpersonal punishments and rewards that maintain traditional roles. *Journal of Applied Psychology, 92*(6), 1499–1511. doi: 10.1037/0021-9010.92.6.1499.

Hewlett, S. A. (2007). *Off-ramps and on-ramps: Keeping talented women on the road to success.* Boston, MA: Harvard Business School Press.

Hochschild, A. (1989). *The second shift: Working families and the revolution at home.* New York: Penguin Books.

Hodges, M. J. & Budig, M. J. (2010). Who gets the daddy bonus? Organizational hegemonic masculinity and the impact of fatherhood on earnings. *Gender & Society, 24*(6), 717–745. doi: 10.1177/0891243210386729.

Hoobler, J. M., Wayne, S. J., & Lemmon, G. (2009). Bosses' perceptions of family–work conflict and women's promotability: Glass ceiling effects. *Academy of Management Journal, 52*(5), 939–957. doi: 10.5465/AMJ.2009.44633700.

Kanter, R. M. (1977). Some effects of proportions on group life: Skewed sex ratios and responses to token women. *American Journal of Sociology, 82*(5) 965–990.

King, E. B. (2008). The effect of bias on the advancement of working mothers: Disentangling legitimate concerns from inaccurate stereotypes as predictors of advancement in academe. *Human Relations, 61*(12), 1677–1711.

Medved, C. E. (2016a). The new female breadwinner: Discursively doing and undoing gender relations. *Journal of Applied Communication Research, 44*(3), 1–20. doi: 10.1080/00909882.2016.1192286.

Medved, C. E. (2016b). Stay at home fathering as a feminist opportunity: Perpetuating, resisting, and transforming gender relations of caring and earning. *Journal of Family Communication, 16*(1), 16–31. 10.1080/15267431.2015.1112800.

Meisenbach, R. J. (2010). The female breadwinner: Phenomenological experience and gender identity in work–family spaces. *Sex Roles, 62*(2), 2–19. doi: 10.1007/s11199-009-9714-5.

Parker, K. (2015, October 1). Women more than men adjust their careers to family life. *Pew Research Center.* www.pewresearch.org/fact-tank/2015/10/01/women-more-than-men-adjust-their-careers-for-family-life/ (accessed January 23, 2017).

Peck, E. (2015, July 14). Do you realize how few women CEOs exist? These executives don't. *The Huffington Post.* Retrieved from www.huffingtonpost.com/2015/07/13/ weber-shandwick-female-ceo_n_7771608.html (accessed January 23, 2017).

Pew Research. (2007, July 18). Modern marriage: "I like hugs, I like kisses. But what I really want is help with the dishes. *Pew Research Center.* Retrieved from www.pewsocialtrends.org/2007/07/18/modern-marriage/ (accessed January 23, 2017).

Ridgeway, C. & Correll, S. J. (2004). Motherhood as a status characteristic. *Journal of Social Issues, 60*(4), 683–700. doi: 10.1111/j.0022-4537.2004.00380.x.

Rosin, H. (2012). *The end of men and the rise of women.* New York: Riverhead Books.

Sabat, I. E., Lindsey, A. P., King, E. B., & Jones, K. P. (2016). Understanding and overcoming challenges faced by working mothers: A theoretical and empirical review. In C. Spitzmueller & R. A. Matthews (Eds.), *Research perspectives on work and the transition to motherhood* (pp. 9–31). Switzerland: Springer International Publishing.

Samuelson, R. J. (2016, April 24). What's the real gender gap? *The Washington Post.* Retrieved from www.washingtonpost.com/opinions/whats-the-real-gender-pay-gap/2016/04/24/314a90ee-08a1-11e6-bdcb-0133da18418d_story.html (accessed January 23, 2017).

Sotomayor, S. (2013). *My beloved world.* New York: Alfred A. Knopf.

Stone, P. (2007). *Opting out? Why women really quit careers and head home.* Berkeley, CA: University of California Press.

Stone, P. & Hernandez, L. A. (2012). The rhetoric and reality of "opting out": Toward a better understanding of professional women's decisions to head home. In B. D. Jones (Ed.), *Women who opt out* (pp. 33–56). New York: New York University Press.

Tinsley, C. H., Howell, T. M., & Amanatullah, E. T. (2015). Who should bring home the bacon? How deterministic views of gender constrain spousal wage preferences. *Organizational Behavior and Human Decision Processes, 126,* 37–48. doi: 10.1016/j.obhdp.2014.09.003.

Tracy, S. J. & Rivera, K. D. (2010). Endorsing equity and applauding stay-at-home moms: How male voices on work-life reveal aversive sexism and flickers of transformation. *Management Communication Quarterly, 24*(3), 3–43. doi: 10.1177/0893318909352248.

U.S. Census. (2011). One-third of fathers with working wives regularly care for their children, Census Bureau reports. Retrieved from https://www.census.gov/newsroom/releases/archives/children/cb11-198.html (accessed January 23, 2017).

U.S. Department of Labor (2016). Women in the workforce: Data and statistics. Retrieved from www.dol.gov/wb/stats/stats_data.htm (accessed January 23, 2017).

Wood, J. T. (2013). *Gendered lives: Communication, gender, & culture* (10th ed.). Boston, MA: Wadsworth.

6   Balancing Family of Choice

Although Trent's mother passed away some time ago, his mother's best friend, Marilou, is still an integral part of his life. Trent has known Marilou since he was a small child, forming an unlikely long connection, given Trent, himself, is in his early 60s. Trent, and his wife, Pam, reason that he has stayed close with Marilou because she helped raise him after his father left him and his mother to fend for themselves.

Trent and Pam pick up Marilou from her assisted living facility, every week, and bring her to their home for Sunday dinner. They also have Marilou over for birthday parties and holidays. In addition to including her in family traditions and celebrations, Trent and Pam occasionally lend a hand in helping Marilou sort her mail and remind her to take her medication. Trent and Marilou joke, to Pam's amusement, that they are one another's honorary mother and son. Trent ponders, to himself, whether his parent/son relationship with Marilou holds more truth than jest.

One morning, Trent received a call from the assisted living facility informing him that Marilou had passed away, peacefully, in her sleep. With differing time zones working to his favor, he was able to speak with some of Marilou's family, who lived on the other side of the country, before leaving for work. On his way to work, Trent tried to fathom how he could function, business as usual, at work when he was feeling as if he had just lost his mother, all over again. Sure, his co-workers would understand that he would want to attend the funeral, but he knew that simply wasn't enough time to grieve. "What am I supposed to tell them?" he thinks to himself, "that I need extra time off because my late mother's *friend* died?" Trent was convinced that no one at work would understand that Marilou *was* family.

***

We likely all have someone like Marilou in our lives who we love, care for, and have fully integrated into our family circle, despite their not meeting the criteria of family by the traditional standards discussed in Chapter 1. This person may supplement or substitute those who we consider family in the traditional sense of the word, or they may be a more convenient alternative to traditional family, who live far away (Braithwaite et al., 2010). We may form family of choice because we are in need of financial, social, or emotional support; or, family of choice may result from cultural norms in which familial care extends beyond those related to us in the traditional sense. Family of choice may be thought of as "those persons perceived to be family, but who are not related by blood or law" (Braithwaite et al., 2010, p. 390), and is built when someone chooses to regard someone with familial commitment and care (Dixon, 2015a). As examined below, delineating between family of choice, close friendships, and community can be difficult, and perhaps even unnecessary. To develop an understanding of family of choice, and the possibilities for caring for chosen familial relationships, this chapter will consider the implications of chosen family terminology, examine some forms of family of choice, and consider the possibility of affirming and advocating for family of choice in one's work–family balance endeavors.

The term "family of choice" isn't widely known. Although some of my participants offered up the term during interviews, most described the concept (if applicable) without actually using the phrase. Furthermore, though I recruited participants using criteria that included family of choice, very few agreed to participate based on a claim of belonging to one. Instead, interviewees would volunteer because they belonged to another family structure (e.g., single), and the experience of belonging to a family of choice would emerge in the interview. This emergent realization of familial belonging and commitment suggests that the number of people who have at least some level of commitment to a family of choice outweigh the number of people who would readily identify as having or being family of choice. As will be discussed later, it is possible that individuals choose not to volunteer information about family of choice out of concern that people will disagree with the designation. People may also closet their family of choice from the workplace out of concern that co-workers and managers will think they are fraudulently seeking accommodation. Regardless of the rationale, not recognizing family of choice as a viable aspect of work–family balance can have implications for the extent to which familial care may be given (and received).

To add to the potential for confusion, family of choice has been discussed as having a number of different meanings. Labeled in communication research as fictive (Lucas & Buzzanell, 2006) or voluntary kin (Braithwaite et al., 2010), I prefer to use *family of choice*[1] because it lends a sense of legitimacy and agency withheld in the word "fictive" and it relays a certain sense of affection missing in the word "kin." And yet, arriving at this decision was tricky in that it is admittedly classist, erasing the experiences of individuals who become family and rely on each other out of necessity, not choice. For example, two single mothers who are neighbors may agree to watch each other's children while the other is at work. They may not like each other, and they may not otherwise choose to include each other as integral parts of their lives, but necessity, born from a financial inability to secure childcare, may dictate otherwise, therefore prompting familial connection and expectations of reciprocity. In situations such as this, where circumstance eliminates the aspect of choice, fictive kin might be a more appropriate term.

The term "fictive kin" emerges frequently in research examining the family dynamics of racial minorities, and African-American families in inner cities in particular (Domínguez & Watkins, 2003; Nelson, 2014; Stack, 1974). As with all families of choice, these relationships are thought to enlarge one's support system (Johnson, 1999; Nelson, 2014; Stack, 1974). For example, studies have examined African-American communities of the 1960s and 1970s, pooling resources for survival (Stack, 1974). Families of all races and ethnicities no doubt continue to form from necessity. However, the term *family of choice* may better serve the needs of those seeking to affirm and advocate for work–family balance needs, because it suggests a deliberate and steadfast familial commitment.

Nelson (2014) found that researchers are more likely to use the term *fictive kin* when describing racial minorities, than they are in describing white and mixed race populations. She explains that, "the language suggests that African Americans 'make up' their relationships through the exercise of imagination while gays and lesbians exercise agency and intention" (Nelson, 2014, p. 216). These misrepresentations suggest that African-American and other racial minorities, form haphazard allegiances that are limited in agency and integrity. At least two implications exist for this racialized framing of family of choice/fictive kin: It can serve to create the illusion that racial minorities create a different, less reliable, form of family of choice (Nelson, 2014), and it can signal that family of choice relationships, among racial minorities, are less worthy of regard. After all, if the "relative" is assumed to only be a member of the family "through the exercise of imagination," how can requests for accommodation compete with the needs of other co-workers with more traditional family ties? At the same time, family of choice that might more accurately be described as family of necessity, should be considered no less of a family structure. Ultimately, despite its limitations, I choose to use *family of choice* over *fictive kin* because misrepresenting one's level of agency in forming family is still closer to accurate than depicting the relationship as fictional or unreal.

Despite the various possible scenarios that may describe family of choice, as Nelson (2013) points out, they all have the common quality of being a positive aspect of someone's life. Unlike the traditionally understood family structures, family of choice "relies on mutual actions and mutual agreements" (p. 262). Family of choice is prompted by a need (such as Marilou being Trent's "honorary mother"), or a cultural commitment, and requires investment that is often reserved for traditional families. Even in the aforementioned example, the two single parents, who wouldn't otherwise interact, see the opportunity for mutual benefit and accordingly agree to a routine. Through this routine, shared experiences of child-raising emerge as does the semblance of a family, complete with obligations and expectations that one can expect from a traditional family structure.

Choice-Based Family Forms

As previously mentioned, family of choice can occur in many forms. As a matter of fact, the argument could be made that family of choice is boundless, and can encompass any of our relationships. With this abundance of familial opportunities in mind, consideration of some common families of choice may help in wrapping our heads around how family of choice may form and why they may be entitled to work–family balance accommodation. In some cases, family of choice is described as an extension (Braithwaite et al., 2010) of a more traditional family structure. For example, Jan, a 45-year-old film editor, and her wife have a friend who they consider to be family and who they care for, when needed, without question:

> I have a friend who is in some financial trouble right now and I am definitely putting my time and energy toward helping her out of that situation. She is chosen family, for sure, we've said it before: if it comes down to it, come live with us. If it means living on the street, that's not going to be an option.

Jan describes opening her home to someone she and her wife consider family. She and other participants discussed extending resources to family of choice while concurrently maintaining a family that appears to be closer to what we think of as traditional. Adding family of choice to more recognizable family structures are often done with the impetus of a particular need, such as Jan's friend who was described as having financial trouble. Family of choice, as an extension of traditional family, may also be the result of support needed as a result of *kin-scription*, defined by Stack and Burton (1993) as power plays in which [traditional] family members hold expectations for one another that derail or (further) complicate the pursuit of personal goals and ambitions. In their study of social support networks among African-American and Latin-American women, Domínguez and Watkins (2003) found that kin-scription resulted in participants seeking familial support and care from outside the traditional family structure. For it was in the traditional family household, it was explained, where support for the individual took a back seat to support and sacrifice for the family unit. An example of kin-scription can also be found in the opening vignette of Chapter 5, when Lisa's brother insisted she move in with, and care for, their ailing mother. Though doing so might contribute to the needs of the family,

Lisa would need to look beyond the traditional family to support her own needs and goals.

In addition to family of choice that extends from a traditional family structure, families of choice also might serve to replace or supplement (Braithwaite et al., 2010) traditional family. Supplemental family of choice can take a number of different forms including LGBTQ networks. Chapter 4 explored work–family balance as experienced by families with one or more LGBTQ working adults. By contrast, LGBTQ communities form families of choice that offer mutual support, especially amid experiences of discrimination and/or rejection from traditionally defined family members. Young people rejected by their parents because of their sexual orientation or gender identity and who seek familial environments elsewhere is a prominent example. In 1997, Kath Weston stated "it's still a 'big deal' to live a life of same sex attraction because very little in society is set up to acknowledge the family ties you propose to make." Thirty years later, despite progress toward equality (see Chapter 4), young people who are LGBTQ are still frequently rejected by their parents and communities (Hirsch, 2015; HRC, 2015). Supplemental families of choice are also likely to form among LGBTQ seniors who are twice as likely to be single, more than twice as likely to live alone, and more than four times as likely to not have children (Gabrielson, 2011). Fear of discrimination may increase social isolation (Gabrielson, 2011), further necessitating a trusted family of choice. LGBTQ communities can also form family of choice through common interests. Allison, a 37-year-old dancer, choreographer, and instructor, describes supplemental family of choice within her community of dancers:

> I like my family here, I feel like [*pause*] I feel like my chosen family here is awesome, and we all take care of each other, and I think the people who are in my, like, ummm [*pause*] my really, like, close circle, here, they're in that close circle because there is a balance of caretaking, and ummm, and I really consider those people to be my family. Like close, close friends who I consider, like sisters and brothers, and we always make jokes about how, like, we're so lucky that we have multiple homes, meaning we each have our own homes, but we're welcome in anyone's, do you know what I mean?

Allison explains a "balance in caretaking" among her chosen family, as well as—while somewhat in jest—the feeling of having "multiple homes." As is discussed below, family of choice living in multiple homes may provide opportunity for thinking about family and care from a community-based lens in which the household is removed from any conceptual prerequisite for deserving care.

In each of the examples provided thus far, family of choice emerges as a result of need: loved ones in need of financial assistance, groups in need of social support, etc. Families of choice are also developed from the needs of the elderly. Allen, Blieszner, and Roberto (2011) examine "kin reinterpretation practices" (p. 1156) among older adults as a means of coping with the impermanence of family ties. Older individuals may enlist friends and colleagues into family roles following the death of traditional family members. They might also engage in kin retention, such as considering an ex-in-law family, following a divorce (Allen et al., 2011). In this chapter's opening vignette, Marilou and Trent consider one another family, and Marilou—who we can assume to be in her eighties—receives care from Trent and his wife, Pam, which she does not receive from her traditional family, who live far away.

Family of choice may also form among U.S. immigrants as well as refugees in need of assistance in cultural brokering. In 2015, the United States resettled 69,933 refugees (Zong & Batalova, 2015). Resettlement[2] organizations seek to provide "complete social life orientation training," such as how to dress for snowy weather and what to expect during American holidays;[3] however, Steimel (2016) found these services to lack appreciation of refugees' cultural norms in addition to difficulties that emerge from language barriers. Refugees communicated a desire to connect with other refugees. Such relationships could foster familial bonds, especially in instances where traditional families are separated. The need for familial bonds, for refugees as well as all immigrants living in the US, is no doubt strengthened as a result of the uncertainty and blatant marginalization coming from Donald Trump's "Muslim Ban." On January 27, 2017, Donald Trump signed an executive order restricting immigration from seven Muslim countries,[4] temporarily suspending all refugee admissions, barring all Syrian refugees indefinitely (Calamur, 2017), and blocking federal funding to "sanctuary cities"—or cities that limit cooperation with federal immigrant agents (Lee et al., 2017). The future of immigration in the U.S. is riddled with uncertainty. Even if the executive order is permanently blocked (Jarrett et al., 2017), needs for social support and cultural brokering, in the face of racism, are no doubt heightened—even for immigrants from countries unaffected by the ban (e.g., Pakistan).

In addition to families emerging from financial, social, or emotional need, family of choice may come from relational dynamics that emerge from cultural norms. Chapter 2 used the work of Pacanowsky and O'Donnell-Trujillo (1982) to argue that organizations are cultures. It makes sense that cultures may emerge in which varying stakeholders within non-profit and for-profit organizations may yield systems of mutual care that render the organization members a family. Domínguez and Watkins (2003) spoke with a woman receiving services from Reardon House—a non-profit that provides childcare through its Early Intervention Program. At first blush, one might assume that the recipient of care was not establishing familial ties with the Reardon staff, but merely availing herself of the services the organization offers. However, the participant developed a relationship with the staff that included assisting management in hiring a new nurse, and taking a job in the kitchen. The participant explains, "I wanted to give back. So not only do I volunteer, I'll work there too and make sure everything I do is a little extra than what's required" (Domínguez & Watkins, 2003, p. 123). Families of choice may also emerge within religious groups as is reflected in the phrase of having a *church family* or having *brothers and sisters in faith*.

Family of choice may also take the form of urban tribes (Watters, 2003). As Watters (2003) explains,

> in the past, urban tribes might have been common among artists, gays, lesbians, bohemians, or hippies, but today it seems that no countercultural credentials were necessary. Tribes were as likely to be made up of ultimate-Frisbee-playing MBAs from Boston as country-music aficionados from Austin, Texas.
>
> (pp. 42–43)

The overall privilege of the "tribe" seemed to have little bearing on the level of interdependency. Watters recounted groups that pooled money to cover medical expenses, attended funerals, and served as sources of protection (e.g., from abusive ex-boyfriends) and comfort.

Family of choice may also take form in relation to the type of romantic relationships one might pursue. Polyamory might be thought of as responsible non-monogamy, and is characterized by the cultivation of multiple intimate relationships with partners who are aware, and perhaps even encouraging, of the other partners (Klesse, 2006; Ritchie & Barker, 2006). Polyamory is distinguishable from open or swinging relationships in that the multiple relationships—while usually sexual—focus on meaningful relational development. Though polyamory has been characterized as an identity, rather than a practice, the family structures yielded from cultivating polyamorous relationships can make family of choice (Dixon, 2015b; Robinson, 2013). For example, one of my participants lived with her two partners. The two partners weren't romantic with each other, but nonetheless lived as a family within the household. Other polyamorous families may not necessarily live together under one roof, but may, nonetheless, be comprised of members who consider their partners' partners family.

Despite the many contexts in which family of choice might take shape, it can be very challenging to communicate it into being, outside the family structure itself. Family of choice has been described as the "poster child" for discourse-dependent families (Braithwaite & DiVerniero, 2014, p. 175), in that there are no constructs, other than communication, that support the notion that the family is indeed family, and accordingly worthy of regard. Consider the family structures discussed, thus far, in this book: Single and childfree adults struggle against a perceived deficit in an otherwise functioning family structure. Families with one or more LGBTQ working adults, and families that resist traditionally gendered distributions of labor, are still traditional families but with a component that renders them uncharacteristic. Family of choice is the only family structure that is, in the purest sense, *family because we say we're family*.

Balancing Family of Choice

Family of choice is difficult to include in work–family balance. This is due, in large part, to the schemas we've created that position traditional immediate family as most important, close family friends as less important, and so forth. DePaulo (2006) discusses the emphasis on providing care within the married unit to the neglect of the community at large, remarking that "[w]e have taken a small set of relationships that deserve to be treasured, and turned them into the only relationships worth valuing at all" (p. 133). Take a moment to think about someone in your workplace. Imagine them disclosing to you that they have been away for some time because their mother passed away. You would likely express sympathy and offer to alleviate a portion of the person's work obligations. Now, imagine someone saying they are struggling upon coming back to work following their mother's friend passing away. You would probably sympathize but also wonder if such a mourning period were necessary. This hypothetical comparison isn't intended to suggest that family, friends, and community are at all times indistinguishable and deserving of equal consideration. What is important, however, is to *honor the possibility* that family of choice is present and worthy of regard.

Affirmation

Even attempting to affirm family of choice in the workplace can be emotionally daunting on account of the likelihood that co-workers and managers will be skeptical of your interpretation of family. As my aforementioned participant, Allison, reflects, "I love my family, my chosen family so much, that I feel like I'm trying to protect that love by keeping it entirely separate." Like Allison, several participants discussed not mentioning family of choice at work in an attempt to avoid speculation. Disagreement regarding who counts as family may surface as a result of organization members who are concerned that work–family balance accommodations are being granted for fraudulent reasons (Dixon & Liberman, 2016). One of the questions I asked research participants was, *Name a time in which you felt someone else took too much time off from work, and how that prompted you to reconsider how you would take time off in the future.* With very little exception, participants were aware of at least one person who they recognized as trying to cheat the system. As Brenda, a 61-year-old mortgage bank manager, exclaimed, "there's always people who want to take advantage of the system."

Also, there can be concerns regarding perceptions of immorality, especially when one's family member of choice is of a different gender.[5] Angela, a 58-year-old actor and model, explained to me her living situation and then doubled back: "I just said I live alone. That is not a reality, I just said that because I don't live with my husband … so it's a good friend of mine". Angela was hesitant to tell me that she was living with a friend. However, upon being asked to talk about her living arrangement, she continued,

> My friend, he feeds me, we went to college together, we've just been the best of friends, and if I'm not there for dinner, he'll call and be like, [Angela], are you coming? What you doing? And he has a girlfriend, but they consider … I'm like their adopted family.

Angela spoke of her long-time friend, and his girlfriend as family—she continued by talking about how thankful she was to have been "adopted" into this existing household. Even in an interview for a study involving family of choice, Angela was very careful to explain that there was nothing romantic going on between her and her friend, or her and her friend's girlfriend. Were Angela to try to represent her family of choice in the workplace, she would likely have to strike a balance between framing the relationship as family (as opposed to a relationship based strictly on the status of being a roommate), and being clear that the relationship is platonic.[6] This sort of arrangement was examined in Domínguez and Watkin's (2003) study in which a participant explained receiving support from a gentleman named Frank only when he is involved in a romantic relationship with another woman. Upending our ideas about family as emerging from romantic relationships, this particular standard emerged from the participant's need to avoid feeling as though she needed to reciprocate Frank's generosity by forging a sexual relationship.

Affirming polyamorous relationships is incredibly difficult and risky, as they are often misunderstood as systems of infidelity. Even in instances where participants were entrepreneurs and/or independent contractors, there was a need to keep polyamorous connections hidden. Jacob, a 43-year-old small business owner from Texas discusses the strain of managing work and relational identities:

> I'm particularly careful to make sure that the people in the town where I live and have my office are not aware that I'm poly to the extent that it actually caused a fair amount of friction in one relationship, because I couldn't be seen with one of my [partners] in this small town, I could get away with that in a big city, but in a small

town where networking is the primary form of advertising ... I have to be sure that people have a good opinion of me and unfortunately for most people, even relatively liberal people, it means believing I'm monogamous.

Here, Jacob felt unable to be seen with his girlfriend out of concern that people would think he was cheating[7] on his wife. Importantly, just because one is in a polyamorous relationship doesn't mean one is in a poly family. However, just as marriage is a goal for many monogamy-preferring adults, the development of a stable, loving family is often the goal of polyamorous individuals as well. As Jacob attests, cultivating relationships that could form families can be tricky for working adults.

In some instances, polyamorous families developed norms of how information about their family structure would be managed in workplace settings. For example, one participant shared that one of her partners always accompanied her to workplace-sponsored family events, because the other partner simply didn't like that sort of thing and was happy to be left out. In other instances, choosing to communicate about one partner but not another can put significant stress on the relationships.

Affirmation can also be tricky when family of choice originates from a time or aspect of one's life that one wishes to keep segmented from the workplace (McCarthy et al., 2002). For example, family of choice developed from time spent at a drug rehabilitation facility may be tricky to represent at work. Recovering from substance abuse often involves severing connections with those who still use, and creating new connections with people one has met on the path to recovery (Ackerman, 2015). Recovery.org even provides advice on knowing when to cut versus cultivate ties upon leaving the structure and safety of a rehabilitation facility (Smith, 2017). Of course, there is the option of simply not disclosing the origins of the relationship, but that can be tricky when information is needed to familiarize co-workers and management with family members.

Finally, affirmation can be difficult when we're accustomed to relegating our family of choice to friendship status. In some interviews, participants referred to someone as a friend throughout most of the interview and then arrived at the conclusion that they were, indeed, family. In other interviews, participants indicated that they care for, and/or are cared for by, a very good friend, but at no point referred to the friend as family. Even if someone devotes a significant amount of time and resources caring for a friend, accommodation for such care may never occur because we (perhaps rightfully) assume that accommodation won't be granted.

Obstacles in affirming family of choice come in the form of preferential regard typically given to traditional family structures, concern that family of choice won't be accepted as "real family," and questions of morality and our own limited experience with family of choice, as a relational possibility. Finding an effective means of affirming family of choice in the workplace may begin with considering how people make sense of their families of choice in general. Braithwaite et al. (2010) interviewed 110 participants to determine how they come to consider family of choice to be a legitimate family structure. Three of the four types of family of choice yielded from the interviews (substitute family, supplemental family, and convenience family) were explained in relation to traditional family. For example, substitute family could be described as family created following the death or estrangement of a blood relative. In the same way Braithwaite et al.'s (2010) participants made sense of family of choice in relation to traditional family, working adults could follow suit. Positioning family of choice as relative to traditional family structures may serve to reify traditional notions of family (Nelson, 2014). However, this may be a necessary first step in planting a seed of familiarity in the workplace.

In addition to talking about family of choice in relation to traditional family, family of choice members can be represented through talk about traditions and time spent together. Consider the opening vignette: had it neglected to mention the Sunday dinners or the occasional help with mail and medications, we likely would not have assumed that Trent would need additional time off to mourn the loss of Marilou.

Advocacy

Family of choice has been described throughout this chapter as involving commitment and responsibility. Tending to responsibilities for family of choice can be difficult if not impossible when family of choice isn't acknowledged in the workplace. It has even been argued that, amid the support received through family of choice, the expectation of reciprocity means added responsibility that can stifle professional success (Domínguez & Watkins, 2003). Given the shaky ground on which family of choice is represented in the workplace, many U.S. workplaces may not be ready to recognize these relationships as a legitimate aspect of work–life balance. Therefore small gestures, that don't extend beyond a discursive auditioning of one's family structure, might be the best first step.

Considering family of choice as a legitimate family form may present an opportunity to problematize the idea that living together under one roof is a prerequisite for the status of being *close* family. Of course, although many a blood- or legally related family member may live separately, family of choice is probably the most likely. Additionally, as mentioned at the beginning of this chapter, family of choice presents an opportunity to blur the line between family and community. Bailyn (2006) astutely observes that "[i]n a society as diverse as ours, where people have a great variety of needs, interests, and values, equal treatment may have unequal consequences" (p. 86). Bailyn not only developed a model in which prioritizing personal needs changes the way we do work and the way we think of workplace commitment, she also sought to expand what we think of to be acceptable personal needs (e.g., to include fellow community members). For now, we may need to rely mostly if not completely on affirmation: Everyday talk about family of choice may go a long way in communicating these families into being.

Conclusion

As we consider the dividing line between family of choice and close friends, we may arrive at the conclusion that no line is necessary. Considerations of family of choice also invite us to look at family through the lenses of need and of cultural norm. Several types of family of choice discussed in this chapter emerge as a result of need—LGBTQ individuals in need of social support in the face of rejection and discrimination, older adults in need of support following the passing of one's immediate family and social circle, and those who have built a support system as a measure of rehabilitation from substance abuse. Family of choice may also emerge from cultural dynamics, such as religious groups based on treating fellow group members with familial care, and polyamorous families in which partners of partners are regarded as family. Of course the interplay of culture and need may also be at play. Taken together, need and culture prompt innumerable types of family of choice, presenting an opportunity to broaden how we consider family in relation to community.

Would it be such an affront on family to include those who we care for and who care for us in the same station of regard that we hold biological and legally-recognized family? As Braithwaite and DiVerniero (2014) attest, family of choice may have the steepest discursive uphill climb with regard to communicating legitimacy into being in the workplace. Affirming family of choice can be difficult when our families emerge from aspects of our lives that we wish to keep separate from the workplace (such as family formed during rehabilitation), when there is concern that our families will be judged immoral (such as polyamorous families), or when there is suspicion that accommodation is being asked for under fraudulent pretenses (such as when one adopts a friend as family, but the legitimacy of the familial status is called into question). Considering the care of a chosen family member as just as worthy of regard as a blood or legally recognized relative may be untenable in most workplace cultures. For now, the best course may be to recognize the value of family of choice and allow workplace discourses about family of choice to begin.

Notes

1 Throughout this chapter, I will use the term *family of choice*, even when referencing literature that uses the terms *voluntary kin* or *fictive kin*. Exceptions are made where I feel the author intends a meaning that is distinguishable from the definition of family of choice provided at the beginning of this chapter.
2 The United Nations defines resettlement as the process of facilitating the transition of someone to a place that is neither the person's country of origin, nor the country to which they pled (UNHCR, 2015).
3 Steimel (2016) conveys a story of one of her participants who stayed in her home, with her spouse, for several days follow Independence Day, because they assumed the sound of the firecrackers to be gunfire.
4 Iraq, Iran, Syria, Somalia, Sudan, Libya, and Yemen.
5 Although, the argument could be made that family of choice of the same gender identity could cause just as much speculation. For example, a woman employee who has a family member who is also a woman, but doesn't fit a typical family designation (e.g., sister) may be speculated to be the employees romantic partner, prompting hypervisibility, as discussed in Chapter 4.
6 See Chapter 3 about the general preoccupation with coupledom.
7 Many polyamorous adults reject the term *cheating*, because it suggests a moral indictment of having multiple partners (Wosick-Correa, 2010).

References

Ackerman, M. (2015, April 24). Post-rehab: 11 things to avoid when a loved one comes home. *Recovery.org*. Retrieved from: www.recovery.org/post-rehab-11-things-to-avoid-when-a-loved-one-comes-home/ (accessed January 23, 2017).

Allen, K. R., Blieszner, R., & Roberto, K. A. (2011). Perspective on extended family and fictive kin in later years: Strategies and meanings of kin reinterpretation. *Journal of Family Issues*, 32(9), 1156–1177. doi: 10.1177/0192513X11404335.

Bailyn, L. (2006). *Breaking the mold: Redesigning work for productive and satisfying lives* (2nd ed.). Ithaca, NY: Cornell University Press.

Braithwaite, D. O. & DiVerniero, R. (2014). "He became like my other son": Discursively constructing voluntary kin. In L. A. Baxter (Ed.), *Remaking "family" communicatively* (pp. 175–192). New York: Peter Lang.

Braithwaite, D. O., Bach, B. W., Baxter, L. A., DiVerniero, R., Hammonds, J. R., Hosek, A. M., ... Wolf, B. M. (2010). Constructing family: A typology of voluntary kin. *Journal of Social and Personal Relationships*, 27(3), 388–407. doi: 10.1177/0265407510361615.

Calamur, K. (2017, January 30). What Trump's executive order on immigration does—and doesn't do. *The Atlantic*. Retrieved from: www.theatlantic.com/news/archive/2017/01/trump-immigration-order-muslims/514844/ (accessed January 23, 2017).

DePaulo, B. (2006). *Singled out: How singles are stereotyped, stigmatized, and ignored and still live happily ever after*. New York: St. Martin's Press.

Dixon, J. (2015a). Polyamory, sex, and the communication of commitment. In J. Manning & C. Noland (Eds.), *Contemporary studies of sexuality & communication*. Dubuque: Kendall Hunt.

Dixon, J. (2015b). *Family*arizing: Work/life balance for single, childfree, and chosen family. *Electronic Journal of Communication, 25*(1–2).

Dixon, J. & Liberman, C. J. (2016). Shedding light on dark structures constraining work/family balance: A structurational approach. In E. S. Gilchrist-Petty & S. D. Long (Eds.), *Contexts of the dark side of communication* (pp. 281–292). New York: Peter Lang.

Domínguez, S. & Watkins, C. (2003). Creating networks for survival and mobility: Social capital among African-American and Latin-American low-income mothers. *Social Problems, 50*(1), 111–135. doi: http://dx.doi.org/10.1525/sp.2003.50.1.111.

Gabrielson, M. L. (2011). "We have to create family": Aging support issues and needs among older lesbians. *Journal of Gay & Lesbian Social Services, 23*(3), 322–334. doi: 10.1080/10538720.2011.562803.

Hirsch, J. S. (2015, April 14). A scientific look at the damage parents do when they bully their gay kids. *The Washington Post.* Retrieved from: www.washingtonpost.com/posteverything/wp/2015/04/14/a-scientific-look-at-the-damage-parents-do-when-they-bully-their-gay-kids/?utm_term=.9a52251aa820 (accessed January 23, 2017).

HRC. (2015). Growing up LGBT in America: HRC youth survey report: Key findings. Retrieved from: www.hrc.org/files/assets/resources/Growing-Up-LGBT-in-America_Report.pdf (accessed January 23, 2017).

Jarrett, L., Marsh, R., & Koran, L. (2017, February 4). Homeland security suspends travel ban. *CNN.* Retrieved from: www.cnn.com/2017/02/03/politics/federal-judge-temporarily-halts-trump-travel-ban-nationwide-ag-says/ (accessed February 2, 2017).

Johnson, C. L. (1999). Fictive kin among oldest old African Americans in the San Francisco Bay area. *The Journals of Gerontology Series B: Psychological Sciences and Social Sciences, 54*(6), S368–S375. doi: https://doi.org/10.1093/geronb/54B.6.S368.

Klesse, C. (2006). Polyamory and its "others": Contesting the terms of non-monogamy. *Sexualities, 9*(5), 565–583. doi: 10.1177/1363460706069986.

Lee, J. C., Omri, R., & Preston, J. (2017, January 30). What are sanctuary cities? *The New York Times.* Retrieved from: www.nytimes.com/interactive/2016/09/02/us/sanctuary-cities.html?_r=0 (accessed February 2, 2017).

Lucas, K. & Buzzanell, P. M. (2006). Employees "without families": Discourses of family as an external constraint to work–life balance. In L. H. Turner & R. West (Eds.), *The family communication sourcebook* (pp. 335–352). Thousand Oaks, CA: Sage.

McCarthy, B., Hagan, D., & Martin, M. J. (2002). In and out of harm's way: Violent victimization and the social capital of fictive street families. *Criminology 40*(4), 831–866. doi: 10.1111/j.1745-9125.2002.tb00975.x.

Nelson, M. K. (2013). Fictive kin, families we choose, and voluntary kin: What does the discourse tell us? *Journal of Family Theory and Review, 5*(4), 259–281. doi: 10.1111/jftr.12019.

Nelson, M. K. (2014). Whither fictive kin? Or, what's in a name? *Journal of Family Issues, 35*(2), 201–222. doi: 10.1177/0192513X12470621.

Pacanowsky, M. E. & O'Donnell-Trujillo, N. (1982). Communication and organizational cultures. *Western Journal of Speech Communication, 46*(2), 115–130. doi: 10.1080/10570318209374072.

Ritchie, A. & Barker, M. (2006). "There aren't words for what we do or how we feel so we made them up": Constructing polyamorous language in a culture of compulsory monogamy. *Sexualities, 9*(5), 584–601. doi: 10.1177/1363460706069987.

Robinson, M. (2013). Polyamory and monogamy as strategic identities. *Journal of Bisexuality, 13*(1), 21–38. doi: 10.1080/15299716.2013.755731.

Smith, A. (2017, February 3). Taking out the trash: How to purge your toxic relationships. *Recovery.org.* Retrieved from: www.recovery.org/taking-out-the-trash-how-to-purge-your-toxic-relationships/ (accessed January 23, 2017).

Stack, C. (1974). *All our kin: Strategies for survival in the Black community.* New York: Harper and Row.

Stack, C. & Burton, L. (1993). "Kinscripts." *Journal of Comparative Family Studies, 24*, 157–170.

Steimel, S. (2016). Negotiating knowledges and expertise in refugee resettlement organizations. *Cogent Social Sciences, 2*(1), 1162990. doi: http://dx.doi.org/10.1080/23311886.2016.1162990.

UNHCR. (2015). UNHCR projected global resettlement needs: 2016. Retrieved from: www.unhcr.org/558193896.html (accessed February 2, 2017).

Watters, E. (2003). *Urban tribes: A generation redefines friendship, family, and commitment.* New York: Bloomsbury.

Weston, K. (1997). (Preface) *Families we choose: Lesbians, gays, kinship.* New York: Columbia University Press.

Wosick-Correa, K. (2010). Agreements, rules, and agentic fidelity in polyamorous relationships. *Psychology & Sexuality, 1*(1), 44–61. doi: 10.1080/19419891003634471.

Zong, J. & Batalova, J. (2015). Refugees and asylees in the United States. *Migration Policy Institute.* Retrieved from: www.migrationpolicy.org/article/refugees-and-asylees-united-states (accessed February 2, 2017).

Conclusion

At its core, this project sought to introduce a dialog in which the politics of what it means to have a family, and to advocate for family needs in the workplace, are explored. Interviews with 26 working adults scattered throughout the U.S., plus supplementary data from a previous study of 60 more yielded ideas, stories, and perspectives that shaped the understanding of family as an emblem of diversity. Ideas such as the *lingering compulsion*, *hypervisibility*, *the culture of care*, and even *family of choice* function to illuminate ways of recalibrating how we view work–family balance and how we might better understand the lived experience of developing family identity in the workplace.

Despite our growing mindfulness of diversity and our expanding options for considering alternative ways of balancing work and family, we still find ourselves in workplaces that favor the needs of traditional families and traditional notions of workplace commitment. While many popular self-help books depict work–family balance in sexist ways, that firmly position women as caregivers and men as unencumbered pursuers of professional success, celebrities show diverse work–family balance but from a standpoint of privilege that few of us can match. In short, U.S. cultures of work give us little in the way of positive, realistic, and inclusive examples of successfully balancing work and family.

Templates for an improved approach to work–family balance can be found in Bailyn's (2006) vision of an alternative way of thinking about the link between public and private lives. This vision seeks to create synergy (as opposed to conflict) between the two spheres. What's more, Bailyn (2006) speaks to the invisibility of the strain of work–family balance—a strain that results from the assumption that time to accommodate family needs a private concern to be negotiated within family structures, rather than a larger, systemic, issue. Viewing the strain of work–family balance as a public, political issue would serve to problematize the prioritization of work and the glorification of workplace commitment. Just as the personal is political, so too is the familial and the expectation that work comes before family needs. As Bailyn (2006) writes, "[w]hat in fact is a societal issue driven by inflexibility in career structures becomes a private issue between husband and wife in which the only possible solution is for one of them to "sacrifice" (p. 68). This sacrifice emerged frequently in my interviews. In some cases, the sacrifice wasn't to any specific person's benefit, but rather a workplace expectation. A logical next step is to examine workplaces reputed to prioritize the needs of the employees.[1] One would have to dig deeper than noting ball pools and nap pods and consider how workplace commitment is (or can be) reshaped in a way that affords commitment to the wellbeing of the employee.

Importantly, looking to companies that look out for the private needs of employees is just the beginning. Coupling Bailyn's upheaval of work–family priorities with Gerson's (2010) departure from structure-bound notions of family, we have a basic philosophical recipe for rethinking the amount of time we relinquish to demonstrating workplace commitment, as well as the present inequalities regarding who is expected to relinquish the most. Interviews provided many instances in which the sacrifices Bailyn (2006) discusses occur not only to the benefit of the workplace but to the benefit of one or more co-workers who's family lives are considered more discursively sound and, therefore, more worthy of accommodation. If family is honored by virtue of its capacity to generate happiness (e.g., two chosen family members who truly bring joy to one another's lives, or the breadwinning mom and the stay-at-home dad, who both love their role in the family and in their communities), rather than its capacity to fit a traditionally familiar form, perhaps a more fair approach to accommodation can be reached.

In considering how we might honor a diversity of family structures, the difference between acceptance and equality should be emphasized, noting that being accepted into a workplace is hardly an assurance that equal regard will be afforded to one's work–family balance needs. In only very few cases did participants describe being actively shunned in the workplace for espousing an identity (family or otherwise) that didn't mesh with the workplace culture. Instead, subtle inequalities emerged as stories told of instances in which the needs of those with traditional families were considered more important. The distinction between acceptance and equality becomes even subtler when needs are generally accommodated, except for when they are in competition with the needs of other co-workers. It is in these situations when we see compromised fulfillment and dignity, and perhaps betrayal of stated commitments to honor diversity.

Curiously, lapses in fulfillment and dignity occur despite a lack of an expanding majority. While the narrative of the traditional family is the most recognized, the traditional family, itself, is only barely the most common. Families, today, are kaleidoscopic (Cohen, 2014) in that there isn't a single, pervasive family form that serves as the ideal. Similarly, family communication scholars have long acknowledged the various ways in which family can be defined, including families that require only the criteria of communicating as families. And yet, it is the needs of traditional families that are given greater regard in the workplace, and that are the point of focus in most family-related research. As reiterated throughout this book, bringing diverse family structure into the realm of legitimacy in the workplace, in research, (and elsewhere) begins with everyday communication.

The workplace may be thought of as an entity separate from communication, an entity continually (re)created by communication, and an entity that is the product of action and discourse (Fairhurst & Putnam, 2004). This book has considered the second and third views—also referred to as the "relativist view" and the "realist view," respectively—in examining how diverse families may be integrated into the workplace. The relativist view accounts for our capacities, as organizational stakeholders, to contribute to meaning-making. The realist view, in contrast, accounts for the possibility for this construction of meaning, but also acknowledges the politics of meaning-construction, and the capacity for voices to be silenced.

With an eye to the relativist view, families can be communicated into being through affirmations of the legitimacy of one's family structure. With the realist view in mind, working adults can weave their family accommodation needs into the tapestry of preconceived notions of what it means to have a family. Of course, resistance can and does occur as co-workers and other organization members have differing ideas of what counts as family. The propositions of Language Convergence/Meaning Divergence Theory (Dougherty et al., 2009) remind us that we may not even be aware of our disagreements about what it means to have a family. Like so many other constructs we engage with in everyday life, it likely doesn't occur to us to question how we define family, or ponder the extent to which our definition of family differs from others' definitions. (Chapter 6 pushed the boundaries of family so far as to blur the line between family and community.) Personal opinions and biases among managers and other gatekeepers may amplify constraints on advocating for diverse work–family balance needs, especially if there is suspicion that one is contriving a familial obligation to use as an excuse to shirk responsibility or betray workplace commitment.

The task of balancing work and family becomes more complex as we attempt to make sense of what it means to be a good employee, and to understand the extent of what is expected of us. The workplace is a culture all its own, however this culture can be integrated, differentiated, and fragmented (Martin, 1992), leaving us with no definitive understanding of the boundaries or even the criteria of work. This ambiguity emerges, in part, from contradicting work expectations that come from modern and postmodern parameters of work, as well as the conflation of productivity and commitment. Postmodern concepts such as the use of technology as a vehicle for demonstrating workplace commitment as well as the (perceived) flattening of hierarchies blurs the boundaries between public and private lives and adds complexity to the task of determining what amount of time away from work, to care for family, is safe. This issue emerged for participants such as Natalie, a customer service representative, who took her work laptop with her when going to care for her mother, and yet the time working on her laptop in the hospital didn't "count" as being "at work." The ambiguity of work expectations is compounded when work, itself, is uncertain. Precarious or no-collar work implies balancing work and family with even less of a dependable workplace culture with which to negotiate accommodation. Several participants relished the life of an independent contractor, because taking the time to affirm and advocate for family wasn't necessary: you work your own hours, and if anyone has an issue with your family life, it doesn't matter. You'll be off to the next job soon enough. But it's important to understand the distinction between intentionally precarious workers—like Bill who worked construction or Adam who is a software developer, and unintentionally precarious workers, like Love who quit working at a social services agency to care for her child, and Candace who is never certain, from one year to the next, whether the public school in her community will need a teacher.[2]

***

Chapter 3 began the tour of varying family structures and roles. Sa/oCf adults make up a significant segment of the workplace population. They are thought to be driven and career-oriented. Yet, the lingering compulsion toward marriage and children leaves this population contending with the perception that they are lacking. Lingering social stigma against never-wed parents and the possibly refurbished stigma attached to divorce may further embolden assumptions that Sa/oCf adults have somehow failed at adulthood. Work–family balance for Sa/oCf adults begins with social inclusion. Talk of children (and, perhaps not as prevalently, spouses) permeates workplace conversation, making it difficult to contribute to existing non-work-related conversations. Inquiries about why an employee has never had children can do more harm than good as such questions suggest that life experiences occur in relation to the lingering compulsion of marriage and/or having kids. In contemplating how to go about integrating more topics into workplace conversation, I considered what participants reported that people talked about, aside from kids, spouses, or work itself. Answers included pets, vacations, extended families, political issues, food/local restaurants, and—a workplace favorite—gossip. One opportunity to create more inclusive conversational spaces is to learn one or more of co-workers' interests and inquire about them on occasion. This may seem like Cultivating Relationships 101, however the common experiences of Sa/oCf working adults would suggest that such prompts for social inclusion are missing or lacking. Importantly, developing inclusive workplace topics is only the beginning.

Honoring non-work life of Sa/oCf employees as being of equal importance and value as employees with spouses and/or children means working weekends, traveling, or taking other undesirable work to accommodate Sa/oCf needs. This isn't to suggest that employees with traditional families should dive headlong into situations of family neglect, but rather be conscientious of the difference between family needs (such as caring for a sick child) and family events (such as attending a soccer game). Such consideration can make room for the needs of other family structures, such as those in which one or more family members are LGBTQ.

Balancing work and family as an LGBTQ working adult means balancing sexual identity. Even as workplaces become increasingly accepting, if not encouraging, of the expression of sexual identities (of varying forms), the bureaucratic/rational norm of the modern workplace makes integrating sexual identity a risky proposition in many workplaces. A key issue for LGBTQ adults is the hypervisibility that comes with co-workers placing sexual attributions on what should be perceived as a social construct. Each identity under the LGBTQ grouping has its own set of stereotypes to contend with, such as the notion that bisexuals are sexually undiscerning and an affront to the professional work environment (Monro, 2015). Despite the negative attributions that still make their way into workplace conversations (HRC, 2014), I am nonetheless surprised by the number of working adults who are still in the closet, or who are hyper-vigilant about how their sexual orientation and/or identity is communicated at work. Those who are "out" at work often feel the need to negotiate sexual and gender identity as an ongoing process as workplaces undergo change (e.g., new management). Though non-discrimination and anti-harassment policies can serve as a hint of whether a workplace includes a culture of acceptance, policy and culture can contradict one another, leaving LGBTQ working adults uncertain of how to affirm their families and advocate for work–family balance needs. In addition to representing LGBTQ families through everyday conversation, it is important to reinforce the reality that the needs of LGBTQ families are strikingly similar to the needs of traditional families (e.g., childcare, eldercare, budgeting, etc.) while also raising awareness of obstacles that are unique to LGBTQ families (e.g., taking time for children who are bullied at school because they have gay parents, a family member undergoing gender affirmative surgery).

Examining the gendering of work–family balance obligations requires acknowledging the lingering dichotomy of women's and men's work and family roles. Despite a "quiet revolution" that began in the 1970s (Goldin, 2006), allowing for the possibility of women to prioritize career goals, both work and family remain highly gendered spaces. This occurs in everyday communication—such as the female employee who acts as a mother to her co-workers—and in statistics that point to wage inequality, and the dearth of women CEOs. Women's added difficulty in balancing work and family is partially the result of the culture of care, in which women are expected to be primary caretakers of children and the elderly, while the male career model (e.g., ongoing, full-time employment; Hewlett, 2007) can push women out of the workplace, altogether. Medved (2016a, 2016b) and others have showcased how female breadwinners and stay-at-home husbands have made strides in discursively *un*gendering divisions of labor. However, work–family balance is still rife with gendered structures that leave women with the pressure of caring for everyone within the family structure while still, for many, pursuing a fulfilling career. Women face a double bind where it comes to affirming family at work: Though communicating family into being is very important, women who talk about family run the risk of affirming the culture of care and compromising their perceived commitment to work. Work should be done to frame family as a diversity issue, rather than a gender issue. Just as we might use a holiday to reflect on the significance the day holds and for whom, we should also look at discourses about family in the same frame. For example, if an employee cares for her parents, sibling, and nephews, as Josephine, a career counselor, does, talking about family creates an opportunity, similar to acknowledging a holiday we might not be readily familiar with, for honoring a diverse perspective.

Finally, interviews conducted for this study suggest that the number of people who actively identify as having a family of choice is far smaller than the number of people in relationships that fit the description. Families of choice are created through need such as LGBTQ families formed through the needs of emotional, financial, and social support as well as families formed from cultural traditions, such as church families. Perhaps people turn away from cultivating familial relationships because the discourse dependency has eluded even them. This isn't to suggest that people should force-conceptualize familial relationships with people who don't fit the criteria, but rather imagine what family relationships would be possible if some of the discursive dependency of family of choice were removed.

Themes & Intersections

This project took place for four reasons: (a) to examine family as an aspect of diversity; (b) to ungender the experience of work–family balance; (c) to locate opportunities for working adults to relate or find common ground in the experience of balancing work and family, amid a diversity of family structures; and (d) to consider practical ways of affirming and advocating for family. The journey of collecting interviews, as well as the contributions of scholars and lay writers provided food for thought on each point.

Family as a Dimension of Diversity

Throughout this book, family has been proposed as an aspect of diversity all its own. Workplaces benefit from diverse workplace members, in part, because diverse perspectives foster more creativity and innovation, cultivate more welcoming work environments resulting in less turnover, and have a greater ability to tap into the needs of a diverse consumer market (Kerby & Burns, 2012). Employees of varying abilities, ages, and nationalities bring different life experiences and standpoints to the workplace. In a comparable way, people from a variety of family structures, who provide a variety of family roles, have their own perspectives and innovations to contribute.

Chapter 3 focused, in large part, on the importance of valuing the non-work lives of Sa/oCf working adults. The discourses that could emerge by widening the topics of workplace conversation hold the potential for stimulating the creativity sought by cultivating a diverse workforce. For example, Leslie and Nora are both single and childfree. Their life experiences run counter to the common narrative of children taking up the majority of their free time. The time otherwise occupied—through emersion into popular culture, insight yielded from taking courses, etc.—can contribute to diverse perspectives that lend to creativity, help reach diverse markets, etc. I'm not suggesting that working adults with children are not engaged in cultural experiences or personal betterment, but rather experiences that occur in the lives of single, childfree adults, that would have otherwise been devoted to coupling and/or child-raising, are fruitful.

Chapter 4 argues that families with one or more LGBTQ working adults are functionally the same as families comprised entirely of straight people. However, the diverse experiences of navigating work–family balance from a historically marginalized standpoint allows for insight into ways in which marginalization can be addressed and perhaps eliminated. This means striking a balance between welcoming family narratives shared by LGBTQ co-workers, all the while being mindful of hypervisibility and its implications.[3] For example, Jeremy was very happy to have his work colleagues in attendance at his wedding to Vlad; however, his experience with the rude client raises questions as to how such hypervisibility can be eliminated from the workplace. Obviously, no one in an organization has control over what customers/clients might say. Policies may be written that require respect of employees as a prerequisite to receiving goods or services.[4] Though, with this solution, a paradox may occur in which hypervisibility is worsened as the process of taking a customer to task for asking rude questions may draw more attention than simply letting it go.

Chapter 5 proposed the positioning of family as an aspect of workplace diversity as a means of coping with traditionally gendered divisions of labor. Participants in this study, as well as others, illustrated how pushing back against gendered notions of work can be risky to one's career. Framing family roles as discursive constructs, equipped with the ability to bring diverse perspectives to the workplace, can cultivate discourses that normalize ungendered care and commitment to work. Female breadwinners and stay-at-home fathers also present important spaces for challenging gendered discourses of work.

Finally, family of choice may be thought of as the most radical call to diversify our notions of family, in that the common assumption that families must be built from blood or legal ties is rejected. Yet it is worth noting that family of choice complies with the academic conceptualizations of family, explained in Chapter 1. So if we begin to honor family of choice in day-to-day workplace interactions, we can get a glimpse of actualized academic notions of family and bring fresh perspectives of life situations involving supplemental, convenient, substitute, or extended family.

Ungendering *the Balance*

The second objective of this project was to ungender work–family balance. As Chapter 5 explored, the male model of success (Hewlett, 2007) renders balance a necessity for women far more so than men. Reinforcing the notion that work–family balance is a "women's issue" only solidifies the male model of success as the correct workplace trajectory and, by extension, confines the culture of care to women. Ungendering work–family balance occurs among Sa/oCf women who have elected not to have children, although, for many women, not having children means being assigned care work for other family members. Additionally, families with one or more LGBTQ adults ungender the distribution of labor, oftentimes by default. Female breadwinners and stay-at-home fathers may feel that their gender is a particularly salient part of their lives because of the pull to reconcile life choices with gender role expectations. Though it has been suggested that millennials aren't rejecting the gendering of chores with the fervor we might expect, change is evident in the everyday discourses of managing work–family balance.

Opportunities to Relate

Though the purpose of this study was to explore and honor how very different our families can be, it is also important to acknowledge the characteristics that tie us all together. First, we all want more time.

Whether it is time with children, time with friends, or time to care for ourselves, the need for more time was a common topic of discussion among participants, as well as the foundation of much of the literature that helped shape this project. Second, people want to live uncloseted lives. Even those who prefer not to disclose an abundance of information about their personal lives still want to feel as though they don't have to perform a familial ideal in the workplace. This unwanted performance could be in the form of pretending to want to have children, pretending that families containing LGBTQ members are in any way lesser, pretending to find joy in divisions of labor thought to be appropriate to one's gender, or pretending that one's family of choice deserves less regard than its biological or legally-sanctioned counterparts. Finally, as reiterated throughout this book, all workplace members of all family structures and roles share the right to an equal attempt at work and family balance. Achieving equal respect for non-worklife means acknowledging that to be inclusive is to understand that no life path is more important, or worthy of regard, than another.

New Ways of Enacting Balance

As explained in the introduction, this is not a "how-to" or a "best practices" book. This is partly because there are no quick fixes to make family structures and roles equal. This is also because the clearest solutions are also unrealistic for most working adults. For example, Chapter 5 echoes the work of Tracy and Rivera (2010), by recommending that female breadwinners find workplaces with managers who support women who choose to devote the majority of their time to their careers. This is virtually impossible. How does one learn of a possible manager's political sensibilities about gender and the distribution of labor? Even if reputation precedes this person, who has the luxury of turning down work on the basis of a manager being rumored to engage in aversive sexism? The suggestions in this section are a little smaller but also a little more feasible.

First, the need-based system should be part of our vocabulary, as working adults. Chapter 3 presented Casper, Weltman, and Kewsiga's (2007) explanation of a need-based system in which work opportunities are given based on need, which is distinguishable from an equality-based system in which everyone is given equal opportunity to work; and an equity-based system in which opportunities are based on employee contributions, such as skills or effort. When all other terms, ideas, and concepts are taken away, the politics of need is the central focal point of this book. The solution is not to advocate for strict equality and the erasure of need-based allocations of resources. All employees have life experiences that merit tipping the scale (e.g., illness, the decision to go back to school, death in the family, etc.). Instead, as we communicate family into being in the workplace, we should be aware of the possibility of expanding need as it is culturally constructed. Rather than taking away the opportunity to be denied resources, it's better and more accommodating for all to expand what counts as need. Looking to the realist view of organizations and communication (Fairhurst & Putnam, 2004), the workplace is a tapestry of preconceived notions about family. Everyday, working adults can integrate practices and discourses to widen the notion of need.

In addition to expanding opportunities for work–family balance accommodation through a broadening of the need-based system, we should answer Bailyn's (2006) call to redesign work for more productive and satisfying lives. In doing so, work–family balance would no longer be a matter of competing for limited kernels of time (away), but rather encouraging one another to take the time we need.[5] This could occur through an expansion of what are considered acceptable reasons to be away, including the acceptability of taking extended time off. If you consider a co-worker taking time away from work for any one of the following activities: volunteering with hospice, leading a civic group, gardening, caring for a child (Wood & Dow, 2010), you may naturally develop a schema, ordering the reasons by level of acceptability. Though there are exceptions, overall we should work to diffuse the schema of *good* and *bad* reasons to be away from work. Communicating one's value of time away can be tricky. As Chapter 2 points out, the precarious nature of work renders asking for time away to be especially risky, as one might depict one's self as less than committed to work. To lessen this risk, instead of making any grand gestures, communication that acknowledges or even celebrates time away from work should be integrated into workplace talk. For example, people sometimes don't take the time away from work afforded to them because of concern for what others might think (Kirby & Krone, 2002). While not encouraging those known to take time off for patently fraudulent reasons (e.g., pretending to be sick; Dixon & Liberman, 2016), supporting co-workers in their endeavors to take time away is a small but influential step toward cultivating a workplace that values time away.

As discussed throughout this book, people may experience difficulty affirming and advocating for family needs, because their families don't fit into workplace conversations as they presently occur. Attempts at inclusion in the conversation can be awkward and even offensive (such as when childfree employees are included in conversations about children with the question of when they plan to have them). One idea is to make micro-inclusions, or small remarks or contributions that integrate family in some small way. For example, in a conversation at work about food allergies, one could contribute about a family member of choice: *Yeah, my good friend, Cecil, is very allergic to avocados.* The word *friend* may seem like a step in the wrong direction, but the otherwise unremarkable remark at least plants a seed that someone named Cecil, with an aversion to avocados, is someone in your life. Though any individual instance of micro-inclusion won't move mountains with regard to meeting work–family balance needs, it can be a positive move toward cultivating familiarity.

Changes can also be made at the managerial/corporate level. First, literature has long advocated for a "cafeteria-style" approach to work–family balance accommodation (e.g., Lucas & Buzzanell, 2006) in which employment benefits are each given a monetary value and employees select from a menu of options up to the total dollar amount allotted to them. Menu items could include tuition reimbursement, life insurance, caregivers' support, etc. Though the success of the cafeteria-style model hinges on the menu items available,[6] having options that also address the needs of non-traditional families can be a step in the right direction for allotting equal opportunities (and equal constraints) to all employees.

Second, family structure should be added, albeit in a small way, to the lexicon of diversity training and to advocacy and mentoring groups already in place in the workplace. As Medved (2016a) astutely writes, "training that encourages all employees to challenge their unconscious biases about gender roles can help develop inclusive work–life policies and supportive daily practices" (p. 252). Depending on the given workplace culture(s), *family structure* and perhaps *family roles* should be added to the list of terms to consider when conceptualizing diversity as a whole. Care should be taken that diversity training doesn't position family structure as an alternative lifestyle that merits excavating and distinguishing from that which is considered normal. Furthermore, resource groups, mentoring programs, and diversity councils should consider how adding issues related to work–family balance might better serve the employees for whom the programs are intended. Considering, specifically, LGBTQ resource groups, Goldberg (2016) asserts that, "[they] send a strong message of acceptance and also may ultimately improve the experiences of sexual-minority employees by increasing wellbeing and decreasing work-family conflict" (p. 1302). Such spaces for affirmation and advocacy should extend to employees belonging to diverse family structures.

Implications & Opportunities

While analyzing interview data and integrating scholarly and popular literature, there were moments when this project could have gone in different yet equally important directions. First, in addition to viewing family as an aspect of diversity, consideration of family structures and roles is a template, or starting point, for better considering other types of diversity. For example, an employee with one or more disabilities may consider a caretaker or aid (whether paid or unpaid) to be family of choice. By first understanding the need to balance work and family with the caretaker acknowledged as family, that particular need may be accommodated. Perhaps a better example focuses on ethnicity. Just as the male model of success assigns masculine standards to workplace success, narratives of family tend to assume white or Euro-American norms. Specifically, the workplace standard of taking time off for immediate family (spouse, children, parents) is a construct that favors the family structures of white working adults. Research has suggested that African-American and Hispanic working adults are more likely to provide direct care for extended family (Dill, 1998; Domníguez & Watkins, 2003). More research is needed on the varying experiences of work–family balance across ethnicities and nationalities, and white privilege as it manifests in work–family balance.

This project also prompts reflection regarding our own individual assumptions of what it means to be family. Single and childfree working adults are sometimes thought to be without families—a familial status that some single and childfree adults, themselves, identify with. Similarly, members of a family of choice are often characterized as friends, often framing the relationship in such a way when talking about it at work (assuming they elect to mention the relationship at all). By becoming acquainted with the idea that family of choice—and regard and accommodation for such family structures—is possible, we may find ourselves redefining some of our current relationships.[7]

Finally, this project prompted consideration of the value of self-care. In addition to the obstacles of negotiating time to tend to the needs of family members, many participants experienced vying for one's own health and personal betterment. Recall Oscar, a case manager for a state agency, who needed time away from work to attend tutoring sessions as he attempted to balance college with work; or Kelly, the college admissions director, who needed time to treat a physical illness. Though the affirmation and advocacy of the self in the workplace is tangential to considerations of family structure, the two endeavors may go hand in hand, especially in instances in which we feel we need to choose between work, family, and self.

Our Time, Our Lives

The book opened with the argument that the familial is political. The politics of family in the workplace become clear when we think about the value of our time and, by extension, the value of our lives. I didn't understand the extent to which our livelihoods are bound to our ability to balance work and family until my study was almost over. I was in my office, listening to the playback of one of my final participants. At the end of the interview, I asked Julio if there was anything else he would like to share. After pausing to collect his thoughts, Julio said:

> When you were explaining your study to me the first thing that came to my mind was *The Cats in the Cradle* ... You make the decision

you have to make and I think I broke their [my children's] hearts for the work instead of having to be the other way around, but if you need the money, sometimes you have to make determinations like that. What can I say? ... Most of the complaints I got were that I was never around. Time spent at the airport, working 18, 20-hour shifts, sleeping overnight at those airports, waiting for that very first fare at 5 or 6 in the morning to come out.

Julio describes his 30 years as a cab driver as the lyrics to *The Cats in the Cradle*, but where expectations were reversed—meaning that work obligations took him away from time that his children expected him to be available. My hope for this book is that it adds to the conversation of work–family balance in such a way that can prevent feelings of regret and lost opportunities that occur, every day, because of the politics of affirming and advocating for family in the workplace. This project was a small step toward realizing lives and times well spent.

Notes

1 For example, Coontz (2006) provides an interesting commentary on gender equality in the domestic sphere and hidden signs of progress: She reports that men tend to embellish when reporting the amount of work they do around the house. Rather than focusing on the inaccuracy in self-reporting, Coontz notes that it was not terribly long ago when men would not admit to doing the housework that they actually did. The idea that men feel compelled to embellish is progress.

2 I neglected to ask Candace about the possibility of earning tenure. Even if tenure is in her future, the precarity for her, and all untenured educators, in the time leading up to earning tenure is not to be discounted.

3 Hypervisibility may result in minority stress, which occurs when "members of stigmatized groups experience a unique form of stress due to their status as a member of the group" (Lavendar-Scott, 2016, p. 839) and can "play out in physical, mental, or emotional strain" (pp. 838–839).

4 I acknowledge that developing policy that requires respect among organizational stakeholders is far easier said than done. Just developing an operationalized definition of respect is tricky. Still, it's a way in which viewing family as diversity can contribute to more welcoming work environments.

5 Admittedly, this brings up the issue of affordability. How can employers, especially in smaller workplaces, afford to allow people to take time off from work? The culture of valuing time off would have to have a boundary. Perhaps, if truly financially necessary, the time off can be unpaid, or partially paid, but the culture of encouraging taking time as needed remains.

6 Examples of menu options include training subsidies, continuing education vouchers, gym memberships, pet care (either routine or during business travel), opportunities for cultural enrichment, etc.

7 I'm in no way trying to advocate for a conceptual overhaul that converts friends to family. Though it is possible for friends to become family as a result of discursively developing the possibility, this conceptual transition should be reserved for friends earnestly regarded with familial love and care.

References

Bailyn, L. (2006). *Breaking the mold: Redesigning work for productive and satisfying lives* (2nd ed.). Ithaca, NY: Cornell University Press.

Casper, W. J., Weltman, D., & Kewsiga, E. (2007). Beyond family-friendly: The construct and measurement of singles-friendly work culture. *Journal of Vocational Behavior, 70*(3), 478–501. doi: 10.1016/j.jvb.2007.01.001.

Cohen, P. (2014, September 14). Family diversity is the new normal for America's children: A briefing paper prepared for the Council on Contemporary Families.

Coontz, S. (2006). *Marriage, a history: From obedience to intimacy or how love conquered marriage.* New York: Viking Penguin.

Dill, B. T. (1998). Fictive kin, paper sons, and compadrazgo: Women of color and the struggle for family survival. In K. V. Hanson & A. I. Gary (Eds.), *Families in the U.S.: Kinship and domestic politics* (pp. 431–445). Philadelphia, PA: Temple University Press.

Dixon, J. & Liberman, C. J. (2016). Shedding light on dark structures constraining work/family balance: A structurational approach. In E. S. Gilchrist-Petty & S. D. Long (Eds.), *Contexts of the dark side of communication* (pp. 281–292). New York: Peter Lang.

Domínguez, S. & Watkins, C. (2003). Creating networks for survival and mobility: Social capital among African-American and Latin-American low-income mothers. *Social Problems, 50*(1), 111–135. doi: http://dx.doi.org/10.1525/sp.2003.50.1.111.

Dougherty, D. S., Kramer, M. W., Klatzke, S. R., & Rogers, T. K. K. (2009). Language convergence, meaning divergence: A meaning centered communication theory. *Communication Monographs, 76*(1), 20–46. doi: 10.1080/03637750802378799.

Fairhurst, G. T. & Putnam, L. (2004). Organizations as discursive constructions. *Communication Theory, 14*(1), 5–26. doi: 10.1111/j.1468–2885.2004.tb00301.x.

Gerson, K. (2010). *The unfinished revolution: Coming of age in a new era of gender, work, and family.* New York: Oxford University Press.

Goldberg, A. E. (2016). Work–family interface, LGBQ parents. In A. E. Goldberg (Ed.), *The SAGE handbook of LGBTQ studies* (Vol. 3, pp. 1299–1302). Thousand Oaks, CA: Sage.

Goldin, C. (2006). The quiet revolution that transformed women's employment, education, and family. *The American Economic Review, 96*(2), 1–21. doi: 10.3386/w11953.

Hewlett, S. A. (2007). *Off-ramps and on-ramps: Keeping talented women on the road to success.* Boston, MA: Harvard Business School Press.

HRC. (2014). HRC study shows majority of LGBTQ workers closeted at the workplace. *Human Rights Campaign.* Retrieved from: www.hrc.org/blog/hrc-study-shows-majority-of-lgbt-workers-closeted-on-the-job (accessed January 23, 2017).

Kerby, S. & Burns, C. (2012, July 12). The top 10 economic facts about diversity in the workplace: A diverse workplace is integral to a strong economy. *Center for American Progress.* Retrieved from: www.americanprogress.org/issues/labor/news/2012/07/12/11900/the-top-10-economic-facts-of-diversity-in-the-workplace/ (accessed August 2, 2016).

Kirby, E. L. & Krone K. J. (2002). The policy exists but you can't really use it: Communication and the structuration of work/life policies. *Journal of Applied Communication Research*, 30(1), 50–77. doi: 10.1080/00909880216577.

Lucas, K. & Buzzanell, P. M. (2006). Employees "without families": Discourses of family as an external constraint to work–life balance. In L. H. Turner & R. West (Eds.), *The family communication sourcebook* (pp. 335–352). Thousand Oaks, CA: Sage.

Martin, J. (1992). *Cultures in organizations: Three perspectives.* New York: Oxford University Press.

Medved, C. E. (2016a). The new female breadwinner: Discursively doing and undoing gender relations. *Journal of Applied Communication Research*, 44(3), 1–20. doi: 10.1080/00909882.2016.1192286.

Medved, C. E. (2016b). Stay at home fathering as a feminist opportunity: Perpetuating, resisting, and transforming gender relations of caring and earning. *Journal of Family Communication*, 16(1), 16–31. doi: 10.1080/15267431.2015.1112800.

Monro, S. (2015). *Bisexuality: Identities, politics, and theories.* London, UK: Palgrave Macmillan.

Tracy, S. J. & Rivera, K. D. (2010). Endorsing equity and applauding stay-at-home moms: How male voices on work-life reveal aversive sexism and flickers of transformation. *Management Communication Quarterly*, 24(3), 3–43. doi: 10.1177/0893318909352248.

Wood, J. T. & Dow, B. J. (2010). The invisible politics of "choice" in the workplace: Naming the informal parenting support system. In S. Hayden & L. O'Brien Hallstein (Eds.), *Contemplating maternity in an era of choice: Explorations into discourses of reproduction* (pp. 203–225). New York: Lexington.

Appendix
Interview Protocol for Primary Study

1 I was hoping we could begin with you telling me a little bit about your role at work. What are your responsibilities? What do you like about your job? Are there any aspects of your job that you can live without?

2 How does your current job stack up against other jobs you've had? Are you happier? Perhaps not as happy?

3 Shifting gears a little bit, please tell me about your family. Who do you take care of and who takes care of you?

4 In what ways are the non-work aspects of peoples' lives talked about in the workplace? When people aren't talking about work, what are they talking about?

5 What is the last thing you've said about your family, at work? This could be a story you told, a piece of information that you gave to contribute to an ongoing conversation, etc.

6 Would you describe for me an experience in which you felt you had to choose between attending to a work obligation and attending to a family obligation? How did you arrive at the choice you made?

7 Please tell me about any policies in place that allow you to take time off work when you need to. When (if ever) did you most recently take advantage of these policies?

8 Please tell me about a time (if any) when you received negative feedback from co-workers or management because you took time off work to attend to a family situation.

9 Please tell me about a time (if any) when you heard co-workers or management criticizing someone else for taking time off work for family-related reasons? In what ways (if any) do you feel this situation caused you to rethink whether you would take time off work for similar reasons?

10 What is your idea of the perfect work/family balance dynamic?

Index

For Product Safety Concerns and Information please contact our EU
representative GPSR@taylorandfrancis.com
Taylor & Francis Verlag GmbH, Kaufingerstraße 24, 80331 München, Germany

www.ingramcontent.com/pod-product-compliance
Ingram Content Group UK Ltd.
Pitfield, Milton Keynes, MK11 3LW, UK
UKHW020944180425
457613UK00019B/519